Y0-AEW-943

For Harold
Ober, the best
back-stop the
Crimson crew ever
had from

The Yale Athletic
Association

(see frontispiece)

George Barton, *The Bell Haven Eight* (Philadelphia; Winston, 1914). Fitzgerald also annotated the frontispiece of this boys' sports novel—see *The Romantic Egoists,* p. 210. Bruccoli Collection.

FITZGERALD/HEMINGWAY ANNUAL 1976

Edited by

MATTHEW J. BRUCCOLI

University of South Carolina

Associate Editors

Margaret M. Duggan

Richard Layman

EDITOR

MATTHEW J. BRUCCOLI
Department of English
University of South Carolina
Columbia, South Carolina 29208

ASSOCIATE EDITORS:

Margaret M. Duggan
Richard Layman

CONSULTING EDITOR: C. E. Frazer Clark, Jr.

EDITORIAL ASSISTANT: Linda Berry

Address all editorial correspondence to the editor.
Address orders and inquiries to Information Handling Services, Library and Education Division, Box 1154, Englewood, Colorado 80110.

Published by Information Handling Services, Library and Education Division, Box 1154, Englewood, Colorado 80110, an Indian Head Company.

Library of Congress Catalog Card Number: 75-83781
ISBN: 0-910972-62-1

Printed in the United States of America.

To Katharine B. Wade
in grateful memory

CONTENTS

F. SCOTT FITZGERALD

ERNEST HEMINGWAY

BIBLIOGRAPHICAL MATERIAL

REVIEWS

ANNOUNCEMENTS

FITZGERALD/HEMINGWAY ANNUAL 1976

F. Scott Fitzgerald

BALLET SHOES

or

BALLET SLIPPERS

by

F. Scott Fitzgerald

THIS IS TO CERTIFY

Harold Ober

HAS REGISTERED IN THE

REGISTRATION BUREAU

OF

THE AUTHORS' LEAGUE OF AMERICA, Inc.

THE {SYNOPSIS / ~~SCENARIO~~} ENTITLED

"Ballet Shoes" by

F. Scott Fitzgerald

"BALLET SHOES": A MOVIE SYNOPSIS

During their North African trip in 1930 the Fitzgeralds met L. G. Braun, manager of ballerina Olga Spessivtzewa. In 1936 Braun came to America to explore a movie contract for Spessivtzewa. Fitzgerald was interested in writing the screenplay, believing that he had special qualifications for the project: ". . . I should be able to deliver something entirely authentic in the matter full of invention and feeling."[1]

On 8 February 1936 Fitzgerald sent Harold Ober three possible ideas for a ballet screenplay. 1) "Zelda's awful experience of trying a difficult art too late in life to culminate with the irony that just before she cracked up she had been hoping to get little 'bits' in Diaghelief's ballet and that people kept coming to the studio who she thought were emissaries of his and turned out to be from the Folies Bergere and who thought they might make her into an American shimmy dancer. . . . One would concede to the picture people the fact that the girl might become a popular dancer in the Folies Bergere. One could conceive of a pathetic ending a la Hepburn in which because of her idealism she went on being a fifth rate 'figurine' in ballets all over Europe—this to be balanced by a compensatory love story which would make up for her the failure of her work. This would seem to me to be much the best treatment of this story."

2) "This idea has to do with an episode of some memoirs of Pavlova. It begins with a little girl briefly glimpsed and dancing in the Imperial ballet before the war. A scene later in Paris at the height of the flurry over the ballet and stranded finally with a ballet company in either Australia or Brazil for lack of funds. The climax would hinge on the catastrophe of the death of Diaghelief. . . . This story would end up in New York or Hollywood, the ballet having a new renaissance under an American growing delight in that particular art. . . ."

3) "A Russian ballet dancer finds herself in the extra line in Hollywood; they pick her out of the crowd for her good looks, give her bits of one kind or another but always on some other basis than the fact that she is a ballet dancer. This treatment of the general subject would have to close with a crash, at least I haven't thought any further than that."[2]

In early March Fitzgerald tried to set up a meeting with Sam Goldwyn to discuss the ballet ideas; and on 12 March 1936 Ober acknowledged receipt of Fitzgerald's treatment here printed, saying that it was being mailed to Goldwyn. Nothing happened.

Like Boxley in *The Last Tycoon,* Fitzgerald was still thinking of movies in terms of cheap stories. "Ballet Shoes" involves a benevolent rum-runner, a "little waif," a long-lost father, and lots of coincidence. He was still saving the sugar for himself.

M.J.B.

---

[1]*As Ever, Scott Fitz—,* ed. Matthew J. Bruccoli and Jennifer Atkinson. New York and Philadelphia: Lippincott, 1972, p. 248. Fitzgerald had already written a ballet synopsis, "Lives of the Dancers."

[2]*Ibid.,* pp. 249-230.

BALLET SHOES*

by

F. Scott Fitzgerald

In 1923 a Russian family (semi-theatrical) arrives at Ellis Island and is interminably detained. Young daughter, 18, has been in Imperial Ballet. She dances for other passengers in steerage to accordian music. She has no idea of New York, and to attract man in small launch, who may get her in before her parents, she throws an old ballet shoe at him.

He is an adventurous young rum runner coming in from the fleet -- and says that if she'll slip over the side he'll run her to New York.

They get there, but next day they can't get back. So she loses her family. He accompanies her to debarkation docks without success, and sadly she concludes they've been deported back to Europe.

The rum runner accompanies her to theatrical agencies interpreting the ways of New York to her. No go. On one pilgrimage she saves a little waif from traffic and in doing so breaks her ankle. She goes to emergency hospital and rum runner takes care of little girl. But she finds out she can never dance again. The ankle doesn't last.

Meanwhile the father <u>has</u> been admitted to U. S. but has changed his name from Krypioski to Kress, on advice received in first sequence on boat and Ellis Island by comic figure, not mentioned further in this sketch but running through picture as father's friend. He is a man who

*Published with the generous permission of Scottie Fitzgerald Smith; all rights to "Ballet Shoes" are retained by Mrs. Smith.

thinks he knows all about U. S. but never finds out anything. Father prowls streets looking for his daughter, thinking she has gone loose, stopping other girls. He speaks some English and becomes in course of time a theatrical booking agent.

On emerging from hospital heroine has decided to make little girl a great dancer as she can never be. She paints barn-like studio herself and starts ballet class with help of rum runner. He has inherited a small shoe factory and gone respectable. But she doesn't marry him, her only deep passion being for the ballet and the little girl's future, a substitute for her own.

Six years pass while the little girl grows up. The school struggles on. The great Pavlova comes to New York but she and the little girl can't afford seats. The heroine has also changed her name on her beau's advice. Frequently she has talked to her father on the phone, he asking her to supply a dozen dancers for such and such a ballet and having no idea that "Madame Serene" is his own daughter.

The time for the little girl's debut has arrived. By sacrificing everything they have the money for it. The little girl sits in their apartment at 125th Street and sends her last pair of shoes to the cobler because the ex-rum runner is to bring her some from his own little factory. She does not know that with his arms full of shoe boxes (including some ballet shoes he has made) he has been stopped at 48th Street by a detective who wants him as witness for some misdemeanor, committed six years before in his rum running days.

The time has grown short -- the young protegé finds that a pair of worn ballet shoes are the only shoes in the apartment. Putting them on she starts for the theatre with one nickel for subway. She loses it in a grating and has to walk from 125th Street to the theatrical section. She reaches there exhausted and crying, and, to the Russian girl's horror, with her feet in awful shape.

They try it however. The curtain goes up on her number and the Russian woman (the heroine) dances in the wings in time with the young girl, to keep her morale up. The number goes over.

There is a sudden interruption to the second number. The hero, intent on delivering the shoes, has broken away from the detective, but has been followed.

Now meanwhile, in the audience, the father has been impressed with young girl and gone behind scenes to engage her. He comes in on the row and in the course of it finds that his daughter is the teacher. It is implied that he can bring pressure to bear to exonerate the young man from what were only false charges.

The show is over, the stage is cleared. The Russian girl dances alone on the stage before her father who sits at the piano and plays for her. The hero and the young girl watch from the wings. The music of St. Saens, The Swan rises to a crescendo and there are tears in the father's eyes --

-- as the picture ends.

Dear Bob:

Keep reading and you'll finally come to your own adventures which you told to me one not-forgotten summer night.

Your Friend

F. Scott Fitzgerald

The Great Gatsby. Courtesy of Doris Kerr Brown.

JOSEPH CORSO

One Not-Forgotten Summer Night: Sources for Fictional Symbols of American Character in *The Great Gatsby*

"One day I was out in the Bay when I noticed a handsome, big yacht had come into the harbor—one of the finest I'd ever seen and, with a kid's curiosity, I made for it.

"I noticed they'd run it in so the stern was up and I realized that when the tide ran out, as it was sure to do, the yacht would tilt more and more and probably break in two. So I rowed along side and yelled to one of the crew, "Hey, Mister, you're going to break your boat!"

The Captain waved the boy away, but the owner told the boy to come on board.

' "What do you do?' he asked, and I told him.

' "How'd you like to work for me?' he next asked. 'I'll give you $25 a week." '

> "I was barefoot and in old clothes, tanned and dirty. . . . I had only old clothes at the beach . . . so he took me to Jim Bell's . . . and had me outfitted completely, with blue coat with brass buttons and white flannels. O, it was great!"

These curiously familiar recollections might belong to a diary account by James Gatz of North Dakota, or to a draft of the scene F. Scott Fitzgerald put into Chapter VI of *The Great Gatsby*. But they are from a *Great Neck News* account of the adventures of fourteen-year-old Robert Crozier Kerr, Jr., on Sheepshead Bay in Brooklyn, New York. The year is 1907 and the yacht belonged to Edward Robinson Gilman, general manager of the Iron Clad Manufacturing Company, among other things, of 23 Cliff Street, Brooklyn, New York.

Bob Kerr was a Great Neck resident who became Fitzgerald's friend during 1922-23. Kerr, a jeweler, philanthropist, singer, piano player, and engaging personality, exchanged stories with Fitzgerald, one of which the author immortalized. That situation, which will be dealt with in detail in section II below, is a vivid illustration of how Fitzgerald utilized such phenomena in his fiction. Like the pearl-bearing Mollusk, Fitzgerald absorbed the life flowing around him, particularly on the North Shore of Long Island in 1923, to help formulate characterizations and settings in his fiction.

Fitzgerald, in his own writings, alluded to the various influences on his fiction. With regard to *Gatsby,* he was very explicit. The most famous example is the notes he wrote on the endpaper of Andre Malraux's *Man's Hope* in 1938:

I. Glamor of Rumsies & Hitchcocks
II. Ash Heaps Memory of 125th Gt Neck
III. Goddards Dwanns Swopes
IV. A. Vegetable days in N.Y.
B. Memory of Ginevras Wedding
V. The Meeting all an invention. Mary.
VI. Bob Kerr's story. The 2nd Party.
VII. The Day in New York
VIII. The Murder (inv.)
IX. Funeral an invention

Fitzgerald had ruminated over the sources he recalled for the highlights of each chapter. However, until now, the meaning of the reference to chapter six, "Bob Kerr's story," was not known.

Robert C. Kerr, Jr. Courtesy of Doris Kerr Brown.

I. The Four Faces of James Gatz

A. The early youth of James Gatz belongs partially to Francis Scott Key Fitzgerald of St. Paul, Minnesota. Fitzgerald's own life provided the idea for his attribution to Gatsby of the belief that he "sprang from his platonic conception of himself." This idea was developed in Fitzgerald's first attempt at a third novel, a piece which, in substance, became the story "Absolution," published in June 1924 in *The American Mercury.* Its young protagonist is a Dakota farm boy named Rudolph Miller who had, as Fitzgerald had once done (see Fitzgerald's *Ledger,* p. 162), lied in confession. While talking to a priest, Father Schwartz, and attempting to tell of his mortal sin, Rudolph also confesses the following:

> "Of—of not believing I was the son of my parents."
>
> "What?" The interrogation was distinctly startled.
>
> "Of not believing that I was the son of my parents."
>
> "Why not?"
>
> "Oh, just pride," answered the penitent airily.
>
> "You mean you were too good to be the son of your parents?"
>
> "Yes, Father."

Years later, in a piece called "Author's House," Fitzgerald has an autobiographical character write in remembrance of "my first childish love of myself, my belief that I would never die like other people, and that I wasn't the son of my parents but the son of a king, a king who ruled the world."

B. It is with the second face of James Gatz that the amalgam of his early life begins to solidify. Fitzgerald introduces us to James Gatz as a restless youth from North Dakota who eschewed an education at St. Olaf Lutheran College for the promise of the open road.

In a letter to John Jamieson, dated 15 April 1934, Fitzgerald said in reference to Gatsby:

> He was perhaps created on the image of some forgotten farm type of

> Minnesota that I have known and forgotten, and associated at the same moment with some sense of romance. It might interest you to know that a story of mine, called "Absolution," in my book *All The Sad Young Men* was intended to be a picture of his early life, but that I cut it because I preferred to preserve the sense of mystery.[1]

There is evidence, however circumstantial, which points to a well-known Minnesotan who may have been the "farm type" from Dakota who attended St. Olaf College that Fitzgerald fused into the second face of young James Gatz. Old Edvart Rölvaag, (1876-1931), the Norwegian-American novelist, best remembered for his *Giants In The Earth,* appears to be the prime candidate.

Leaving his life in a fishing fleet, the adventurous Rölvaag sailed from Norway for New York in 1896, the year of Fitzgerald's birth, and eventually crossed westward to work on a relative's farm in South Dakota. Working there, he earned enough money to continue his education. He attended St. Olaf College, the Lutheran school in Northfield, Minnesota. Rölvaag did so well that he went from student to faculty member one year after his graduation in 1905. While all his fiction was originally written in Norwegian, one of the subjects he taught at St. Olaf, and an English translation of his works did not appear until the spring of 1926, Rölvaag was widely read and famous throughout Minnesota and the Middle West. He died in 1931, and his fiction today is usually relegated to the Middle-West schoolroom. That Fitzgerald knew of Rölvaag seems very likely, and that Rölvaag served some purpose in the creation of the young James Gatz as far as the "Dakota" and "St. Olaf" elements are concerned is quite possible.

C. The next face of Gatsby is the seventeen-year-old tramp searching for his fortune on the shores of Lake Superior in Michigan.

In June 1975, The Great Neck Library sponsored an exhibition entitled "F. Scott Fitzgerald And Great Neck In The 1920's." I had the honor and pleasure of contributing to the exhibition and addressing Great Neck residents one evening on the subject. On the last night of the exhibition, I was talking with various people when I was approached by two women. One of them introduced herself, and after confirming that I was Mr. Corso, she introduced the other:

"Mr. Corso, I would like you to meet the daughter of The Great Gatsby."

In fact, I had been introduced to the charming Mrs. Doris Brown, daughter of Robert C. Kerr, Jr., who as a child grew up amidst the zany doings in Great Neck during the Roaring Twenties. The exhibition had brought Mrs. Brown out with some memorabilia that had once belonged to her father. She produced for me several documents which not only illuminate Fitzgerald's reference to "Bob Kerr's story," but provide significant insights into the creative process in the making of "Jay Gatsby of West Egg, Long Island."

The most significant is Fitzgerald's letter to Kerr, the date of which can be placed around July 1924, when the Fitzgeralds were living at the Villa Marie in St. Raphael, France. This letter has not been previously published and appears now with the kind permission of Mrs. Brown.

Great Neck—I mean
St. Raphael, France
Villa Marie

Dear Bob:

Thanks for your letter & for selling the membership many thanks indeed. One hundred and fifty is more than I expected. I hope some time that I may be able to return the favor.

The part of what you told me which I am including in my novel is the ship, yatch I mean, & the mysterious yatchsman whose mistress was Nellie Bly. I have my hero occupy the same position you did & obtain it in the same way. I am calling him Robert B. Kerr instead of Robert C. Kerr to conceal his identity (this is a joke—I wanted to give you a scare. His name is Gatsby).

Best to you all from all of us and again thanks enormously for your courtesy & your trouble.

Sincerely,

Scott Fitzg ——

The reference in the first paragraph is to Fitzgerald's membership in a local country club. The balance of the letter reveals that Kerr had related to Fitzgerald a story about a yacht and a "mysterious yatchsman whose mistress was Nellie Bly."

To further clarify her father's story, Mrs. Brown produced an inscribed first edition of *Gatsby,* as well as clippings from two Great

Great Neck — Imean
St. Raphael, France
Villa Marie

Dear Bob:

Thanks for your letter + for selling the membership many thanks indeed. One hundred and fifty is more than I expected. I hope some time that I may be able to return the favor.

The part of what you told me which I am including in my novel is the ship, yatch Imean, + the mysterious yatchsman whose mistress was Nellie Bly. I have my hero occupy the same position you did + obtain it in the same way. I am calling him Robert B. Kerr instead of Robert C. Kerr to conceal his identity (This is a joke—I wanted to give you a scare. His name is Gatsby).

Best to you all from all of us and again thanks enormously for your courtesy + your trouble

Sincerely
Scott Fitzg

Courtesy of Doris Kerr Brown.

Neck newspaper articles.[2] Around April of 1925, Fitzgerald sent Bob Kerr a copy of *Gatsby,* acknowledging his debt to Kerr once again. The inscription reads:

> Dear Bob:
>
> Keep reading and you'll finally come
> to your own adventures which you told to
> me one not-forgotten summer night.
>
> Your Friend
>
> F. Scott Fitzgerald

According to the first news article, Kerr met up with a Major Edwin R. Gilman in Sheepshead Bay almost exactly the way James Gatz met with Dan Cody in Little Girl's Bay on Lake Superior. The second article[3] paraphrases some of the first but further states:

> Yes sir, it was regular Horatio Alger stuff. . . . That was "From Rags to Riches" for fair, from a dirty dory to an immaculate yacht. Bob Kerr lived on board the boat acting as his employer's secretary for three and a half years, until Mr. Gilman died. At that time he was getting $75 a week and found. In time he developed his skill at the piano and in singing. Mr. Gilman had a fine entertainer as well as secretary on board. Also the youth had a fine training in business.

The stories do contain a number of inaccuracies, which I shall set straight when I discuss the "Three Faces of Dan Cody" below.

Before we leave the young Gatsby, there is one other matter worth exploring. We are told in *Gatsby* that James Gatz had left behind him an old copy of a book called *Hopalong Cassidy* in which is inscribed the date September 12, 1906, followed by a number of resolutions the young Gatz was presumably laboring to keep. The behavior associated with these resolutions belonged to the influence of the dime-novel adventures of Horatio Alger (á la Bob Kerr) and Frank Merriwell. As a teen-ager, James Gatz, like thousands of American male youths around the turn of the century was reading publications called dime novels, particularly one called *Hopalong Cassidy.* Why did Fitzgerald choose the *Cassidy* book and not one of those of the well-known adventurers of the time to comment on the American character of

James Gatz? It seems clear that Fitzgerald saw in *Cassidy* an association with the illusory romantic American West which served to symbolize the milieu in which James Gatz was spinning his own dreams. This was the milieu later to be alloyed with Dan Cody's—that of the real American West of savage violence.

Fitzgerald was probably familiar with Clarence E. Mulford's novels about the American West, although he may never have actually read any. His citing of *Cassidy* with relation to 1906 is an error, since Mulford did not publish his novel of that name until early 1910. The first novel in which Cassidy appeared was Mulford's *Bar-20* of 1907, but it was in *Hopalong Cassidy* that Mulford's new character came into his own. Mulford, who was never west of Chicago until 1924, published twenty-seven volumes in which Cassidy appeared, including two published in 1924: *Rustler's Valley* and *Cassidy Returns.*

The significance of the *Cassidy* reference is in the fact that it serves to expose the whole area of the dime novel to review—that medium which was responsible for creating in American youth so many illusions and myths about Democracy and the American character emerging from the pioneer west. E. F. Bleiler, an authority on the American dime novel, has made observations remarkably relevant to Fitzgerald's purpose in *Gatsby* in his introduction to *Eight Dime Novels:*

> During the years of its heyday . . . the dime novel permeated young America, molding folkways in the same manner that television does today. It influenced the popular stage, and in turn was counter-influenced. Its plots affected the early movies. . . . They also offered a picture, perhaps distorted, of what was going on in otherwise inaccessible parts of the country. . . .
>
> The dime novels also reflected and served to reinforce the general cultural "myths" of the period: the ambivalence felt toward the successful criminal; admiration for the violent egotist; worship of physical strength; the Puritan ethic about wealth; the upward dynamism of progress; the righteousness of expansion; and a simplistic morality.[4]

D. The mature Jay Gatsby owes much to the personalities of two people, one of whom was, again, Fitzgerald himself. The other, we now know for certain, was Max Gerlach, a bootlegger whom Fitzgerald knew in and around Great Neck in 1922-24. Matthew J. Bruccoli has published his discoveries concerning Max Gerlach who used the term "old sport" in his conversation. But long before we knew the man's

CRABS AND KEDGE ANCHORS GAVE R. C. KERR, JR. BIG START AT 14

A Brooklyn Boy and Spent Vacations at Sheepshead Bay—Showed Major Edwin R. Gilman He Knew About Yachts—Various Routes to Maiden Lane—Gives His Two Reasons for Success

By DORIS FLEESON

REMEMBER in F. Scott Fitzgerald's "The Great Gatsby," first a novel, which the noted author wrote in Great Neck and which Owen Davis brought to the stage, that Gatsby told of being picked up as a barefoot kid along the coast by a rich yachtsman who took him about with him everywhere for a few years?

"You see," said Robert C. Kerr, Jr., to me the other evening, in talking of his early days, "Scott and I were 'buzzing' one evening and I told him what I'm telling you."

I knew with that start I ought to have the whole story for—yes, indeed—the speaker's the very same R.C.K., Jr., of the beautiful brick house on the hill on Cedar Drive, the Estates, and of No. 37 Maiden Lane, diamonds, jewelry and silverware.

"I was born in Brooklyn, October 7, 1892," Mr. Kerr told me. "I went to public school and to high school. There wasn't much money in my family and so my schooling ended with high school. I began as office boy for the American Surety Company and graduated into senior office boy for J. Charles O'Brien, Brooklyn real estate broker.

"Then I was a stenographer-typist in the Brooklyn Edison Company where I was promoted to confidential secretary to the Vice-President.

"In the Summer I'd spend my two weeks' vacation at Plum Beach, off Sheepshead Bay, with the folks. You know, that's where the old famous race-track was and it was a great amusement place in those days.

"I was still just a kid and I'd always spent vacations and Summers there, played around with the boats and fished a lot. Well, one of my stunts was to find softshell crabs and sell them to all the eating places thereabouts. It's quite a tricky task and I made good money at it for I was pretty skillful—sometimes $10 and $14 a week, which was real money for me then.

"One day I was out in the Bay when I noticed a handsome, big yacht had come into the harbor—one of the finest I'd ever seen and, with a kid's curiosity, I made for it.

"I noticed they'd run it in so the stern was up and I realized that when the tide ran out, as it was sure to do, the yacht would tilt more and more and probably break in two. So I rowed alongside and yelled to one of the crew, 'Hey, Mister, you're going to break your boat!'

"He told me to 'beat it' and then I saw the captain and repeated my advice. He joined the sailor in ordering me away when the owner appeared. He called out, 'What does the boy want?'

"And I, being a 'fresh kid,' said, 'Mister they're going to break your boat in two because they're too lazy to put down kedge anchors.'

"'Is that so? What are kedge anchors?' he asked, so I explained. (Mr. Kerr had to explain to us, too. Anyway, they hold the stern down so the boat remains on even keel.)

"Then he ordered the crew to put down the kedge anchors and invited me aboard.

"'What do you do?' he asked, and I told him.

"'How'd you like to work for me?' he next asked. 'I'll give you $25 a week.'

"I thought I could bear to quit my $16-week job for that."

An interesting and intimate view of the very well-known trio, the Bob Kerrs and Doris, in the living room of their charming home on the hill on Cedar Drive, the Estates. It's the home that Mr. Kerr bought in 1918 when visiting in Great Neck five minutes after he saw the "For Sale" sign. Which has brought here one of our most prominent and best liked families who are hard-working members in our activities and good friends to all. Mr. Kerr made a story-book start which we're sure you'll be interested to read about. (By GERMAINE KELLERMANN)

"Thus," continued Mr. Kerr, "Major Edwin R. Gilman, for it was he, hired his secretary. "I was barefoot and in old clothes, tanned and dirty. I remember that he drove me home in his car—a Thomas Flyer—and my mother came running out, scared to death.

"'How dare you ride in one of those automobiles, Bob Kerr!' she scolded me.

"I only had old clothes at the Beach and the Major wanted me to start at once so he took me to Jim Bell's—he was Fifth Avenue's big tailor then—and had me outfitted completely, with blue coat with brass buttons and white flannels. O, it was great!"

And that's what Mr. Kerr did from 1906 to 1909. It was Major Gilman's business to inspect canteens—he was in the regular army service—and the pair traveled all over and up and down the coast in the Major's yacht.

"Major Gilman died in 1909 and I had to fare forth in quest of another job." I sold Blau-Gass plants for a year, the first gas Long Island had, and I covered the Island with plants, a lot of 'em in Great Neck. Then I went into the automotive business and was Sales Manager for the Dorian Demountable Rims Company in the days when rims were manufactured separately.

"When the factories equipped their own cars, that business faded away. I became a jewelry salesman for Dieges & Clust and after a year had an opportunity to buy into a firm established for fifty years, John B. Murphy, Inc., and I became President of that.

"I resigned after eight years and in 1922 went into business for myself. I had studied gemology at Columbia for two years and worked to perfect myself in the jewelry business."

It seems strange to talk to Mr. Kerr for so many paragraphs and not mention

(*Continued on page 8, column 2*)

The Great Neck News—unlocated clipping, c. 1929. Courtesy of Doris Kerr Brown.

identity, Fitzgerald had alluded to him in correspondence with his editor at Scribner's, Maxwell Perkins:

> *I myself didn't know what Gatsby looked like or was engaged in* & you felt it. If I'd known & kept it from you you'd have been *too impressed with my knowledge to protest.* This is a complicated idea but I'm sure you'll understand. But I know now—and as a penalty for not having known first, in other words to make sure, I'm going to tell more.
>
> It seems of almost mystical signficance to me that you thot he was older—the man I had in mind, half unconsciously, *was* older (a specific individual) and evidently, without so much as a definate word, I conveyed the fact. Or rather I must qualify this Shaw Desmond trash by saying that I conveyed it without a word that I can at present and for the life of me trace.[5]

This is further emphasized in a letter Fitzgerald wrote to John Peale Bishop in August 1925:

> Also you are right about Gatsby being blurred and patchy. I never at any one time saw him clear myself—for he started out as one man I knew and then changed into myself—the amalgam was never complete in my mind.[6]

Ultimately, of course, a significant aspect of the young man called Jay Gatsby was derived from the psyche of the author. Fitzgerald had a fascination with the self-made man, as well as with the romantic with "heightened sensitivity to the promises of life . . . an extraordinary gift for hope, a romantic readiness. . . ." The months in Great Neck had given Fitzgerald the opportunity to shape the experience of his twenty-seven years into the microcosm of East Egg and West Egg life; the opportunity to sum up his own disillusionment with the American Dream against the backdrop of the northeast, examining symbolically three centuries of American history during one short summer of 1922.

II. The Three Faces of Dan Cody

A. Of course, like most other lovers of *Gatsby,* I had noted the obvious relationship between Dan Cody and Colonel William F. Cody, the famous "Buffalo Bill" of the American West. That Fitzgerald intended such an association with his "pioneer debauchee, who during one phase of American life brought back to the Eastern seaboard the savage violence of the frontier brothel and saloon," is apparent.

It should be noted that William F. Cody spent many years traveling throughout Minnesota, appearing particularly in Minneapolis and Duluth. In fact, Cody owned property in Duluth, an estate he named "Codyview" and kept from 1899–1910. His sister, Wellie Cody Westmore lived there. Today in Duluth there is a Cody Street commemorating the Colonel. It was to Duluth from Lake Superior that Dan Cody took James Gatz "and bought him a blue coat, six pairs of white duck trousers, and a yachting cap." For the geographically curious, there is a spot on the Michigan end of Lake Superior called Little Girls Point. According to Mr. Ray Maurin, of the Ironwood Area Historical Society of Ironwood, Michigan, Little Girls Point ". . . has no bay. There is no way any yacht could anchor in this place. There is no marina at Little Girls Point. It is just a river mouth into Lake Superior with no anchoring facilities."

Fitzgerald was careless at times about facts of nature and locality. In one draft of *Gatsby* he had the hero "standing on the shore" watching the *Tuolomee* and seeing that the "very dressy little ship was going to be broken up by the tide within two hours." This was true of the yacht in Sheepshead Bay, but not at all true of Lake Superior where there are no tides, as Ring Lardner pointed out in a list of corrections he provided Maxwell Perkins after reading the proof of the novel.

B. I was surprised to learn that there once was a real Dan Cody. There are two references to this Dan Cody in print. The first, somewhat veiled, is in Fitzgerald's *Ledger,* appearing on page 177 under 1923 which reads: "March-Sold This Side of Paradise and South to Montgomery. Dapper Dan. The Whitfields. . . ." The second reference appears in Sara Mayfield's *Exiles From Paradise,* in which we learn that Dan Cody was one of Montgomery's most eligible and well-to-do bachelors in 1919 and also one of Zelda Sayre's favorite beaux. In fact, Dan Cody, a strikingly handsome young man, had been one of several beaux pressing Zelda for her hand in 1919 when she had temporarily broken her engagement with Fitzgerald. By March 1923, Dan Cody had married and the visit by the Fitzgeralds was presumably cordial; but in retrospect, Fitzgerald may have linked Dan Cody of Montgomery, Alabama to the "pioneer debauchee" in *Gatsby,* not just because the allusion to Cody suited the situation but because, psychologically, the wealthy Dan Cody of Montgomery represented someone rich who

Dan Cody, 1920. Courtesy of Miss Virginia Cody.

almost stole Zelda from Fitzgerald, just as surely as Tom Buchanan of Chicago was to steal Daisy Fay of Louisville from Jay Gatsby. The reference seems to have been intended to edify one person: Scott Fitzgerald.

C. And then there was "Major Edwin R. Gilman." As I stated above, the newspaper accounts of this man attributed to Bob Kerr were not entirely accurate. For one thing, Edward Robinson Gilman was not an army Major, although he did have a commission as a Second Lieutenant from West Point in 1885.[7] Gilman was born in Pennsylvania on 13 October 1863. His West Point biography reads as follows:

> He was the son of the late Colonel Jeremiah H. Gilman, of the Class of 1856, and was appointed to the Military Academy from Maine, his father's native state. He entered the Academy July 1, 1881, graduated June 13, 1885, and was thereupon appointed Second Lieutenant, Fifth Infantry. He joined his regiment at Fort Keogh, Montana.
>
> He resigned in June, 1888, to enter business at St. Paul, Minnesota, as representative of the Thompson-Houston Electric Company (now General Electric Company) and established a large and prosperous business for his company in the Northwest.
>
> In 1890 or 1891 he went to Chicago and there organized the Great Western Electric Supply Co., of which he was president and general manager. In the financial panic in 1893 the company went out of business. Following this he took up his residence in New York City, and for a time was connected with the Merriam Publishing Co. and in promoting various concerns. In 1899 he was employed to re-organize the Iron Clad Manufacturing Co. of Brooklyn, N.Y., of which he became general manager in 1900 and later, also of the American Steel Barrel Co. With these two he remained until his death.
>
> He was Democratic candidate for Congress from the Sixth District of New York in 1908 and was defeated. The nomination again was offered to him in the fall of 1910, but his health made acceptance impossible.
>
> Mr. Gilman was a member of the Army and Navy Club and Lawyers' Club of New York City, New York Yacht Club, The Canarsie Yacht Club, The Automobile Club of America and the Aero Club. He was vice-president of the Brooklyn Democratic Club and president of the Waterway League of Greater New York and Long Island.

He never married, and was buried beside his father and mother, at Kensico, N.Y.

His sister Katherine, (the wife of Dr. John E. MacKenty of New York City), survives him.

Edward Gilman was a self-made man, very successful and well-known along the east coast of America, and prior to his death on 9 February 1911, at Sheepshead Bay, he apparently had some relationship with that most famous of early female reporters, Elizabeth Cochrane Seaman, popularly known as Nellie Bly. The only allusion to the alleged liaison we have is Fitzgerald's, in his letter to Bob Kerr. Presumably, had Gilman and Mrs. Seaman been having an affair, Kerr would have been privy to it in his capacity of secretary to Gilman. Now we can fully understand Fitzgerald's reference to "Ella Kaye, the newspaper woman" in *Gatsby,* and why her relationship with Cody would have been "common knowledge to the turgid sub or suppressed journalism of 1902." However, there are no references to it in books and articles on Nellie Bly published over the last 53 years, since her death on 27 January 1922 at St. Marks Hospital in New York.

Elizabeth Cochrane, like Gilman, was born in Pennsylvania, and it was she, as a reporter for the *New York World,* who made headlines with her exposé in 1887 of the lunatic asylum on Blackwell's Island (later Welfare, now Roosevelt Island, and the same one Nick Carraway alludes to in Chapter IV of *Gatsby*). Her greatest claim to fame, though, was her trip around the world, alone, from 14 November 1889 until 25 January 1890. The trip lasted a bit more than 72 days, breaking the fictional trip of Jules Verne's Phineas Fogg. She was greeted first in Jersey City and then elsewhere in America with the hoopla accorded today's astronauts. In 1895 at the age of 28, somewhat inexplicably, she married Robert L. Seaman, a Brooklyn manufacturer, who was over 70 years old at the time. That the marriage raised eyebrows is quite likely. In fact, it was not long before newspaper stories cast shadows over the relationship between Nellie Bly and her husband. The *New York Times* printed the following article on 10 November 1895, less than six months after the wedding:

> Robert Seaman, old and a millionaire, married Elizabeth Cochrane better known as "Nellie Bly" last Spring. Mrs. Seaman last night caused the arrest of Robert Hanson, Superintendent of a private detective agency in Catskill, N.Y.

Edward R. Gilman, c. 1903. Courtesy of the U.S. Military Academy, West Point.

Hanson, in a cab, had been following Mrs. Seaman, also in a cab, the greater part of the day. He said, when he was arrested at Thirty-fourth Street and Broadway, that he had been employed by Mr. Seaman to follow Mrs. Seaman. He made a note of her every stopping place.

After the arrest, Mrs. Seaman called to her driver "Barney! To the Imperial Hotel!"

Her husband, whose home is at 15 West Thirty-seventh Street went to the West Thirtieth Street Station and gave bail for Hanson.

This story indicates two significant things: first, that Seaman had ıspicions concerning Nellie's behavior and secondly, that the Seaans may not have been living together. However, not all the controv'sy surrounded Nellie, as is indicated in another *Times* article printed n 24 November 1895:

Chicago. Nov. 23. The litigation between L. H. Bisbee, a Chicago Attorney, and Robert Seaman, the New York millionaire, and husband of "Nellie Bly," involving the recovery of $50,000 from the lawyer, assumed a sensational phase yesterday in the Court of Master in Chancery Leaming, before whom evidence is being taken.

In a long cross-examination conducted for the millionaire, Mr. Bisbee stated that he visited New York in 1887 and effected a settlement between Mr. Seaman and Ernestine Sanderson who claimed to be Mr. Seaman's common-law wife, whereby the woman was to go away and cease to be a burden upon his mind. The defendent said he had a verbal agreement with the millionaire that his services in effecting a release of the woman's claims were to liquidate any amount of money for which Mr. Seaman might hold Mr. Bisbee's notes.

John C. Patterson, counsel for Mr. Seaman, was surprised at the revelation of the "woman in the case." Mr. Bisbee said Mr. Seaman deeded property to the woman, and a lot of jewels, and that Mr. Seaman agreed to relinquish all claims against the defendent on the further payment of $5,000.

How and when Nellie Bly and Edward Gilman met is not yet known, ut we do know from the *New York Times* obituary for Nellie Bly on

28 January 1922, the following: "In 1895 she married Robert L. Seaman, forty years her senior, President of the American Steel Barrel Company and the Iron Clad Manufacturing Company." This is a confirmation of what appears in another *New York Times* article announcing Seaman's death in March of 1904:

> Robert Seaman, President of the Iron Clad Manufacturing Company, died yesterday at his home, 15 West Thirty-seventh Street. Mr. Seaman, who was eighty years old, was knocked down by a horse three weeks ago, and died from the injuries received. Mr. Seaman's wife was with him at the time of his death. She was Miss Elizabeth Cochrane, and was widely known at the time of marriage in 1895 as "Nellie Bly." Mr. Seaman was at one time a Director of the Merchant's National Bank.

It was noted above that in 1899 Edward Gilman "was employed to re-organize the Iron Clad Manufacturing Co. of Brooklyn, N.Y., of which he became general manager in 1900 and later, also of the American Steel Barrel Co." We may surmise from this information that by 1899 or 1900 Gilman and Mrs. Seaman had met. Whether this was their first contact remains unknown. Gilman came to New York City around 1894 and could have known Nellie Bly before her marriage. It is also possible that he and Nellie were the source of Robert Seaman's concern in November 1895, but it is not likely that Seaman would trust and hire Gilman several years later if he knew of any such affair.

When Robert Seaman died in 1904, very advanced in age and blind, Elizabeth Seaman was still young at 38 and Gilman was 40. Their liaison probably peaked between then and 1910. We know that he declined to run for Congress out of New York in 1910 because "his health made acceptance impossible," and he must have been inactive during the last year or so of his life. This was not the "physically robust" Dan Cody of *Gatsby* but could have been the Dan Cody "on the verge of soft-mindedness. . . ." On the other hand, Fitzgerald may have been aware, possibly through Bob Kerr, that Robert Seaman was extremely infirm and blind during his last years, although it was an accident which killed him, and that there was a struggle over the estate left by Seaman. In fact, two wills were set forth within months of his death. According to *New York Times* articles of 17 June and 2 September 1904, Nellie Bly was able to make claim to everything Seaman left:

> The will of Robert Seaman was filed yesterday in the office of the

Courtesy of the New-York Historical Society, New York City.

Surrogate. He leaves the bulk of his estate, of which the value is not stated, though it was believed to be large, to his widow, Elizabeth C. Seaman, and some nephews, grand-nephews, and grand-nieces. He makes bequests of shares of stock in the Iron Clad Manufacturing Company to a number of its employes.

To Sarah Fawcett, who was "in his household," he leaves $10,000; to a friend, Ester A. Savage, $15,000; to Ernestine Sanderson, $5,000; to Catherine B. Lockwood, $5,000.

His grand-nieces, Arlisle and Nellie Young, will each receive $10,000, and the residuary estate will go to his nephew, William H. Seaman and his nieces, Elizabeth S. Johns and Emma S. Bennet. Mr. Seaman's wife was once a newspaper woman known as "Nellie Bly."

Through her counsel, Robert W. Hardle, Mrs. Elizabeth Cochrane Seaman, also known as "Nellie Bly," widow of Robert Seaman, who died on March 11, last, filed a second will executed by Mr. Seaman on November 29, 1897, in the Surrogate's office yesterday. This will leaves all the property to the widow.

On June 16 last David Otis, an executor and residuary legatee of Robert Seaman, filed a will bearing date of December 24, 1895, in which Mrs. Seaman got only the bulk of the estate, specific bequests being left to a nephew, two nieces, and several grand-nephews and grand-nieces, amounting to $80,000. The second will is dated in Wiesbaden, Germany.

These circumstances indicate that Seaman made the first will out shortly after the incident with Nellie and the detective in November of that same year. It also provides the setting for what Fitzgerald may have had in mind when he alluded to Ella Kaye's attempts at separating Dan Cody from his wealth. The second will, which was made in Germany during one of several trips the Seamans are known to have made early in their marriage, gave Nellie full control of Seaman's fortune upon his death. Seaman was 73 at the time and was experiencing approaching blindness. It is not difficult to imagine Nellie working her will on the aged millionaire, resulting in her becoming the sole beneficiary of his estate. The will reads:

> I give and bequeath all my property personal and real of any kind and in any place whatsoever to my wife Elizabeth C. Seaman and hereby appoint her sole Executrix.
> This is my Last Will and Testament.
>
> Robert Seaman
>
> Witnessed:
> Carl Ebbighausen
> Alfred Raab
>
> Wiesbaden 29 November 1897

The interesting circumstance concerning this will is that its authenticity was contested by Seaman's relatives, those who had been cut out altogether. However, it was not until 21 May 1909 that the Honorable Abner C. Thomas, Surrogate for Manhattan County, ruled the following:

> Now, therefore, upon all the papers and proceedings herein, it is hereby Ordered Adjudged and Decreed that said instrument purporting to be the last will and Testament of said Robert Seaman deceased bearing date the 29th day of November, 1897 was properly executed and is genuine and valid; that the said Robert Seaman at the time of the execution of said instrument was in all respects competent to execute the same and was not under restraint or undue influence. . . .

Nellie had attempted to assume her husband's responsibilities during his incapacity before death, with the help, no doubt, of Edward Gilman. However, by the time the estate was settled and Gilman had himself died, Nellie had had little success with her properties. Her obituary in the *New York Times* of 28 January 1922 reads:

> . . . on Mr. Seaman's death . . . she took entire charge of the properties. Luck turned against her, however, and a series of forgeries by her employes, disputes of various sorts, bankruptcy and a mass of vexations and costly litigation swallowed up Nellie Bly's fortune, however, and she returned to journalism with her old spirit. At the time of her death she was a member of the staff of the New York Evening Journal.

The one aspect of this situation that remains unclear is what Gilman's role in the operation of the Iron Clad Manufacturing Company was between Seaman's death and his own.[8] We are told in his West Point biography that he remained with the company until he died. However, the fact that Seaman's estate was not finally settled until May of 1909 indicates that the problems Nellie had with her husband's fortune and businesses may not have begun until after Gilman was already terminally ill, or perhaps, after his death in 1911. It is not likely that the businesses would have faltered while Gilman, an astute businessman, was still alive and managing them. It is also probable that the years between Seaman's death and Gilman's (1904-1911) were those when the relationship was stabilized and young Bob Kerr learned of it. Since Kerr allegedly spent the three and one-half years prior to Gilman's death on Gilman's yacht, it is likely that the affair was either still a fact or was waning during the last part of the same period. The known facts in the matter, when compared with Kerr's story, tend to substantiate Kerr's thorough knowledge of the situation, an awareness due perhaps to Gilman's trust or Kerr's alertness, or both.

It is purely coincidental, I believe, that Gilman was employed in Saint Paul, Minnesota when Edward Fitzgerald and Mollie McQuillan were married there in 1890; but it is nonetheless interesting to note that both mentor and parent of Gatsby and Fitzgerald were salesmen in the Middle West (Gilman with the Thompson-Houston Electric Company, and Fitzgerald with the American Rattan & Willow Works and Proctor & Gamble) who came east to New York (Gilman to New York City and Fitzgerald to Buffalo), one to succeed and one to fail.

D. The remaining elements of the Dan Cody characterization are interesting in themselves for their elucidation of another aspect of *Gatsby*. I noted earlier that Gilman's yacht was allegedly called the *Kemah,* although this appears to have been a fabrication on Kerr's part. Whatever its actual name, Fitzgerald chose the name *Tuolomee* for Dan Cody's yacht. It was an apt choice since Tuolumne County in California was the scene of considerable gold mining in the 1850's and 1860's. But the key to understanding Fitzgerald's choice lies in the awareness that Mark Twain once lived in a mining camp on Jackass Hill in Tuolumne County, which he wrote about in *Roughing It.* Fitzgerald was probably also aware of a much publicized event which took place at Jackass Hill on 10 June 1922 while he was at Dellwood Lake in Minnesota. The *St. Paul Dispatch* was the only Minnesota paper to carry the story, headlining the A.P. dispatch "TWAIN'S CABIN DEDICATED. Author Lived in Shack During California Gold Rush." The *New York Times* story did make mention of the fact that William D. Stephens, Governor of California, dedicated the sight as a landmark in Tuolumne County. But the other significant aspect of this matter is the fact that the largest gold mine south of the town of Tuolumne is the *Buchanan* Mine which has yielded over $2 million. Fitzgerald may have intended a link between the fortune of Dan Cody and the wealth associated with the Buchanan family of Chicago.

III. Tommy Hitchcock, Allan Dwan, The Wilsons, Daisy, Jordan, and The Owl-Eyed Man

Back in Great Neck, New York where Fitzgerald lived at 6 Gateway Drive in the Great Neck Estates, the social life was thriving, and from October 1922 to May 1924, Fitzgerald absorbed much that was subsequently reflected in *Gatsby*.

To begin with, in the list in Malraux's book, Fitzgerald attributes elements of the Buchanans' high life in Chapter I to the "Glamor of Rumsies and Hitchcocks." Charles Cary Rumsey and Tommy Hitchcock, Jr. had large estates in Old Westbury, Long Island (actually, Thomas Hitchcock, Sr. was still alive at the time), and Hitchcock was noted as one of the country's best polo players at age 23. He and Fitzgerald were friendly, and in a letter to his daughter Scottie in 1939, Fitzgerald praised Hitchcock:

> . . . who came back from England in 1919 already a newspaper hero in his escapes from Germany and the greatest polo player in the world—and went up to Harvard in the same year to become *a freshman*—because he had the humility to ask himself "Do I know anything?" That combination is what forever will put him in my pantheon of heroes.[9]

It is not too difficult to see how Tom Buchanan became a polo player, nor how the young military hero Jay Gatsby went to Oxford after the war. Tommy Hitchcock was one of the few very wealthy people Fitzgerald was close to in his lifetime, and one that along with Gerald Murphy, Fitzgerald admired.

The first party at Gatsby's in Chapter III was one Fitzgerald created out of experiences he had at those given by the "Goddards. Dwanns. Swopes." Movie director Alan Dwan and editor Herbert Bayard Swope were well-known personalities of the 1920's, but the Goddard alluded to is not. For the record, Charles Harold Goddard, like Bob Kerr, was a Great Neck Estates neighbor of Fitzgerald's. Goddard had large real estate holdings, and he and his wife Grace lived with their two children and five servants in a large home a couple of blocks from Fitzgerald's place. With regard to Dwan, there is a good possibility that he was the model for the movie director referred to in the scene at Gatsby's second party in Chapter VI. Dwan was working very closely at that time with Gloria Swanson. An entry for July 1923 in the *Ledger* reads "Parties at Allan Dwanns. Gloria Swanson and the movie crowd."

On the subject of Daisy and her friend Jordan Baker, I suggest a connection with Father Fay. Jordan Baker's Aunt in *Gatsby* is Mrs. Sigourney Howard, and Daisy Buchanan's maiden name is Fay. One of Fitzgerald's early and most influential mentors was Monsignor Sigourney Fay; he was used for a character in *This Side of Paradise.*

Finally, we come to the Owl-Eyed man we meet twice in *Gatsby.* As I previously suggested to the audience in Great Neck at the Fitzgerald Exhibition, my belief is that the Owl-Eyed man was based on Ring Lardner, Fitzgerald's only close friend in Great Neck. That Lardner and Fitzgerald shared a taste for literature, practical jokes, and liquor while together in Great Neck is a matter of record. It is also true that Lardner was one of the few people to have read, contributed to and otherwise criticized the proofs of *Gatsby.* There is some evidence that the men shared certain of the ideas on the American character seen in *Gatsby.*

The reference to "owl eyes" is one clearly associated with Lardner: it was a nickname he picked up while following the White Sox in Chicago as a sportswriter during the early 1900's—the team that Meyer Wolfshiem fixed.

This concludes a first examination of some of the experiences of Scott Fitzgerald, spanning the first 27 years of his life, which helped shape *The Great Gatsby.* It seems fitting in this Bicentennial year, the year in which we will celebrate the 80th anniversary of Fitzgerald's birth, that we can say with more certainty and understanding of his great American novel, "So that's what he was thinking—that's what was on his mind when he wrote it." The creative process is a bit clearer. If nothing else, I hope that I have conveyed with some clarity how this literary genius took the many disparate elements of his time and forged a fable that remains the most compelling examination of the illusion-studded ethos of the American Republic written to date.

---

[1]*The Letters of F. Scott Fitzgerald,* ed. Andrew Turnbull. New York: Scribners, 1963, p. 509.

[2]Doris Fleeson, "Crabs and Kedge Anchors Gave R. C. Kerr, Jr. Big Start At 14," undated clipping from the *Great Neck News;* John Yard, *Duograph,* undated pamphlet published by the *Great Neck News.*

[3]The second article includes the following pertinent material:

> When Bob was fourteen, his parents had a dory at Sheepshead Bay. One day he was rowing into Sheepshead Bay inlet when he saw the famous schooner yacht "Kemah" stranded on a bar. He yelled to those on deck to get out a kedge anchor from the mast or the craft would break in two. The captain waved the boy away but the owner, Edwin R. Gilman, then President of the Guarantee Trust Company, told the boy to come on board.
>
> Bob put out the kedge anchor where he thought it should be and then Mr. Gilman wanted to know all about him.

[4]New York: Dover, 1974.

[5]*Letters,* pp. 172-173.

[6]*Letters,* p. 358.

[7]Besides the discrepancies in first name and military rank, the Kerr articles include the following errors:

A. The reference to Gilman's being the President of the Guarantee Trust Company. Sources at the Morgan Guaranty Trust Company, 15 Broad Street, N.Y., advised that Alexander J. Hemphill, not Gilman was the company's leader during the period in question.

B. The reference to Gilman's owning the yacht *Kemah.* Based on research by Ms. Elsa Resnick, Reference Librarian at the Great Neck Library in New York, the yacht *Kemah* was owned by Thomas Alsop of Connecticut in 1908 and 1909. The ship was built in 1906 and was first named *America,* a fact which along with the other points appears in *Lloyd's Register of American Yachts.*

C. The reference to Gilman's death in 1909. Edward R. Gilman died on 9 February 1911 of carcinoma of the prostate and chronic hepatitis at his home in Sheepshead Bay, Brooklyn, N.Y.

D. The reference to Gilman's occupation as a canteen inspector for the Army. All factual information known about Edward R. Gilman establishes that he left the military in 1888 and was involved in numerous business ventures until his death. The reference to canteen inspection is either a complete fabrication or there may be a remote chance that the Iron Clad Manufacturing Company produced canteens under a government contract.

[8]For the record, Edward Gilman did not appear to benefit in any unusual way from his position with Seaman's companies or his relationship to Nellie Bly. Gilman never became an officer of Seaman's companies, and at the time of his death in 1911, he left less than $1,000 in his estate. There was a search for his will but none was found. In May, 1913, Letter of Administration were granted to J. Holly Clark, Jr. of Flushing, N.Y. who had a claim of $330.22 against Gilman's estate. Clark had assumed the bill due the Stephen Merritt Burial and Cremation Company for materials furnished and services rendered for Gilman's funeral. It appears that Gilman and Nellie Bly may have ended their liaison or that Nellie could not come forth at the time of Seaman's death. In any event, since Clark and Gilman's survivors could not locate a will, Clark's petition was granted and the matter closed. Strange as it may seem, Edward Gilman was nearly poor when he died.

[9]*Letters,* p. 49.

DOROTHY BALLWEG GOOD

"A Romance and a Reading List": The Literary References in *This Side of Paradise*

"Tis the good reader that makes the good book; in every book he finds passages with confidences or asides hidden from all else and unmistakably meant for his ear."

Emerson

Lionel Trilling has written that "it is hard to overestimate the benefit which came to Fitzgerald from his having consciously placed himself in the line of the great. He was a 'natural,' but did not have the contemporary American novelist's belief that if he compares himself with the past masters, or if he takes thought—which for a writer, means really knowing what his predecessors have done—he will endanger the integrity of his natural gifts . . . and to perceive how continuously he thought about literature, is to have some clue to the secret of the continuing power of Fitzgerald's work."[1] Concurring with Trilling's analysis and "demonstrating its rightness" in his article "Scott Fitzgerald's Reading," John Kuehl examines the books and authors with which Fitzgerald was familiar to prove that he had "intellectual courage" and energy as well as "a connection with tradition and with mind."[2] Critics such as Alfred Kazin, Paul Rosenfeld, Malcolm Cowley, and Edmund Wilson have disparaged Fitzgerald's intellectual capacities, and Kuehl quotes Glenway Wescott as stating: ". . . I think Fitzgerald must have been the worst educated man in the world."[3] After analyzing Kuehl's article and Trilling's assessment, one must conclude that Wescott has made an erroneous judgment. Fitzgerald was well-read; had "an unwavering conviction that he could produce out of his own head stories as entertaining as any he had read";[4] and was capable of intelligently utilizing in his own writings what he had read. *This Side of Paradise* is, in part, a product of Fitzgerald's prodigious reading habits.

Fitzgerald once termed his first novel "a Romance and a Reading List"; it is an apt description, but easily misinterpreted. Perhaps a more precise title would read "a philosophy and a reading list." Fitzgerald is indeed a romantic in the purest sense of the word, which is reflected through the literary references made in the novel. Within the pages of *This Side of Paradise* the author mentions, or quotes from, some 70 literary works including novels, non-fiction, plays, and poems with such diverse titles as *Little Women, Faust, Mrs. Warren's Profession,* and *For the Honor of the School.* Fitzgerald not only names individual works but some 100 various authors and philosophers, both historical and contemporary. Plato is mentioned, as well as Huysmans, Nietzsche, and Chesterton. Prominent poets such as Byron, Browning, Shakespeare, and Tennyson find their way into the text in addition to more obscure novelists such as Fannie Hurst, John Fox, Jr., and Jeffery Farnol. An analysis of the works and authors cited provides one with a literary yardstick of the pre-World War I generation of readers. The critical reader must ask why the literary references are so numerous, and if they serve a thematic function in the novel. Why, for example, does the narrator see Amory as a modern Heraclitus at one point in his development or why does Amory read *Vandover and the Brute* and *A Portrait of the Artist as a Young Man* when he is rejected by Rosalind Connage? Why is he not reading Robert Chambers or Booth Tarkington? What is indicated to the careful reader concerning Amory's state of mind at these times? Amory's reading tastes at particular periods reveal a good deal about his developing character and philosophical outlook; they are not solely literary padding.

It should be remembered that an immature F. Scott Fitzgerald wrote

This Side of Paradise; he was striving to have a work accepted for publication and yearning to establish a literary reputation. It seems natural that he would want to impress his readers and critics with his literary background, or to at least let them know how much he knew. Fitzgerald is, like Amory when he first encounters Thomas Park D'Invilliers, attempting to impress. Amory at this meeting is reading George Bernard Shaw's originally banned play, *Mrs. Warren's Profession,* and obviously enjoying what he is reading although ignorant of Shaw's reputation; the subject matter of the play is of interest to the young reader who soon discovers that he is no literary match for Tom, but undauntedly "discussed books by the dozens—books he had read, read about, books he had never heard of, rattling off lists of titles with the facility of a Brentano's clerk. D'Invilliers was partially taken in and wholly delighted."[5] The word "partially" is important. His anticipated audience for *This Side of Paradise,* like Tom, will not be "taken in" totally by his literary allusions, but they will be "delighted" with what these allusions indicate to the reader concerning Amory, and also Fitzgerald. By examining these selections, one can see that a very subtle commentary on the main character is provided throughout the novel. Fitzgerald's craft would grow beyond this technique, but in his first full-length work he is attempting to reveal the character of Amory Blaine, and perhaps his own character, by showing the literature and philosophies that influenced the protagonist's development. Fitzgerald writes of Amory that he "had grown up to a thousand books, a thousand lies. . . ."[6] To a great extent Amory's personal history is the history of the books he has read. *This Side of Paradise* indeed reveals an education of a personage through reading lists.

As Trilling has stated, Fitzgerald "consciously placed himself in the line of the great." He, like his earliest protagonist, Amory Blaine, has a code to live by, "which, as near as it can be named, was a sort of aristocratic egotism."[7] Each sees himself as unique, and at the conclusion of *This Side of Paradise* Amory "was where Goethe was when he began *Faust;* and where Conrad was when he wrote *Almayer's Folly.*"[8] Why is the comparison with these particular authors and works made? *Almayer's Folly* was Conrad's first novel and the start of an important literary career. Conrad was at that time similar to Amory: "An intellectual personage not very well known at present,"[9] but anonymity was to be short-lived.

Amory is also where Goethe was when he began his greatest accomplishment which was to become his life's work; *Faust* was not completed until immediately before his death. Amory has such a commitment to creativity. It was not necessary for Fitzgerald to relate this information to his readers; his literary references make the more subtle commentary, and disprove Kazin's statement that "Fitzgerald's actual intelligence was never equal to his talent."[10] Although immature, Fitzgerald was a skilled craftsman aware of the manipulative powers of the adept author. Through a simple technique of citing book titles, the complex philosophy and personality of a character become intelligible.

Like Fitzgerald in 1920, Amory is inaugurating his adult life; "it was the becoming he dreamed of," and, similar to Burne Holiday who "was so evidently developing," Amory "considered that he was doing the same."[11] He "was proud of the fact that he could never become a mechanical or scientific genius,"[12] but from no other heights is he debarred. *This Side of Paradise* describes an education for greatness, and that education includes prolific reading.

The Kuehl article is helpful in understanding the significance of the works and authors cited in *This Side of Paradise*. Kuehl's sources include "Fitzgerald's published canon, his notebooks, his letters, the volumes he gave to Miss Sheilah Graham during the late '30's (about 200), and the volumes he owned (about 1,000)."[13] Kuehl concludes that although Fitzgerald's reading was fairly wide, it was "quite selective" in that "he picked the periods, the artists, and the genres that were necessary to his own particular genius—the lyric poetry of the English Renaissance (Shakespeare), the early nineteenth century (romantic poets, especially Keats), the late nineteenth century (French symbolists, Browning, Swinburne, Kipling), the twentieth century (Brooke, Eliot); the novel of social realism (Thackeray, Butler, Norris, Dreiser, Proust, Wharton), the 'novel of selection' (Flaubert, James, Joyce, Conrad, Cather, Hemingway). When he outgrew certain authors, for example Wilde, Wells and Mackenzie, he found new, more helpful models."[14] These selective periods and authors are reflected in Amory's reading habits.

Commencing his education with books that differ from the average child's reading, and consuming them profusely and heterogeneously, Amory is continually attracted to the romantics. He knows that he is an atypical person and must find a method of expressing this knowledge to the world. Like William Benham in *The Research Magnificent* Amory "spent the greater part of his life studying and experimenting in the noble possibilities of man. He never lost his absurd faith in that conceivable splendour."[15] In a dialogue with himself, Amory reveals that he has found that he can always do the things that people do in books; they have profoundly influenced him. The annotated lists appended here will perhaps provide insights into the novel and into the characterization of Amory Blaine which cannot be gained elsewhere.

Through the random literary references and the five extensive reading lists, Amory's maturing reading acumen, intellectual growth, and moral development are reflected. They suggest the influences that are forming his impressionable personality, and as James E. Miller has commented: "Like many of Fitzgerald's technical devices, the reading list has a quality of enumeration which suggests documentation."[16] It would have been quite dull to read descriptions of the various stages of Amory's intellectual and personal development; the reading lists subtly provide this information and also tantalize the reader to investigate the significance of the references. They also provide a testament to Fitzgerald's adeptness as a young author.

In his notebooks, Fitzgerald wrote "books are like brothers" and he once referred to an early version of *This Side of Paradise* as a prose, modernistic *Childe Harold.* The author often thought of Amory in connection with the books he had read, and an awareness of Fitzgerald's accomplishment in *This Side of Paradise* is gained through an examination of the literary references made throughout the work. A study of them is an education, for one discovers that Fitzgerald understood the implications of the references he made, and these implications add much to the work. Fitzgerald was equal to the books he read, and Edmund Wilson did him a serious disservice when he stated: "He has been given imagination without intellectual control of it."[17] *This Side of Paradise* is evidence of his control, and further investigation is needed regarding the references made to fully appreciate their import.

---

[1]Lionel Trilling, "F. Scott Fitzgerald" in *F. Scott Fitzgerald: The Man and His Work,* ed. Alfred Kazin (Cleveland: World, 1951), p. 201.

[2]*Ibid.*

[3]Glenway Wescott, "The Moral of F. Scott Fitzgerald" in *F. Scott Fitzgerald: The Man and His Work,* ed. Alfred Kazin (Cleveland: World, 1951), p. 122.

[4]Donald A. Yates, "The Road to 'Paradise': Fitzgerald's Literary Apprenticeship" in *F. Scott Fitzgerald,* ed. Kenneth Eble (New York: McGraw-Hill, 1973), p. 19.

[5]F. Scott Fitzgerald, *This Side of Paradise* (New York: Scribners, 1920), p. 56 (51—Page references to the Scribner Library edition follow in parentheses).

[6]*Ibid.,* p. 282 (262).

[7]*Ibid.*, p. 19 (18).
[8]*Ibid.*, p. 284 (264).
[9]*Ibid.*, p. 290 (269).
[10]Alfred Kazin, "An American Confession" in *F. Scott Fitzgerald: The Man and His Work*, ed. Alfred Kazin (Cleveland: World, 1951), p. 179.
[11]*This Side of Paradise,* p. 136 (124).
[12]*Ibid.*, p. 20 (18).
[13]John Kuehl, "Scott Fitzgerald's Reading" in *Profile of F. Scott Fitzgerald,* ed. Matthew J. Bruccoli (Columbus: Charles E. Merrill, 1971), p. 60.
[14]*Ibid.*, p. 59.
[15]H. G. Wells, *The Research Magnificent* (New York: Macmillan, 1915), p. 4.
[16]James E. Miller, *F. Scott Fitzgerald: His Art and His Technique* (New York: New York University, 1967), p. 18.
[17]Edmund Wilson, "Fitzgerald Before The Great Gatsby" in *F. Scott Fitzgerald: The Man and His Work,* ed. Alfred Kazin (Cleveland: World, 1951), p. 77.

TITLES MENTIONED IN *THIS SIDE OF PARADISE*

The first page reference is to the 1920 text; the Scribner Library page reference follows in parentheses.

Asterisks indicate an inaccurate title or a misspelling of a title by Fitzgerald in *This Side of Paradise;* the correct form is given in parentheses.

In every case, the edition cited in this list is an edition Fitzgerald could have seen; I have no way of determining the edition he actually read.

Page 3 (3) *Encyclopedia Britannica*

Page 4 (4) *Do and Dare,* 1905
Novel by Horatio Alger
New York, Hurst

Page 4 (4) **Frank on the Mississippi,* 1867
(*Frank on the Lower Mississippi*)
Novel by Charles Austin Fosdick [Harry Castlemon]
Cincinnati, Carroll

Page 5 (5)	*Fêtes Galantes*, 1869 Poetry collection by Paul Verlaine
Page 17 (16)	*Arsene Lupin,* 1909 Play by Francis de Croisset and Maurice Leblanc
Page 18 (17)	*For the Honor of the School*—unidentified children's book
Page 18 (17)	*Little Women,* 1901 Novel by Louisa May Alcott Boston, Little Brown
Page 18 (17)	*The Common Law,* 1911 Novel by Robert W. Chambers New York, Appleton
Page 18 (17)	*Sapho,* 1905 Novel by Alphonse Daudet New York, Societé des Beaux-Arts
Page 18 (17)	*"Dangerous Dan McGrew," 1907 ("The Shooting of Dan McGrew") Poem by Robert W. Service
Page 18 (17)	*The Broad Highway,* 1911 Novel by Jeffery Farnol Boston, Little Brown
Page 18 (17)	"The Fall of the House of Usher," 1839 Short story by Edgar Allan Poe
Page 18 (17)	*Three Weeks,* 1907 Novel by Elinor Glyn New York, Duffield
Page 18 (17)	*Mary Ware, the Little Colonel's Chum,* 1908 Novel by Annie Fellows Johnston Boston, L.C. Page
Page 18 (17)	*"Ghunga Dhin," 1892

	("Gunga Dhin") Poem by Rudyard Kipling
Page 18 (17)	*Police Gazette*—Gaslight era American magazine
Page 18 (17)	*Jim-Jam Jems*—joke magazine edited by Captain Fawcett
Page 29 (27)	*The Beloved Vagabond,* 1906 Novel by William J. Locke New York, Lane
Page 29 (27)	*Sir Nigel,* 1906 Novel by Sir Arthur Conan Doyle New York, McClure, Phillips
Page 32 (29)	*The White Company,* 1891 Novel by Sir Arthur Conan Doyle New York, Lovell
Page 32 (30)	*The Little Millionaire,* 1911 Muscial play by George M. Cohan
Page 36 (33)	"L'Allegro," 1632 Poem by John Milton
Page 36 (33)	*The Gentleman from Indiana,* 1899 Novel by Booth Tarkington New York, Doubleday and McClure
Page 36 (33)	*The New Arabian Nights,* 1882 Short story collection by Robert Louis Stevenson New York, Holt
Page 36 (33)	*The Morals of Marcus Ordeyne,* 1909 Novel by William J. Locke New York, Lane
Page 36 (33)	*The Man Who Was Thursday: A Nightmare,* 1908 Novel by Gilbert Keith Chesterton New York, Dodd, Mead

Page 36 (33) *Stover at Yale,* 1911
Novel by Owen Johnson
New York, Stokes

Page 36 (33) *Dombey and Son,* 1848
Novel by Charles Dickens

Page 52 (47) *Golden Treasury of the Best Songs and Lyrical Poems of the English Language,* 1899
Poetry collection edited by Francis Turner Palgrave
New York, Stokes and Brothers

Page 55 (49) *Mrs. Warren's Profession: An Unpleasant Play,* 1905
Play by George Bernard Shaw
New York, Brentano's

Page 55 (50) "Marpessa," 1897
Poem by Stephen Phillips

Page 55 (50) "Come Into the Garden, Maude," 1855
Poem by Alfred Tennyson

Page 56 (51) *Patience,* 1881
Opera by Gilbert and Sullivan
New York, Hitchcock

Page 56 (51) *The Picture of Dorian Gray,* 1910
Novel by Oscar Wilde
Paris, Carrington

Page 57 (51) *"Mystic and Somber Dolores," 1866 ("Dolores")
Poem by Algernon Charles Swinburne

Page 57 (51) *"Belle Dame Sans Merci," 1819
("La Belle Dame Sans Merci")
Poem by John Keats

Page 59 (53) **Poems and Ballades,* 1866
(Poems and Ballads)

Poetry collection by Algernon Charles Swinburne

Page 93 (84) *"The Ode to a Nightingale," 1819
("To A Nightingale")
Poem by John Keats

Page 116 (106) **What Every Middle-Aged Woman Ought to Know,* 1918
(What Every Woman Knows)
Play by Sir James Matthew Barrie
New York, Scribner

Page 116 (106) *The Spell of the Yukon and Other Verses,* 1916
Poetry collection by Robert W. Service
New York, Dodd, Mead

Page 130 (119) *The New Machiavelli,* 1910
Novel by H. G. Wells
New York, Duffield

Page 131 (120) *None Other Gods,* 1911
Novel by Robert Hugh Benson
St. Louis, Bitterder

Page 131 (120) *Sinister Street,* 1919
Novel by Compton Mackenzie
New York, Appleton

Page 131 (120) *The Research Magnificent,* 1915
Novel by H. G. Wells
New York, Macmillan

Page 134 (123) *Masses*—socialist magazine

Page 135 (123) *Varieties of Religious Experience: A Study in Human Nature,* 1901-1902
William James
[Gifford Lectures on natural religion delivered in Edinburgh]

Page 135 (124) *Anna Karénina,* 1918

Novel by Lev Nikolaevich Tolstoi

Page 135 (124) *The Kreutzer Sonata and Other Stories,* 1890
Short story collection by Lev Nikolaevich Tolstoi

Page 149 (136) *The Life of St. Teresa*—unidentified

Page 164 (150) "Locksley Hall," 1886
Poem by Alfred Tennyson

Page 165 (151) "A Song in the Time of Order," 1866
Poem by Algernon Charles Swinburne

Page 171 (157) *Agamemnon,* 458 B.C.
Play by Aeschylus

Page 203 (190) **Et Tu, Brutus,* 1917
(Dear Brutus)
Play by Sir James Matthew Barrie

Page 216 (202) "Clair de Lune," 1869
Poem by Paul Verlaine

Page 224 (209) *A Portrait of the Artist as a Young Man,* 1916
Novel by James Joyce
New York, Huebsch

Page 224 (209) *Joan and Peter,* 1918
Novel by H. G. Wells
New York, Macmillan

Page 224 (209) *The Undying Fire,* 1919
Novel by H. G. Wells
New York, Cassell

Page 224 (209) *Vandover and the Brute,* 1914
Novel by Frank Norris
Garden City, Doubleday, Page

Page 224 (209) *The Damnation of Theron Ware,* 1896
Novel by Harold Frederic

Chicago, Stone and Kimball

Page 224 (209) **Jenny Gerhardt,* 1911
(Jennie Gerhardt)
Novel by Theodore Dreiser
New York, Harper

Page 239 (223) "Ulalume," 1847
Poem by Edgar Allan Poe

Page 241 (225) "Manfred," 1817
Poem by Lord Byron

Page 241 (225) *Don Juan,* 1819-1824
Poem by Lord Byron

Page 248 (231) "Triumph of Time," 1866
Poem by Charles Algernon Swinburne

Page 284 (264) *Faust* (1871-English translation)
Play by Johann Wolfgang von Goethe

Page 284 (264) *Almayer's Folly,* 1895
Novel by Joseph Conrad
London, Unwin

AUTHORS MENTIONED IN *THIS SIDE OF PARADISE*

The first page reference is to the 1920 text; the Scribner Library page reference follows in parentheses.

Asterisks indicate that the work is also mentioned in *This Side of Paradise.*

Where Fitzgerald misspelled a name, the correction follows in parentheses.

Page 2 (2) George Gordon Noel Byron, Lord Byron
1788-1824
English Romantic poet
**Don Juan,* 1819-24

Page 18 (17) George Alfred Henty
1832-1902
English author of historical novels for boys
Dr. Thorndyke's Secret, 1898

Page 18 (17) Mary Roberts Rhinehart (Rinehart)
1876-1958
American novelist and mystery writer
The Circular Staircase, 1908

Page 29 (26) George Bernard Shaw
1856-1950
Irish dramatist and philosopher
**Mrs. Warren's Profession,* 1905

Page 36 (33) Robert Chambers
1865-1933
American novelist and short story writer
The King in Yellow, 1893

Page 36 (33) David Graham Phillips
1867-1911
American novelist, journalist, and reformer
Susan Lenox: Her Fall and Rise, 1917

Page 36 (33) E. Phillips Oppenheim
1866-1946
English novelist of international intrigue
The Man and His Kingdom, 1901

Page 36 (33) Alfred Tennyson
1809-1892
English Victorian poet
*"Come Into the Garden, Maude," 1855

Page 36 (33) Rudyard Kipling
1865-1936
English imperialist, poet, and novelist
*"Gunga Dhin," 1892

Page 45 (41) Booth Tarkington

1869-1946
American novelist
**The Gentleman from Indiana,* 1899

Page 49 (44)	Niccolo Machiavelli 1469-1527 Florentine statesman and political theorist *The Prince,* 1513
Page 55 (50)	William Shakespeare 1564-1616 Elizabethan dramatist and poet *Sonnets,* 1609
Page 55 (50)	John Milton 1608-1674 English Puritan poet *"L'Allegro," 1632
Page 56 (51)	John Keats 1795-1821 English Romantic poet *"La Belle Dame Sans Merci," 1819 *"To A Nightingale," 1819
Page 56 (51)	Oscar Wilde 1854-1900 Irish author, playwright, and wit **The Picture of Dorian Gray,* 1890
Page 57 (51)	Algernon Charles Swinburne 1837-1909 English lyric poet and critic **Poems and Ballads,* 1866
Page 57 (51)	Gilbert Keith Chesterton 1874-1936 English essayist, novelist, and man-of-letters **The Man Who Was Thursday,* 1908
Page 57 (51)	Sir James Matthew Barrie

1860-1937
English dramatist and novelist
**What Every Woman Knows,* 1908
**Dear Brutus,* 1917

Page 57 (51) Sir Arthur Wing Pinero
1855-1934
English dramatist of sentimental comedy
The Freaks, 1918

Page 57 (51) William Butler Yeats
1865-1939
Irish poet and dramatist
Poems Written in Discouragement, 1913

Page 57 (51) John Millington Synge
1871-1909
Irish dramatist
The Playboy of the Western World, 1907

Page 57 (51) Ernest Dowson
1867-1900
English poet of the 1890's
The Pierrot of the Minute, 1897

Page 57 (51) Arthur Symons
1865-1945
English poet and critic
Studies in Prose and Verse, 1904

Page 57 (51) Hermann Sudermann
1857-1928
German dramatist
Magda, 1896

Page 57 (51) Robert Hugh Benson
1871-1914
English novelist and Catholic apologist
**None Other Gods,* 1911

Page 88 (79) Pierre Corneille

1606-1684
Father of French tragedy
The Cid, 1637

Page 88 (79) Jean Racine
1639-1699
French dramatist
Andromaque, 1667

Page 103 (94) Robert Browning
1812-1889
English Victorian poet
Poems, 1849

Page 116 (106) Joris-Karl Huysmans
1848-1907
French decadent novelist and critic
Marthe, 1876

Page 116 (106) Walter Pater
1839-1894
English essayist and critic
Marius the Epicurean, 1885

Page 116 (106) Theophile Gautier
1811-1872
French decadent poet, critic, and journalist
Albertus, 1832

Page 116 (106) Francois Rabelais
1494?-1553
French satirist
Gargantua, 1534

Page 116 (106) Giovanni Boccaccio
1313-1375
First great writer of modern Italian prose
The Decameron, 1349-1351

Page 116 (106) Gauis Petronius Arbiter
?-66 A.D.

Roman satirical novelist
Satyricon, first century A.D.

Page 116 (106) Gauis Suetonius Tranquillus
?69-140 A.D.
Roman biographer
Lives of the Caesars, second century A.D.

Page 116 (106) O. Henry [William Sydney Porter]
1862-1910
American short story writer
Cabbages and Kings, 1905

Page 116 (106) John Fox, Jr.
1863-1919
American novelist and best selling author
The Little Shepherd of Kingdom Come, 1903

Page 116 (106) Richard Harding Davis
1864-1916
American romancer and journalist
Captain Macklin, 1902

Page 116 (106) James Whitcomb Riley
1849-1916
American "hoosier" poet and journalist
Rhymes of Childhood, 1890

Page 116 (106) Rupert Brooke
1887-1915
English Georgian poet
**Selected Poems,* 1917

Page 117 (107) Alexander Pope
1688-1744
English poet and essayist
The Rape of the Lock, 1712

Page 119 (109) Immanuel Kant
1724-1804
German philosopher

Critique of Pure Reason, 1781

Page 129 (118) H. G. Wells
1866-1946
English novelist, historian, and scientific writer
**The New Machiavelli,* 1910
**Joan and Peter,* 1918
**The Undying Fire,* 1919

Page 134 (123) Lyoff (Leo) Tolstoi
1828-1910
Russian novelist
**Anna Karenina,* 1918
**The Kreutzer Sonata,* 1890

Page 135 (123) Edward Carpenter
1844-1929
English poet and essayist
Narcissus and Other Poems, 1873

Page 135 (124) Walt Whitman
1819-1892
American poet
Leaves of Grass, 1855

Page 136 (125) Paul Charles Joseph Bourget
1852-1935
French novelist, dramatist, essayist, and naturalist
The Cruel Enigma, 1887

Page 136 (125) Ralph Adams Cram
1863-1942
American author and church architect
The Gothic Quest, 1907

Page 141 (129) Ralph Waldo Emerson
1803-1882
American transcendental poet and essayist
Poems, 1847

Page 162 (149) Friedrich W. Nietzsche

1844-1900
German philosopher
Thus Spake Zarathustra, 1883-1892

Page 163 (150) Johann Wolfgang von Goethe
1749-1832
German poet, novelist, and dramatist
**Faust:* Part 1, 1808
Part 2, 1832

Page 163 (150) Johann Christoph Frederick von Schiller
1759-1805
German dramatist
William Tell, 1804

Page 164 (151) Charles Robert Darwin
1809-1882
English biologist
On the Origin of the Species, 1859

Page 164 (151) John Henry Newman [Cardinal Newman]
1801-1890
English theologian, poet, and ecclesiastic
The Idea of the University Defined, 1873

Page 171 (157) Aeschylus
525-456 B.C.
Greek dramatist
Agamemnon, 458 B.C.

Page 175 (161) Charles Baudelaire
1821-1867
French decadent poet and critic
Les Fleurs du Mal, 1857

Page 176 (163) James Boswell
1740-1795
Scottish author and biographer
Life of Samuel Johnson, 1791

Page 176 (163) Samuel Johnston (Johnson)

1709-1784
English biographer, essayist, and lexicographer
Dictionary of the English Language, 1755

Page 208 (194) Ella Wheeler Wilcox
1850-1919
American verse writer
Poems of Passion, 1883

Page 224 (209) H. L. Mencken
1880-1956
American journalist, critic, and essayist
The American Language, 1918

Page 224 (209) Compton McKenzie (Mackenzie)
1883-1972
Popular English novelist
**Sinister Street,* 1913-1914

Page 224 (209) John Galsworthy
1867-1933
English novelist
The Man of Property, 1906

Page 224 (209) Arnold Bennett
1867-1931
English novelist and dramatist
The Matador of Five Towns and Other Stories, 1912

Page 226 (211) Stephen Vincent Benét
1898-1943
American poet and novelist
Five Men and Pompey, 1915

Page 229 (214) Thomas Carlyle
1795-1881
Victorian essayist and historian
The French Revolution, 1837

Page 230 (214) Percy Bysshe Shelley
1792-1822

English romantic poet
Prometheus Unbound, 1820

Page 232 (217) Edna Ferber
1887-1968
American novelist
Dawn O'Hara, 1911

Page 232 (217) Gouveneer (Gouverneur) Morris
1752-1816
American author, essayist, and diplomat
Observations on the American Revolution, 1779

Page 232 (217) Fanny (Fannie) Hurst
1889-1968
American novelist and short story writer
Gaslight Sonatas, 1918

Page 232 (217) Irvin S. Cobb
1876-1944
American humorist and novelist
Back Home, 1915

Page 232 (217) Harold Bell Wright
1872-1944
American novelist
The Calling of Dan Matthews, 1909

Page 232 (217) Zane Grey
1875-1939
American writer of western romances
Riders of the Purple Sage, 1912

Page 232 (217) Rupert Hughes
1872-1956
American novelist, dramatist, and biographer
Empty Pockets, 1915

Page 233 (217) Ernest Poole
1880-1950
American novelist

His Family, 1917

Page 233 (217) Dorothy Canfield [Fisher]
1879-1958
American novelist
Home Fires in France, 1918

Page 233 (217) Joseph Conrad
1857-1924
English novelist
**Almayer's Folly,* 1895

Page 233 (218) Walter Arensberg—unidentified

Page 233 (218) Alfred Kreymborg
1883-1966
New York poet and dramatist
Mushrooms, 1916

Page 233 (218) Carl Sandburg
1878-1967
Free verse poet of Chicago school
Chicago Poems, 1915

Page 233 (218) Louis Untermeyer
1885-
American poet and critic
First Love, 1911

Page 233 (218) Eunice Tietjens
1884-1944
Free verse poet of Chicago school
Profiles from China, 1917

Page 233 (218) Clara Shanafelt—unidentified

Page 233 (218) James Oppenheim
1882-1932
American novelist and poet
Songs for the New Age, 1914

Page 233 (218) Maxwell Bodenheim
1893-1954
American poet and novelist
Minna and Myself, 1918

Page 234 (218) Richard Glaenzer—unidentified

Page 234 (218) Scharmel Iris—unidentified

Page 234 (218) Conrad Aiken
1889-1973
American poet and critic
Earth Triumphant, 1914

Page 234 (218) Vachel Lindsay
1879-1931
American poet
The Chinese Nightingale and Other Poems, 1917

Page 234 (218) Edgar Lee Masters
1869-1950
American poet, novelist, and biographer
Spoon River Anthology, 1915

Page 239 (223) Edgar Allan Poe
1809-1849
American poet and short story writer
*"Ulalume," 1847

Page 241 (225) Paul Verlaine
1844-1896
French lyric poet associated with symbolists
**Fêtes Galantes,* 1869
*"Clair de Lune," 1869

Page 255 (238) Plato [Aristocles]
?427-347 B.C.
Greek philosopher
The Republic, c368 B.C.

Page 284 (264) Samuel Butler

1835-1902
English author of satirical novels
The Way of All Flesh, 1903

Page 284 (264) Ernest Renan
1823-1892
French historian and critic
Vie de Jesus, 1863

Page 284 (264) Voltaire [Francois-Marie Arouet]
1694-1778
French poet, historian, and philosopher
Candide, 1759

Page 285 (265) Henrick Ibsen
1828-1906
Norwegian dramatist
A Doll's House, 1879

Page 285 (265) Arthur Schopenhauer
1788-1860
German philosopher
The World as Will and Representation, 1819

Page 290 (269) Jean-Jacques Rousseau
1712-1778
French philosopher
Emile, 1762

OTHER LITERARY REFERENCES IN *THIS SIDE OF PARADISE*

Page 34 (31) Roland:
character in "Chanson de Roland," part of *Chansons de Geste* (12th-15th centuries)

Page 34 (31) Horatius: Roman war hero

Page 57 (52) Savoy Operas:
operas by Gilbert and Sullivan performed at the

Savoy Theatre in London (1844-1901)

Page 67 (60) *Thais:* historical novel by Anatole France set in fourth century Egypt and based on the tale in the *Golden Legend* of the courtesan who became a saint (1890)

Page 67 (60) *Carmen:* opera by Bizet (1875)

Page 84 (76) Ganymede: a beautiful youth of Phrygia who was carried up to heaven by angels and became cupbearer to the gods in place of Hebe

Page 87 (78) Norse Sagas: prose narrative recorded in Iceland in the 12th and 13th centuries of Norwegian historic or legendary figures and events of the heroic age of Norway and Iceland

Page 151 (139) Puck: mischievous sprite from Shakespeare's *A Midsummer Night's Dream* (1596)

Page 168 (154) Heraclitus: philosopher of Ephesus who wrote *Concerning Nature* (c 500 B.C.); known as the "weeping philosopher"

Page 253 (236) Dark Lady of the Sonnets: un–named woman who is addressed in some Shakespearean sonnets (1609)

WORKS QUOTED IN *THIS SIDE OF PARADISE*

First page reference is to the 1920 text; the Scribner Library reference follows in parentheses.

Asterisks indicate an inaccurate quotation by Fitzgerald; the correct text follows in parentheses.

Title Page

". . . Well this side of Paradise!. . .
There's little comfort in the wise."
Rupert Brooke
"Tiare Tahiti" from *1914 and Other Poems,* 1915

*"Experience is the name so many people give to their mistakes." (Experience is the name every one gives to their mistakes.)
Oscar Wilde
Lady Windermere's Fan, 1892

Page 58 (53)

"Asleep or waking is it? for her neck
Kissed over close, wears yet a purple speck
Wherein the pained blood falters and goes out;
Soft and stung softly-fairer for a fleck. . ."
Algernon Charles Swinburne
"Laus Veneris" from *Poems and Ballads,* 1866

Page 82 (74)

"Oh, winter's rains and ruins are over,
And all the seasons of snows and sins;
The days dividing lover and lover,
The light that loses, the night that wins;
And time remembered is grief forgotten
And frosts are slain and flowers begotten,
And in green underwood and cover,
Blossom by blossom the spring begins
The full streams feed on flower of ——"
Algernon Charles Swinburne
Atalanta in Calydon, 1865

Page 87 (78)

*"Beaches of Lukanon before the sealers came." (The Beaches of Lukannon—before the sealers came!)
Rudyard Kipling
"Lukannon" from *The Jungle Book,* 1894

Page 103 (94)

"Each life unfulfilled, you see,

It hangs still, patchy and scrappy;
We have not sighed deep, laughed free,
Starved, feasted, despaired—been happy."
Robert Browning
"Youth and Art" from *Dramatis Personae,* 1864

Page 208-209 (194–195)

"For this is wisdom—to love and live,
To take what fate or the gods may give,
To ask no question, to make no prayer,
To kiss the lips and caress the hair,
Speed passion's ebb as we greet its flow,
To have and to hold, and, in time—let go."
Laurence Hope
"The Teak Forest" from *India's Love Lyrics,* 1902

Page 240-241 (224-225)

"Les sanglots longs
Des violins
De l'automne
Blessent mon coeur
D'une langueur
Monotone.

Tout suffocant
Et blême quand
Sonne l'heure
Je me souviens
Des jours anciens
Et je pleure . . ."
Paul Verlaine
"Chanson D'Automne" from *Poémes saturniens,* 1866

Page 244 (228)

"And now when the night was senescent
And the star dials pointed to morn
At the end of the path a liquescent
And nebulous lustre was born."

Edgar Allan Poe
"Ulalume," 1847

Page 247 (230) "Blind on thy sandals, oh, thou most fleet.
Over the splendor and speed of thy feet——"
Algernon Charles Swinburne
Atalanta in Calydon, 1865

Page 249 (232) "Is it worth a tear, is it worth an hour,
To think of things that are well outworn;
Of fruitless husks and fugitive flower,
The dream foregone and the deed foreborne?"
Algernon Charles Swinburne
"Triumph of Time" from *Poems and Ballads,* 1866

POEMS, OR EXCERPTS OF POEMS, IN *THIS SIDE OF PARADISE* ATTRIBUTED TO FITZGERALD

Page 18 (16) "Marylyn and Sallee . . ."

Page 51 (46-47) "A serving lady speaks . . ."
[Presumably by Fitzgerald, but possibly by John Peale Bishop]

Page 94 (85) Untitled prose-poem

Page 117-119 (108-109) "In a Lecture-Room"

Page 164-165 (151) "Victorians, Victorians . . ."

Page 165-166 (152) Untitled poem

Page 173-174 (159-160) "A Lament for a Foster Son, and He goin
War Against the King of Foreign"
[Presumably by Fitzgerald, but could poss
have been sent to Fitzgerald by Signourey

Page 174 (160-161) "Embarking at Night"

Page 187 (175) Untitled poem

Page 233-234 (218) "Boston Bards and Hearst Reviewers"

Page 235 (219-220) Untitled prose-poem

Page 238-239 (222-223) Eleanor's poem

Page 253 (235-236) Eleanor and Amory's prose-poem

Page 258-259 (240-241) "A Poem That Eleanor Sent Amory Several Years Later"

Page 259-260 (241-242) "A Poem Amory Sent To Eleanor and
Page 259-260 (241-242) Which He Called 'Summer Storm' "

Page 273 (254) Untitled poem

FITZGERALD'S PREVIOUSLY PUBLISHED POEMS IN *THIS SIDE OF PARADISE*

Page 147 (134-135) ["On A Play Twice Seen"]
The Nassau Literary Magazine, June 1917

Page 154 (141) From "The Cameo Frame"
The Nassau Literary Magazine, October 1917

Page 160 (146-147) From "The Cameo Frame"
The Nassau Literary Magazine, October 1917

Page 168 (154) ["Princeton—The Last Day"] Revised
The Nassau Literary Magazine, May 1917

SONGS QUOTED IN *THIS SIDE OF PARADISE*

The first page reference is to the 1920 text; the Scribner Librar reference follows in parentheses.

Page 17 (15)	"Casey Jones"
Page 33 (30)	Lyrics from George M. Cohan's *The Little Millionaire* which was first produced on Broadwa in 1911
Page 45 (40)	Unidentified popular song
Page 46 (41-42)	"Going Back to Nassau Hall"
Page 76-77 (69)	"Babes in the Woods"

University of South Carolin

MEREDITH CARY

Save Me the Waltz as a Novel

It has proved all too easy to read Zelda Fitzgerald's novel, *Save Me the Waltz,* in terms of illness, seeing in the metaphoric style primarily the reflection of a diseased imagination and discounting the content as being so neurotically antagonistic to men and so contentiously autobiographical as to be of no value except to biographers.[1] Such a view is understandable if the novel is considered to be on the losing side of a kind of novelistic duel between Zelda Fitzgerald's *Save Me the Waltz* and F. Scott Fitzgerald's *Tender Is the Night*—an approach which is tempting because of the flamboyance of the personalities, the commonality of the artistic material drawn upon, and the conjunction of the actual writing of the two novels. However, it is necessary to observe that whereas it is Zelda Fitzgerald's novel which is usually condemned as excessively autobiographical, it is Scott Fitzgerald's novel which in fact details the lives of an alcoholic and a mental patient.[2] Since an easy recognition of the personalities and problems has not caused *Tender Is the Night* to be simplistically assigned to a sub-literary category, it should be possible to approach *Save Me the Waltz* as something other than an associational curiosity. The reward for doing so is the discovery of a work exhibiting impressive artistic control of both form and content—the patterns of metaphor, the narrative structure and the character delineations reveal *Save Me the Waltz* to be a thoughtful and carefully balanced study of a search for individuality, social relevance, and order.

The structure of the novel is, appropriately, orderly. Divided into four sections, it treats in two phases—first the training for the experience and then the experience itself—each of the two central concerns of the main character—Alabama Beggs. There is the childhood which is the only training offered the young girl for the marriage which represents her life. And when she becomes disillusioned with the marriage and retreats from "life" to "art," there is her training in the dance and finally her career as a ballerina. The events which flesh out these four sections depict the will to succeed and the recognition of failure of a talented woman driven to excel in both areas.

Alabama's childhood is influenced primarily by the personalities of her father and her mother, and by the expectations of the society in which she grows up. Opening the novel with a description of the character of Judge Beggs in the metaphor of a castle, Zelda Fitzgerald suggests the crucial importance of both the negative and positive implications of his personality as a father. "Impregnable" because of his intellect, his integrity and his unapproachability, he is a "living fortress" for his children, who, as long as they belong to him rather than to themselves, are convinced they can "do anything and get away with it."[3]

While he protected his children from society, he also protected himself from them, however, declaring "without humor, 'I will build me some ramparts surrounded by wild beasts and barbed-wire on the top of a crag and escape this hoodlum' " (p. 4). This extension of the castle metaphor for his private use within the family enclosure suggests the inevitability of his children's reactions to him as to fragments of a personality beyond their reach. When they were small, he seemed to be "the personification of an extra penny, a street-car ride to whitewashed picnic grounds, a pocketful of peppermints," (p. 5). As teenagers, they perceived him as "a retributory organ, an inexorable fate, the force of law, order, and established discipline" (p. 5). In both stages, they grasp only the function, having no means of approaching close enough to perceive the man. They therefore learn only his rules, not his values, and so they are hampered by his remoteness from them just as they are "crippled" by the family remoteness from society.

Inevitably, the girls "seek respite in their mother" from so unyielding a presence. Their mother, Millie, is an "emotional anarchist" of "wide and lawless generosity" (p. 11). In contrast to the paternal view of them as "hoodlum," Millie announces that "If my children are bad . . . I have never seen it" (pp. 4-5). Unjudging either of her husband or her children, she urges the girls to avoid confrontations with their father, not through obedience but through "making their arrangements outside" (p. 11).

For Alabama, this model of femininity as accommodating rather than judging is reinforced by the observation of her older sister's behavior on dates. Her sister changes into a "more fluctuating, more ingratiating person, as she confided herself to the man. She wished it were herself. There would be her father at the supper table. It was nearly the same; the necessity of being something that you really weren't was the same. Her father didn't know what she really was like" (p. 21).

Unlike Millie, whose personality really did disappear into her wifehood even to the abandonment of her own family in favor of her service to her husband's people, Alabama learns to conceal, not to cancel, what she is "really like." In a phrase the repetition of which measures the development of Alabama's growing perception of the discrepancy between the ideal and the possible, she convinces herself that "the only thing of any significance was to take what she wanted when she could" (p. 29). But even from the beginning, the ruthlessness of such a plan is modified by her counter-drive toward "paying for things I do—it makes me feel square with the world" (p. 30). Thus, by the time her introductory portrait is complete, what she "really" is emerges as a chaotic mixture of the will and self-righteous integrity of her father and the yieldingness and non-judging sympathy of her mother. If her mother perceives Alabama's characteristic drive to be "more conquering" than her sister, still, Alabama's childhood concept of what makes people interesting is that "things happen" to them. Such a blend of dominance and passivity, embodied in the extremes of her parents, becomes the framework on which the individual Alabama matures.

Her maturation is, inevitably in such an environment, marked in sexual rather than vocational terms. Her inspection of her mother and sisters leads the teenaged Alabama to conclude that there is "nothing to do but drink and make love" (p. 31). However, such a conclusion is only partially appropriate. At first Alabama submits herself to David, imagining herself being "pulled finer and smaller like those streams of spun glass that pull and stretch till there remains but a glimmering illusion" (p. 38). So totally is she subsumed by her lover's personality that she seems to herself to have "crawled into the friendly cave of his ear" where she becomes lost among "the deep trenches of the cerebellum," the desolate "mystic maze" of "vast tortuous indentations" which lead her round and round until she becomes hysterical (p. 38). The metaphor suggests both the concept of femininity which her childhood has given her and her inability to fit its pattern: it is not really within her character to disappear into David as Millie disappeared into the Judge.

In the footsteps of her mother, however, she masks her reaction well enough that David and her father dispose of her as if she were uncomplicatedly her mother's child. David's view of the relationship is the conventional one, and so he asks her father, not Alabama herself, about the marriage. To Alabama, he observes merely that "you are my princess and I'd like to keep you shut forever in an ivory tower for my private delectation" (p. 40). Her submissiveness is quite casually assumed by the egotistical young artist, who has linked the name of "Miss Alabama Nobody" with that of "David David Knight Knight Knight." But Alabama, who has just escaped her father's "fortress," is not charmed by the image. The "real" Alabama, whom neither her father nor her young lover perceives, asks David not to mention the ivory tower again. And on her honeymoon, she tells herself that "no power on earth could make her do anything . . . any more, except herself" (p. 42).

The conflict between their views of their relationship is not immediately disastrous, partly because both seem to assume the establishment of a new home something on the order of the Beggs'. The differences, however, are significant. The judge has so fixed a sense of place that he does not even momentarily consider moving from his home when it becomes too large on the departure of his children. In contrast, David and Alabama drift among hotels and rented houses, changing not only addresses, but cities and even countries. That they are working not on a fortress but on an encampment that cannot be defended is suggested by their inability to repel invasion even temporarily. For example, Alabama brings her parents to her home only to discover "drunks in the hammock" who invade the diningroom during dinner and who, even when paid to leave, can not be prevented from reeling back into the kitchen during the night.

Similarly, Provence, where they settle for a time, seems to Alabama to be a place where keeps and battlements crumble and moats fill harmlessly with honeysuckle. The metaphor recalls most immediately the image of the Judge—appropriately, since it is at this stage in her life that Alabama faces the extent to which her father's pattern of marriage is inappropriate to her character. Further, Provence is in Europe's "south," a concept of locale which David sees as appropriate to Alabama but not to himself. The notion that it is congenial to one but not to the other emblemizes the crumbling of their relationship, for it was with their acute sense of closeness that they expected to replace the geographical sense of home which was a major portion of the Judge's strength.

In the beginning, they are agreed that their joint personality should be David's. David's fame emphasizes Alabama's observation that it is "a man's world," and she makes an effort to be "feminine" in her mother's way, expressing a longing to live "without premeditation," insisting that she will be content to "luxuriate in this voluptuous air and grow fat on bananas and Chablis while David Knight grows clever" (p. 80). But even her declarations of dependency embody an ominous ambivalence. She remarks to her daughter that "I am so outrageously clever that I believe I could be a whole world to myself if I didn't like living in Daddy's better" (p. 82). David is to *grow* clever while Alabama *is* clever: it is a strikingly poor basis on which to submerge Alabama's personality. Further, it suggests that another of the difficulties facing the marriage is the extent to which David's character differs from that of the Judge.

David does not tower over Alabama in maturity any more than in cleverness. For example, he indulges in tantrums over minor irritations such as his ranting that it "ruined his talent to have his buttons torn off in the laundry" (p. 50). But the problem is not altogether David's. Her recognition of David's limitations does not prevent Alabama from casting him as a kind of father substitute when she finds it convenient. She assumes that he will organize their life and then blames him for her boredom, as she blamed her father during her childhood. To be sure, the charge is not wholly irresponsible since David's view of a woman's role is a devastatingly limiting one. He assumes that Alabama will find some painless way of going into cold storage while he works and emerge as a compliant feature of his social life when he wishes to be amused. And when she complains of boredom to him, his notion of a solution is to suggest a party.

As was prefigured by the metaphors of their courtship, Alabama makes an attempt at the sort of life David imagines, with endless reading and abortive attempts to sew. But the "female role" is simply inappropriate to her. She cannot keep the servants from stealing, she cannot dominate the cook sufficiently to get any variety into the family meals, she cannot keep the house free of insects. The passage in which she discovers her pregnancy embodies the various elements of her problem. In an "incompetent" discussion of the problem, David suggests that Alabama ask her mother for advice. But Alabama objects: "Oh, David—don't! She'd think I wouldn't know how" (p. 47). In fact, of course, no matter what may be her family's view of the normal and basic function of womanhood, she doesn't "know how."

Her lack of an instinctive understanding of the conventional role is further illustrated in the flirtation which overtly triggers the breakdown of the marriage. She has been accustomed to attention for her wit in her own language. But at the party which was to relieve her boredom, she discovers that she does not understand French well enough to be clever. And noticing that it is David alone, rather than the pair of them, who receives the attention, she turns to the international form of communication—falling into a love affair out of boredom and a demolished sense of worth.

However, love affairs between people who cannot talk to each other are predictably useless. Alabama buys a French dictionary and her lover buys an English dictionary, but she does not really want to sneak to his apartment to consummate the flirtation, and his final letter is in interminable French which Alabama can only destroy unread. It was an affair of appearances only—they are both blond and brown and beautiful—and so it is the photograph which accompanied the letter which has meaning for Alabama: "Though it broke her heart, she tore the picture too. It was the most beautiful thing she'd ever owned in her life, that photograph. What was the use of keeping it?" (p. 98).

The implications are complex. She has no instinct to clutch the past. She has discovered something—in the realm of appearances, at least—more beautiful than David and his painting. That the relationship has been a matter of surfaces only is not in itself a basis on which to turn away from it, for the affair constitutes an admission that her life with David does not make room for the "real" Alabama either. She concludes that "Jacques had passed over that much of their lives like a vacuum cleaner" (p. 96) not entirely because David is repellently outraged—yelling about "foreigners," "wops" and "kikes"—but because, for her as well, the experience has "vacuumed up" the idle happiness of her marriage to David, just as her marriage had cancelled the security derived from her father. Recognizing a turning point, she re-edits her earlier understanding of life's process: "You took what you wanted from life, if you could get it, and you did without the rest" (p. 98).

It is in response to this new insight into the necessity of sometimes doing without that her solution emerges from the tangle of emotions embodied in the episode which closes the marriage section of her story. Having retreated to Paris to escape the "south" which has become symbolically obnoxious to David, they attend a party where David flirts with the guest of honor. The hostess describes Gabrielle Gibbs to Alabama as a "half-wit" who has a body like marble. David supplies the speculation that her marble is arrestingly covered throughout with blue veins. To Alabama, who is introduced to her as she is being sick in the bathroom, Gabrielle is simply a blonde drunk on the bathroom floor, so disorderly that "a platinum wisp floated in the bowl of the toilet" (p. 107). But to the rest of the party, Gabrielle is "the center of something" and Alabama feels painfully inferior. Although it is Gabrielle who is wallowing around the bathroom floor, it is Alabama whom the hostess ushers out of the room "like a maid gathering dust off the parlor floor" (p. 108). While David tries to impress the dancer by speculating that she wears something "boyish underneath your clothes," it was Alabama who gave him the idea by actually wearing silk BVDs. To add to her sense of outrage at David's use of her, Alabama is advised by others in the party as to her wifely role. She is told of her "need to be bossed," and when she objects that she wants to direct her own life, if she could only find its direction, she is reminded: "You've a child, haven't you?" (p. 115).

The conventional role has its appeals for her, and so she whimpers to David that she wishes she could "live in your pocket," but David sensibly objects that she would slip through a hole she had forgotten to darn. The normal is simply not her role, a difficulty echoed in the hostess' remark that dancing "would be the very thing for Alabama. I've always heard she was a little peculiar—I don't mean actually batty—but a little difficult. An art would explain" (p. 113). It is a view which finally makes sense to Alabama. She has come to realize that she cannot rest as a function of her husband and her daughter. And yet she is sufficiently convinced by her mother's type of femininity to agree that her failure to adapt to the image requires an "explanation." She therefore vows to become "as famous a dancer as there are blue veins over the white marble of Miss Gibbs" (p. 118). Her intention is to justify her character, lend direction to her life, and compete with "the center of something."

Alabama plunges into her training for the dance as deliberately and as wholeheartedly as she had pursued the other phases of her life. Although the original decision was made somewhat on the spur of the moment and resulted at least superficially from her taking seriously the idle flippancy of a social wit, Alabama works out a careful rationale for her new pursuit. "She tried to weave the strength of her father and the young beauty of her first love with David, the happy oblivion of her teens and her warm protected childhood into a magic cloak" (p. 129). She was determined, having despaired of "careless" happiness, to "command her emotions, to summon love or pity or happiness at will," to "drive the devils that had driven her" (p. 124). Because the dance demands self-discipline and represents ordered beauty, she pursues it as a means of forcing those missing qualities onto her unsatisfactory life.

Since the qualities at issue are those which have triggered David's irritation with their marriage, Alabama's studies at first seem to promise rescue for the foundering marriage as well as release for the "real" Alabama. But David very soon stops being pleased at the increased free time Alabama's absorption gives him and turns instead to complaints about the loss of home life. The inevitable recriminations quickly billow into brutal competition. Each feels the other is incapable of understanding the rival art. And instead of shifting their ground to the larger idea of a general concept of art which would include both painting and the dance, David develops a pattern of undercutting Alabama's efforts as those of the permanent amateur in contrast to the professionalism he has the income to document. Although he says he will help her become a dancer, he "did not believe that she could become one," and he continues to treat her like one of his possessions, exhibiting her to his friends "as if she were one of his pictures" and inviting them to feel her muscle.

When, despite his interference and complaints, Alabama does receive an offer to dance professionally, David is convinced there is "something accidental" about the offer and refuses to allow her to consider taking it. Further, since the offer is from a company in Naples—the "south"—David will not consider moving the household even though Alabama's work is geographically tied while his is not: he could paint anywhere, if he would.

The passage with which the third section of the novel concludes sums up this tangle of conflicting influences on Alabama and on the marriage. As long as Alabama was merely training for the dance, she could avoid a confrontation over the deterioration of her marriage by spending more and more time at the studio. But the job offer precipitates a decision. Since it negates David's most vocal claim to dominion over Alabama—that she is ineradicably an amateur and therefore beneath his professionalism—it triggers a greater insistence on his part for some symbolic submission from her in other ways. Always to some extent her mother's daughter, Alabama at no time seems to question David's right to make the rules applicable to the marriage. Therefore she does not challenge his notion that her becoming a professional dancer will require their separation. Nor does she contradict his decision that Bonnie must stay in Paris rather than accompany her mother to a region where there will be no French schools.

The marriage has for a long time seemed so bankrupt to her that she may be responding principally to their mutual sense of "unconscious relief" at the separation. However, her obedience in the disposition of Bonnie is not so willing. She has tried to involve Bonnie in the dance with her in order to overcome the child's objection that "it is too 'sérieuse' to be the way Mummy is" (p. 147). But Bonnie continues to feel that her mother was nicer before she began to dance, and Alabama recognizes in her child the longings which she herself felt so overwhelmingly for something "pretty and stylized in her life" (p. 161). When she finds in Bonnie's drawing book a picture in which "two figures held hands gingerly," and which Bonnie has labeled "c'est trés chic, mes parents ensemble" (p. 161), Alabama is defeated. She cannot turn away from her daughter's family view. Bonnie wants her parents together no matter how "gingerly" the alliance. It is appropriate that the recognition should make Alabama feel "sick and middle-aged" since her choice involves setting aside her own drive for beauty and order in favor of the same drive in the coming generation.

If the matter had rested there, the dancer's defeat would have been uncomplicated. However, family life is organized by David's opinions and not by Bonnie's. And David's response to her giving up makes clear that he is not thinking of them as "parents together" but as a man with his subsidiaries. He consoles Alabama by promising to "try to arrange something" in America. The patronizing reminder that he expects to organize her opportunities as well as set up her limitations makes clear that he sees the decision as a contest which he has won. Before the job offer, Alabama had no real choice but to submit to David's demands for obedience and subservience, for even if David had been able to accept a relationship of equals, Alabama's own view of marriage was too like that of her parents to allow her to demand or even visualize such an arrangement. Therefore, when David's arrogance rouses her from the temporary delusion of Bonnie's view of them together, she recoils into the dance. For the first time, she has a choice.

The result of the choice is far from clear cut, however. She is an undoubted success, professionally. And although she misses Bonnie, she is not really a competent parent, as is symbolized by the disastrous party she gives Bonnie during the child's visit to Naples. Nor does she feel much kinship to her daughter, who has stopped her dancing lessons as soon as Alabama is no longer there to require them of her, and whose increasing snobbishness brings forth complaints that Italian trains de luxe are not sufficiently luxurious. David is really no better a parent than is Alabama, as is indicated by the parallel inept party he arranges for Bonnie upon her return to France, but her snobbishness motivates the child's preference for living in her father's wealthier, more social world in Paris.

In contrast to the society which collects around David, Alabama is "always alone." Even her fellow dancers cannot understand her reasons for dancing when she has a husband and child. The complete isolation which her choice has brought upon her is emphasized in the hospital sequence with which her independence ends. Though she is alone—remote from society and family, as her father was—she is not impregnable as he was. Her career stops when the tendons in her foot are cut as a result of the blood poisoning she develops from the effects of the glue of her dancing slipper which invades a neglected blister on her toe.

The disaster is not simply bad luck. Having started too late to train for the dance—partly because of her own waywardness and partly through her parents' lack of ambition for a daughter—she must work too hard to recover the time. Self-controlled only through decision and not through basic personality, she is undisciplined in areas her attention does not touch, and therefore she neglects the blisters she sees as simply one element of the central masochism of any discipline. Unsure of the exclusive value of building a "whole world to herself" as opposed to living in David's world, she is insufficiently egotistical—in contrast to Gabrielle Gibbs, or Arienne, a less talented but more dedicated fellow student at ballet school—to secure her future through attention to inartistic detail. She has pursued the dance because it is beautiful and because it represents order—in other words, because it is not life for her. Her father's impregnability came from "paring your perceptions to fit into the visible portion of life's mosaic" (p. 24), whereas Alabama, believing in the "infinite promise of American advertising" (p. 210), remains vulnerable to reality.

In contrast to her childhood intention to "bring forth sweet-smelling blossoms from the hardest of rocks, and night-blooming vines from barren wastes" (p. 7), she confronts in the hospital a different kind of unnatural growth: "Nebulous weeds swung on the current: purple stems with fat animal leaves, long tentacular stems with no leaves at all, swishing balls of iodine and the curious chemical growths of stagnant waters" (p. 194). Where she had intended extraordinary beauty, she concludes in her delirium that her struggle toward differentness has produced only grotesque and repellent abnormality. The distressed imagery merges into David's reassurance that "it has brought us together again." The meaning of that palliative to the demoralized Alabama is the silent revision of her life's rule: "she had always meant to take what she wanted from life. Well—she hadn't wanted this" (p. 195).

When Alabama rises from the hospital bed which signals the end of her dreams of the dance in order to attend her father's deathbed, the novel returns to the imagery of its opening scenes. Alabama considers that she is returning to the "peaceful" place where she "was little," but the differences in her perceptions indicate the extent of her change. The final series of images involving parents and home is pervaded by her "shocked" realization: "without her father the world would be without its last resource. But . . . it will be me who is the last resource when my father is dead" (p. 195). The man who had, in the beginning, been a "living fortress" now lies "withering on the bed." Alabama at last remembers how she used to "gloat when something went wrong" as a symbolic breaching of her father's invulnerability. Though still sensitive to the "noble completeness" of her father's life, she now understands the mechanism of that completeness. Her father's house is small—smaller than those the grown up children live in. Its size is an equivalent of the less tangible curtailment which is his life method.

Money is the image which most clearly represents his limitations. He has saved the first coins he ever earned. His response to the early death of his only son is to ask in a "heartbreaking" cry how he can be expected to pay for the funeral. His parallel response to his own death is to hand Millie a check to cover his funeral expenses, stipulating that he wants it back if he doesn't die. "We can't afford this sickness," he says, "over and over," as he languishes toward death, and his last words are, "this thing is costing money" (p. 204). The accumulating references build an image of a man who limits his perceptions of life to tangible elements.

It is to such an individual that Alabama turns, seeking "some kind of shelter" from her prolonged struggle with life's less tangible results. Failing to allow for the discrepancy of their life methods, she formalizes her own experience into a final question for the "infallible" man who symbolizes justice, both publicly, as a judge, and personally, as her father. She asks if "our bodies are given to us as counterirritants to the soul," and why, in that case, bodies "fail" when they should bring surcease from "tortured minds," just as souls "desert us as a refuge" when "we are tormented in our bodies" (p. 199). Why has the dance failed to relieve her of the disappointments of marriage; why has her body failed her in the dance? "Ask me something easy," answers the dying man (p. 199).

The ritual of transmission is complete. Alabama recalls her childhood rage at discovering that Santa Claus could exist as a myth that was not true. Yet she "feeds" on memories of her father "like converts imbibing a cult" (p. 205), even while she recognizes his small house, his failure to leave a final message, his limitation to the realm of "easy" questions. This resignation where once she would have been enraged marks the beginning of a new attempt to bring order and meaning to her life. She explains to David that "the object of the game" is to create "a beautiful harmonious mosaic of two gods of the hearthstone" so that when Bonnie is adult she will feel "less cheated" and will "believe that her restlessness will pass" (p. 206). She will attempt to set aside her own despair by deliberately creating an illusion for Bonnie. She will cherish the "cult" of parenthood—as distinct from the father who bequeathed her "many doubts"—by turning her attention to Bonnie's impression of their world.

Her vision is an attempt at compromise. Alabama recalls that "when she had wanted her own way about things," her father had told her that "if you want to choose, you must be a goddess" (p. 204). Her invocation of "two gods" echoes the language of the Judge's remark at the same time that her calling for "gods of the hearthstone" shows her effort to "choose" limitation in the form of the "conventional" role she recognizes as suitable for her mother and sister.

Domesticity does seem to be the only role left open to Alabama, and yet her ability to "choose" it appears to be limited by more than the difficulty implied by her father's attitude toward choice. David objects to what he considers "middle-aged moralizing." Bonnie misunderstands Alabama's concern with good manners. And the family "hearthstone" is a rented house through which the twilight flows like the "clear cold current of a trout stream" (p. 212). This final image, which incorporates a state of flux into the basic conditions of life, emphasizes the contrast between the perpetually moving household Alabama offers Bonnie and the "fortress" her father had seemed to create for her.

The possibility for success of Alabama's new "choice" is spelled out in the exchange which ends a party she and David have given on the basis of their re-established marriage:

> "I'm going to air the room a little," said Alabama. "I wish people wouldn't set wet glasses down on rented furniture."
>
> "Alabama," said David, "if you would stop dumping ash trays before the company has got well out of the house we would be happier."
>
> "It's very expressive of myself. I just lump everything in a great heap which I have labelled 'the past,' and, having thus emptied this deep reservoir that was once myself, I am ready to continue." (pp. 211-212).

She has remained a person "to whom things happen," but because of her own character and because of the society in which she lives, the happenings have served to cancel, to vacuum up, to empty the reservoir which she had hoped would prove a collecting pool. Compelled by energy and a dream of order, she applies herself to the role her family and society offer her. Searching for a life method whereby housework will prove "expressive of herself," she imagines she will order the past by dumping ashes. But David's complaint is justified regarding both housework and marriage. It is true that they would both be "happier" if she could resign herself to simply cleaning up instead of symbolizing order, if she could stop noticing that David is being courted for his remarkable artist's insight into the ballet—an insight which is derived from her own defeated efforts.

However, the "devils" which drive Alabama make such capitulation impossible to her. Torn between her father's inflexible will and her mother's conventional role, her own creativity and her society's norm, she is bound for defeat in every realm of life, from dancing to cleaning ashtrays. Her realism forces her to a recognition of the discontinuity between her present desire for resignation and the quality of her past integrity which produced the struggle that "was once myself." It is only her gallantry which allows her, though "empty," to continue.

From the beginning, Alabama's assumption of her own competence is clear. Her childhood contribution to her family's conversation on the awkwardness of crabs is to say "I believe I could make one . . . if I had the material" (p. 25). Such a God-complex might have been offensive in a more self-serving individual. But this drive is modified in Alabama by a remarkable honesty in analyzing the creature she did help to create: herself. In giving Alabama a part to play in her own making, Zelda Fitzgerald avoided the bathos which is a danger in the representation of defeat. Alabama's own personality, character and biology contribute centrally to her downfall. Her flamboyancy prevents her from succeeding at wifely things. Her lack of self-discipline defeats her talent. Her motherhood, her age and vulnerability to disease focus her other difficulties into a pattern of despair. Her biology is important also in that it informs her relations with her family and her society. The people with whom Alabama deals—her father, mother, husband, daughter, friends and colleagues—present a united view of the female role. And Alabama shares their view of normal womanhood. An additional part of her difficulty, then, is her conception of her own helpless abnormality.

In structuring Alabama's problem in this way, Zelda Fitzgerald avoided the polemic common in representations of the female version of defeat. The function of the novel is to trace the causes of Alabama's downfall, but the pattern of causation is so intricate and diversified and the responsibility so inadvertent that no villain is produced. Rather than assigning blame, Zelda Fitzgerald fleshes forth a situation and its results. This avoidance of oversimplification is the key to the novel's power. Dispassionately evoking the intricacy of the counterbalancing and contradicting elements of character and environment, Zelda Fitzgerald creates a convincing pattern out of apparent chaos and happenstance. In this lies the literary value of the work.

Western Washington State College

---

[1]For example, see Geoffrey Hellman, "Beautiful and Damned," *Saturday Review*, IX (October 22, 1932), 190; Andrew Turnbull, *Scott Fitzgerald* (New York: Scribners, 1962), pp. 191, 207; Arthur Mizener, *The Far Side of Paradise* (Boston: Houghton Mifflin, 1951), p. 220. Even Henry Dan Piper, in his more sympathetic discussion of the novel, dots his analysis with metaphoric references to disease and uncontrol. See his *F. Scott Fitzgerald A Critical Portrait* (New York: Holt, Rinehart and Winston, 1965), pp. 193-204.

[2]Nancy Milford, *Zelda a Biography* (New York: Harper & Row, 1970), pp. 139-140, 286-287.

[3]Carbondale: Southern Illinois University Press, 1967, p. 231. References in the text are to this edition.

JUDITH WILT

The Spinning Story: Gothic Motifs in *Tender Is the Night*

After completing in relatively short order the exquisite cameo of *The Great Gatsby* F. Scott Fitzgerald spent seven difficult years putting together *Tender Is the Night,* a novel alive with deeper, rougher magic than any of his other works. He was headed toward "the crack-up," which would come to a crisis directly after the publication of *Tender Is the Night,* 1934-36, and which he would later describe, with nervous bravado, in a piece by that name in *Esquire*. Three signs he saw in himself as prelude to the crack-up: increasing detachment from all but the guilty rote pretense of relating to other people "in order to preserve something—an inner hush maybe, maybe not"; a corresponding paradoxical secret dependence on four contemporaries for the very stuff of his political, social and aesthetic thought, to the point where "there was not an 'I' any more"; and, by the merciless logic of mind, which will not stand the condition of "not being I," a terrifying vertiginous fall into becoming "identified with the objects of my horror or compassion." "All rather inhuman and undernourished, isn't it?"

commented the jauntily re-patched Fitzgerald of February, 1936, like a great doomed daddy telling his horrible fairy tale: "well, that, children, is the true sign of cracking-up."

In "The Crack-Up," Fitzgerald said he found one principle to help keep the cracked plate together, and serviceable: closing all the channels from himself to others, no more "giving of myself," no more money in the account, no more water in the well. One channel of relationship was still open, however: "Trying to cling to something, I liked doctors and girl children up to the age of about thirteen and well-brought-up boy children from about eight years old on. I could have peace and happiness with these few categories of people."[1]

One ought to be as chaste as possible in applying the Gothic measure to works of fiction. Few novels are entirely without the apparatus of suspense, hidden violence, ritual obsession, hideous pursuits and secret monstrousnesses which we want vaguely to call "Gothic." Trace Gothic outlines in most American novels especially and the new gestalt leaps up to consciousness immediately. Hold the novel away for a rereading and often the outline will sink back into triviality or whimsicality.

The Great Gatsby is like that, I think. Draw heavy lines around the ash-wasteland passages, shrink all of Long Island and New York into a tiny space under the mad faceless gaze of Dr. T. J. Eckleburg, count up the verbal notes of "ghost" and "apparition" sounded through the pages, and the novel becomes "Gothic." Read it again and the Gothic apparatus seems somehow peripheral, not "realized," held off. It is held off, in fact, by the narrator, that "figure of reason," who enters on the scene of the horrid and in a true Gothic novel is drawn in and transformed by it. Nick Carraway, like that other important American fictional Nick whom he so closely resembles, simply and powerfully will not allow the Gothic in, either as dream or nightmare, and so the landscape slumbers as metaphor and Gatsby himself, "haunting the East," remains an even dreamier metaphor for the homebound midwesterner.

Only if the new Gothic gestalt really lives beside and within the older conventional one after the most honest reappraisal, only if the reasoner is drawn into the haunted landscape and escapes to tell a real tale, beyond metaphor, does the novel become part of that other "great tradition." And *Tender Is the Night* is such a novel. Within the conventional paradigm of the novel as American social history lives a true Gothic novel.

I want to pull out three major strands from the tradition of Gothic fiction and trace their weave in this novel. The first is that peculiarly Gothic narrative strategy, perfected in the "classical" Gothic period by Maturin in *Melmoth the Wanderer,* of drawing in, often through two or three loops of storytellers, towards the unthinkable act, the unsayable desire, the unbearable bargain, the "unhuman" mystery that generates the story. The second is a specially Gothic "matter" exploited in *The Castle of Otranto,* perfected in Radcliffe's *The Italian,* standardized in the line of "female Gothic" running from LeFanu's *Uncle Silas* to Victoria Holt and Mary Stewart, and given a subtle and wrenching twist in Joyce Carol Oates' newest, *Do With Me What You Will,* a matter elementally and fixedly at the center of Fitzgerald's novel as it is of much of his work including "The Crack-Up," a matter explosively compressed in *Tender Is the Night* into the banal film-title phrase, "Daddy's Girl." The third is that wonderfully Gothic setting, the madhouse, transmuted during the nineteenth century into the laboratory (or as in *Dracula* and in *Tender Is the Night,* the laboratory-madhouse), with its cast of attendant victim-ghouls, and its ambiguously dreadful presiding spirit, the scientist, and above all its constant nightmare dissolving of the boundaries of madness and reason.

One of the most interesting and fruitful controversies about *Tender Is the Night* is the severe qualm Fitzgerald suffered about the arrangement of the narration, the "angle" of attack on the story. Unlike *Gatsby, Tender Is the Night* has no first-person narrator; it is "unrolled" by an omniscient and "scientific" narrator who has chosen, in a way many critics think artificial, even "artsy," to begin not at the beginning, where an "unrolling" should begin, but in the middle, and at an angle slanting in from an outsider's observation of the central personality, Dick Diver. Rosemary Hoyt is a seventeen-year-old movie-kitten visiting the Riviera at a time in the 1920's when the beach still had that special dream atmosphere of mystery, natural grandeur and privilege, when it was myth kingdom enough to have a king and Dick Diver was that king. A relationship starts between them, working itself out under the burning Mediterranean sun in a trance-like fashion not unlike some of the crisis moments in Camus' *The Stranger.* Halfway through this first book, however, it becomes evident that the Rosemary-Dick relationship is only a preparation for, perhaps a distraction from, perhaps even a counter in, the "real" concern of the novel, which is the fierce and deadly struggle going on inside that entity that Rosemary and all their other friends see as Dick-and-Nicole-Diver, or as we later ominously learn they themselves have named it, "Dicole." Book Two gives us, in a business-like fashion that seems both a relief and an imposition, the story behind, or inside, or around, "Dicole." Dick Diver, from a line of Southern rural semi-clerical American gentry, grew up in the North and graduated from Yale during the first world war and spent the time off the battlefield training himself as a psychiatrist. Nicole Warren, from a line of Chicago robber barons, lost her mother early, grew close to her father and was seduced by him, some years later suffered a breakdown diagnosed as schizophrenia by the head of the "clinic for millionaires" to which Doctor Diver was attached. They meet, love and marry, cure, are cured, are sickened, not necessarily in that order, fight gamely the stresses from inside their psyches and outside, finally achieve, or sustain, or suffer, the crack-up of that entity, Dicole, and separate, she to another, more brutal man, and another marriage, and he to New York and obscurity, or possibly to "bide his time . . . like Grant at Galena," last visible to the narrator of the book in an embarrassing "entanglement" with "a girl who worked in a grocery store."

If the narrative began with Book Two, so Fitzgerald after initial publication ruminated, it would arch cleanly and swiftly through its "main" theme—a man of high scientific ideals and great intellectual gifts is destroyed by that weakness for the love of women which in Fitzgerald's world is always indistinguishable from the corruption of wealth. In this world the dreamer is an ironic Midas; no matter what he reaches for he touches only gold, which chokes and does not nourish. Even the touch of love leads only to a gold bride, so that marriage is ultimately, in one of Diver's most terrible visions, an endless "making love to dry loins." In that fearful chemistry, love-money-destruction, Rosemary and even Nicole herself have subordinate place as characters and influences on the reaction, and the outer, circumstantial drama whose major figures are Doctors Dohmler and Gregorovious and the successful scientists, as opposed on the battlefield of Diver's destiny to "Baby" Warren and "the Warren money," dominates the narrative. In that narrative, as John Callahan among others demonstrates,[2] the acutely historical, the American, tragedy, the American masculine tragedy, of the novel is well and clearly served. Near the end of the novel Nicole approaches Dick's workroom "sanctuary," the one room he had successfully paid for and isolated to himself against the powerful currents of her love and Warren money, and sees him, rather astonished, as something separate from herself:

> He was thinking, he was living a world completely his own and in the small motions of his face, the brow raised or lowered, the eyes narrowed or widened, the lips set and reset, the play of his hands, she saw him

progress from phase to phase of his own story spinning out inside him, his own, not hers.[3]

That story spinning out, unrolling his own fate, "his own, not hers," is the book Malcolm Cowley published after Fitzgerald's death, which starts with the original Book Two, fitting in "Rosemary's angle" comfortably where she belongs in the chronology of his story. That story is the one to be expected inside the covers of the Scribner reprint of 1962, whose blurb reports "the story of Dick Diver, a young psychiatrist whose career was thwarted and his genius numbed through marriage to the exquisite and wealthy Nicole Warren."

But in fact the novel inside that cover, the major popular and teaching text, is the original arrangement, the apparently distorting arrangement which starts with the young girl's perceptions. And in that arrangement the story is not one that conveniently passes "from phase to phase" under the strenuous efforts of a trained analyst. It is more like "an incalculable story was telling itself inside him, about which she could only guess at in the moments when it broke through the surface" (p. 345). Or even more, the novel reads like "tearing the words from some story spinning itself out inside her, too fast for him to grasp" (p. 246). Inside him, inside her, the "story" spins, too hot to touch, too quick to hold. It needs to be approached warily.

If we look at this oblique and wary approach, the approach of the healthy girl-child, fascinated, towards the mysterious and fatal object, Gothic structural parallels abound. Landing at "an isolated railroad stop," Rosemary and her mother are dismayed by the heat and emptiness of the beach: "Something tells me we're not going to like this place." There are the usual tense-making oblique Gothic warnings from friendly strangers: "They have sharks out behind the raft. Yesterday they devoured two British sailors. . . . We wanted to warn you about getting burned the first day. . . ." The ostentatious attention to the healthy glow, the "thrilling flush" of the girl sets up the sort of disturbing relationship we find often in vampire stories:

> Dick Diver looked at her with cold blue eyes; his kind, strong mouth said thoughtfully and deliberately: 'You're the only girl I've seen for a long time that actually did look like something blooming.' (p. 27)

There are the usual "village characters" in the path between the girl and the mysterious object, Riviera visitors half repelled, half fascinated by the ambience around "Dicole" who are, unlike Rosemary, somehow barred from advancing on the mystery, the castle, as they well know:

> 'We thought maybe you were in the plot,' said Mrs. McKisco. . . . 'We don't know who's in the plot and who isn't.'
> 'The plot?' inquired Rosemary, half understanding. 'Is there a plot?'
> 'My dear, we don't *know,*' said Mrs. Abrams, with a convulsive, stout woman's chuckle. 'We're not in it. We're the gallery.' (p. 9)

Gazing at the man in the center of the plot, Dick Diver, "all complete there," the girl feels the pull of personality—"I fell in love on the beach," Rosemary tells her mother. Since Dick is, as the narrator says significantly, "already possessed" by his wife, Rosemary's love falls perforce upon the couple. She makes the usual young girl's wrong guess about the nature of the attraction she feels, and the narrator quietly undermines the guess:

> Her naïveté responded whole-heartedly to the expensive simplicity of the Divers, unaware of its complexity and its lack of innocence . . . and that the simplicity of behavior also, the nursery-like peace and good wili, the emphasis on the simpler virtues, was part of a desperate bargain with the gods and had been attained through struggles she could not have guessed at. (pp. 26-27)

"Desperation" enters her love, and with her mother's calm permission Rosemary sets out to engage the mysterious hero in a love affair. Meanwhile the narration shifts to the Diver's "castle" on a hill to paint a scene of "faintly rotten" gardens and the false "impression of repose," where the husband and wife communicate by megaphone about giving a party: " 'I want to give a really *bad* party . . . where there's a brawl and seductions and people going home with their feelings hurt and women passed out in the cabinet de toilette' " (p. 35). Making his sinister parallels perfectly clear, the narrator concludes this introduction to his hero's parties, given to exercise an "extraordinary virtuosity with people," "He sometimes looked back with awe at the carnivals of affection he had given, as a general might gaze upon a massacre he had ordered to satisfy an impersonal blood lust." Not even when we understand better his "lust" does Dick Diver quite recover from pictures like this; meeting these pictures immediately in this arrangement of the novel makes it impossible to regard him uncritically as a scientific genius numbed by women.

Two memorable things happen at this carnival-party; in purest

Gothic tradition one is onstage and Romantic—Rosemary declares her love for Dick and is gracefully not turned down, only "passed along to Nicole"; and one offstage and mysteriously "horrid":

> 'What's the matter, Vi?'
> 'My dear—' she said at large, and then addressed Rosemary, 'my dear—it's nothing. I really can't say a word.'
> 'You're among friends,' said Abe.
> 'Well, upstairs I came upon a scene, my dears— '
> Shaking her head cryptically she broke off just in time, for Tommy arose and addressed her politely but sharply: "It's inadvisable to comment on what goes on in this house.' (pp. 46-47)

What Violet McKisco saw in the bathroom and Tommy Barban, the mercenary, fights a duel to make her keep silent about, haunts the first book until the end, when the scene is repeated before Rosemary's eyes. It effectively breaks apart the new unit which has been tentatively forming, Dick-and-Rosemary. Like the child she is, Rosemary has simply wanted Dick, followed him, offered herself. Like a father, Dick has soothed her, petted and complimented her and humorously evaded her; like a doctor he has studied, diagnosed and dismissed her case. Holding the girl off, keeping his innocence with the help of these two roles, Dick is yet "suddenly confused . . . simply confused" by Rosemary's insistence. The story spinning inside him and Nicole, symbolized by "what Violet McKisco saw in the bathroom," clearly makes Rosemary an object at once of desire and of horror to Dick. "Shaken by the impetus of his newly recognized emotion" (p. 111), Dick begins to lose grace, judgment and "repose," and at the start of a scene which will find the former virtuoso of people literally lost and wandering in the streets the narrator tells us again that this disaster of emotion Dick feels is not, cannot, simply be a husband's regret at the entrance of a new love. Some Secret Sin is at stake: "Dick was paying some tribute to things unforgotten, unshriven, unexpurgated" (p. 119).

Dick and Rosemary are saved from that, this time, by a series of ludicrous incidents which redramatize before them the circumstance of the Secret Sin. Rosemary finds the dead body of a Negro in her bloodstained bed and calls in Dick. Rushing to "save" Rosemary from scandal, Dick competently hands the bloody spread to Nicole to remove, and arranges the "scene" around the dead man so that Rosemary will appear not to be involved. In a sway of "wild worship" when the crisis is over the man and girl move toward each other. But they are torn away by a sound from the bathroom: "a verbal inhumanity that penetrated the keyholes and the cracks in the doors, swept into the suite and in the shape of horror took form again" (p. 147). It is Nicole, kneeling by the tub, "swaying sideways and sideways," clutching the stained spread around her and looking in terror, in humiliation, in abject love, in outraged accusation at the man who enters: "It's you!—with your spread with red blood on it. I'll wear it for you—I'm not ashamed." And from the man comes only, three times, the harsh, perhaps necessarily harsh, command, "Control yourself!"

As if in obedience to that command, the narrative switches in Book Two from the language of Romantic lyric and Gothic intimation to the detached ironic voice of the historian with "the ring of a biography" to establish. The historian focuses away from women, "tired of women's worlds" like the rotting musician, Abe North. The scene is a psychiatrist's clinic, the doctors are men, the patients seem largely to be women; the word is a man's world, the story is a man's: "—Dick Diver's moment now began. . . . It was a damp April day, with long diagonal clouds over the Albishorn. . . . To-day he went out to see Franz Gregorovious at Dohmler's clinic on the Zurichsee" (pp. 155-57).

If, as some readers wish, Mary Shelley had begun her novel when the creature's moment began—"It was on a dreary night of November that I beheld the accomplishment of my toils. With an anxiety that almost amounted to agony, I collected the instruments of life around me, that I might infuse a spark of being into the lifeless thing that lay at my feet"—then the novel would have been, as most films are, the creature's story spinning itself out. Instead, it is a novel about how the story or motive or disease spinning in the mind and actions of the explorer Walton is both transformed into and confirmed by the story spinning in the mind of the scientist Victor Frankenstein, and how these stories result in and are transformed by and challenged by the story set spinning in the brain of the child-creature at the center of the fiction. If Fitzgerald had in fact begun his novel with Doctor Diver attempting the cure of the girl he sees that April day we should have been without that significant sense of mystery, danger, madness *spreading outward* from the center that makes this book important, and makes it Gothic. Without the special impact and immediacy of Rosemary's innocent-crafty pursuit of the older man, and her happy-cowardly escape, we should not know how terribly and in a sense monotonously the Secret Sin repeats itself, and fastens on everyone in its path in the effort to repeat itself.

Above all, without that climactically placed melodramatic tableau of the girl-child and the red-stained bed and the dead man and the looming commanding man we should have an imperfect rendering of the center secret itself. For in the atmosphere of Book Two, that very carefully maintained atmosphere of rational candor that goes with the ultimate clean, well-lighted place—the asylum, the secret shrinks into the banal, the quietly understood, the casually regretted. The scientists simply want information; the racking agony of the guilty father is irrelevant:

> Half an hour after this second arrival on the Zurichsee, Warren had broken down, his fine shoulders shaking with awful sobs inside his easy-fitting coat, his eyes redder than the very sun on Lake Geneva, and they had the awful story.
>
> 'It just happened,' he said hoarsely. 'I don't know—I don't know. . . . People used to say what a wonderful father and daughter we were—they used to wipe their eyes. We were just like lovers—and then all at once we were lovers—and ten minutes after it happened I could have shot myself—except I guess I'm such a Goddammed degenerate I didn't have the nerve to do it.'
>
> 'Then what?' said Doctor Dohmler. . . . (pp. 170-71)

The final note of broken bathos from Warren is ignored, as it deserves to be, by the scientists. He is not their patient, and it seems not their business to attempt the obvious prognosis about the guilty father, that he *will* achieve his own death somehow, if not by shotgun. Even when Doctor Diver meets him later in the last stages of alcoholic poisoning he makes no connection between the father's story spinning itself out, and the daughter's.

The title of the spinning story, the name of the sin, is not rape, or even incest, or even sex, but Complicity, the desire of the forbidden, desire of the evil, desire of the unnatural, desire of the destructive, the rotten, the dying, desire of death. Complicity, participation in the horror, is at the heart of the real terror in Gothic novels, which is why the most moving portraits of terror in classic Gothic, from Monk Lewis to Mary Shelley to Stevenson, always show the terror of the "villain," not the victim. Even for that greatest of all "Gothic" victims, Clarissa Harlowe, the strongest terror is her terror of complicity. Complicity in this novel links *all* the themes together. Complicity in wealth-the-destroyer nags eternally at Dick Diver as it does at all Fitzgerald's men, complicity in the perils of the poor is part of the nightmare of the rich. Above all, in a novel as explicitly "post-war" as

Hemingway's *The Sun Also Rises* or as Lawrence's *Women in Love,* complicity in that monumental act of self-destruction is the secret terror and exaltation of a whole generation:

> 'This western-front business couldn't be done again, not for a long time. . . . This took religion and years of plenty and tremendous sureties and the exact relation that existed between the classes. . . . You had to have a whole-souled sentimental equipment going back further than you could remember. . . . This kind of battle was invented by Lewis Carroll and Jules Verne and whoever wrote Undine, and country deacons bowling and marraines in Marseilles and girls seduced in the back lanes of Wurtemburg and Westphalia. Why, this was a love battle—there was a century of middle-class love spent here. . . . All my beautiful lovely safe world blew itself up here with a great gust of high explosive love. . . .' (p. 75)

On the most universal scale, the complicity at stake in this novel is that awful love-battle. The doctor says it couldn't be done again. But by the side of the "love story" spinning through Dick and Nicole in *Tender Is the Night* spins the battle story in the life of Tommy Barban, whose life is a shuttle between his love for Nicole and "a war" that he feels he must "go find" after every visit to the couple. Wars are easy to find for this mercenary, with his absolutely simple stock of ideas and his utterly complicated routine of battle readiness. And when at the novel's end Nicole, finally "cured" of Dick and by him, moves to the protection of Tommy, when this whole-souled sentimental equipment triumphantly joins itself to that exquisite training for war, it is a restarting, restaging of that drama of complicity in universal natural-war which amounts almost to prophecy.

On the smallest scale, the inner drama that fuels and is fueled by the outer, there is Nicole, like Rosemary, "Daddy's Girl." In the first book, unknowing, we see Rosemary's performance in that successful film along with Nicole and Dick in a special screening. Of Nicole the narrator reports only that she was restless, of Dick that his analyst's mind "winced for all psychologists at the vicious sentimentality" of a father complex "so apparent" (p. 91). Dick's scientific shield keeps his distaste professional until the shield is shattered by Rosemary's ferociously naive offer to give Dick a screen test, presumably so he can play her father-lover on screen as well as off. There was, says the narrator, "an awful silence."

In that awful silence, it seems clear, Rosemary and Nicole have snapped together in Dick's mind as the girl-child pursuing and fleeing the parent-lover, who was once Warren and is now, fixedly, himself. Of Nicole, the doctor diagnosed, "She felt complicity . . . so from sheer self-protection she developed the idea that she had had no complicity" (p. 173). Schizophrenia results, and finally, crack-up. In the crack-up the story which began as a plot between Nicole and her father escapes to lodge itself inside the already spinning story of Doctor Diver. The young Nicole, Rosemary's age at this time, pursues the new father with a nervous reserve born of that old subterranean terror of complicity, forcing him to accept the responsibility of cure, of initiation, and finally, of love. "I kept waiting for some one to tell me. It was the duty of some one who understood. The blind must be led" (p. 161), she writes to Diver at this period with an instinct which in her never wavers, even to the end when she makes a break for "independence" toward the most powerful, because most single-minded, father in the book, Tommy Barban. And later, still more ominously to those familiar with the Gothic, she writes to Doctor Diver, "I am slowly coming back to life."

Gathering his instruments of life, the phonograph tunes, the meetings and letters, playing with fire and fascinated by "that excitement about her" generated by his own increasingly weak hold on his professional and paternal shield, the scientist fights not to become Daddy, not to become God-the-Father. But his profession offers him both these roles exactly as "instruments of life" for his patients, and his personal instinct is in these directions too. In fact the personal "bent" led him to the profession, as he recognizes:

> The weakness of this profession is in its attraction for the man a little crippled and broken. Within the walls of the profession he compensates by tending toward the clinical, the 'practical'—he has won his battle without a struggle. (p. 182)

Early in life, sensing that the moral values he was inheriting were unserviceable in the new world, perhaps even weaknesses in it, Dick replaced father and grandfather with himself. Broken, he has moved toward the broken of this world like a homing pigeon and, the narration sometimes suggests, like a vulture, to become, for them, a virtuoso of people, or a clinical psychiatrist. As a psychiatrist, or virtuoso, he must become what the broken people need, temporarily, while retaining a detached personal and professional self. This too is schizophrenia, partially controllable through professional ethics, and with luck. In the case of Nicole Warren, unluckily for the man whom his friends called "lucky Dick," crack fitted crack, need meet need. Dick's secret desire to be father-lover-God, to have all the love in the world, betrays him to the omnivorous girl-child whom Fitzgerald described earlier in terms made for Rosemary but applicable to Nicole: "she wanted for a moment to hold him and devour him, wanted his mouth, his ears, his coat collar, wanted to surround him and engulf him" (p. 87). Personal and professional, conscious and unconscious collapse together in Dick; he cannot achieve for either of them the necessary "divorce" from the girl-child he has made: "He was enough older than Nicole to take pleasure in her youthful vanities and delights. . . . He tried honestly to divorce her from any obsession that he had stitched her together—glad to see her build up happiness and confidence apart from him" (p. 181). They love, and marry, and "he knew her problem was one they had together for good now" (p. 206). They have become a unit, similarly cracked, a unit inside which there is genuine, even romantic love, but which is dominated by the parent-child "story" spinning itself out too quickly to grasp except when it briefly comes to the surface, in three of Nicole's attacks.

The story's terror surfaces after the birth of the Divers' first girl-child, the birth of the first boy was not so disturbing. In the presence of her own daughter, "everything got dark again" for Nicole and she madly lashed out at the eternal betraying lover-father: ". . . If I could get word to my husband who has seen fit to desert me here" (p. 211). We also hear Nicole snap viciously about her daughter: "You tell me my baby is black—that's farcical, that's very cheap," a startlingly Gothic reference to the possible devil-child sired by that ambiguous father-lover which perhaps figures again in Nicole's third "attack" over the dead Negro. The second surfacing of the story happened at the party where Rosemary and Dick began the flirtation that for Nicole even more than Dick seemed to promise the repeat of the Secret Sin, the spreading of the complicity, especially since Nicole's own complicity in whatever is developing is helplessly assured by Dick's habit of "passing on" all people to Nicole as therapy for her and as professional detachment for himself.

It is extraordinary to note this dangerous attraction-repulsion between the older darkly dangerous man and the girl-child in Gothic fiction proper. It seems a reversal of Oedipal anxiety-action: the father's desire to kill his son and rape and destroy his daughter. It is a kind of Titus Andronicus complex except that the hostility seems directed actually at the child, not at the mother-wife. In Walpole's

Castle of Otranto two powerful fathers battle for control of their and each other's children; Manfred's son is murdered and he pursues his son's bride Isabella through labyrinths to the accusing statue of the girl's father; he is foiled in his rape but Destiny or Desire guides his other dagger to the passionate murder of his own daughter, Matilda. In Lewis' *The Monk* and Radcliffe's *The Italian* the ambiguous horror of the older man's passion, murderous and erotic, for the girl-child, a passion provoked by the orphan's innocent pursuit of parent figures, is further complicated by the double burden of fatherhood carried by the priest-villains. Even Jane Austen's *Northanger Abbey* is haunted by an avenging, or at least loveless, father whose antipathy to the girl-child heroine is a transference of his singular antipathy towards his own children. The threat to the young, especially the girl, and the sense of rivalry with the son that we see in General Tilney is not all in Catherine Morland's Gothic imagination. And in *Frankenstein,* where both Victor's adopted sister-lover Elizabeth and the two creatures, male and female, whom he creates, function to some extent as his children, the deadly antipathy between parent and child results first in the destruction of the two women and then in mutual self-destruction, the parent in this case willing, or even anxious, to give up his own life so long as he can compass the death of his created son.

None of the pragmatic issues surrounding these extreme illicit passions, issues of property or reputation or lust or religious principle or even simple life and death, seems a real correlative to the demonic energies released between parent figure and child figure in classic Gothic. Some deep struggle for control of the springs of being itself seems to be the issue, some struggle by the parent to unmake or reabsorb the child, and thus to stop time, keep his own power, freeze his own being into immortality. The most powerfully imagined Gothic "old man" of all, Melmoth the Wanderer, has held all the Being given to his line of the family to himself, has exchanged it with no woman, given it away to no child; as a consequence lives four generations beyond his span, a terror to himself and all his race. And when he finally does, in bitterest reluctance, despair and cynicism, make this transference, lend this power, he knows that in the world that now is, he is buying his own death. The Inquisitors, with Isadora and the child in their prison, speculate: "We hold him by the cords of man—if he burst these cords he is more than man. He has a wife and child, and if there be human elements in him, if there be anything mortal clinging to his heart, we shall wind round the roots of it, and extract it." The dread of letting-go, into death, has fixed itself in Melmoth and turned him to stone; the burden of so much immortal Being clenched in one man is so awful a sight, so painful a thought, that Melmoth cannot rid himself of his excess to child, friend or enemy, though he tries.

Melmoth's is the other agony, the agony of the un-father. Frankenstein's, or Fitzgerald's, is the terror of giving away his power, draining away his vitality. The love-destruction of the girl-child seems at bottom the attempt to take it all back, to cancel out those withdrawals from the spiritual bank account that Fitzgerald spoke of in "The Crack-Up."[4]

Quarrying material for still another treatment of the destructive wealth of the Beautiful Americans, Fitzgerald, in this novel, at this point in his own psychic history, struck deep into this Gothic territory, and produced a work rough, unwieldy, mysteriously violent, and insightful. In the story of Dick Diver, whose ambiguous American yearnings for identification with and freedom from "my father . . . all my fathers" (p. 267) made him take up that role blindly at every turning of his fate, Fitzgerald was dealing with personal and archetypal dynamite. To protect himself from this dimly recognized weakness, this "high explosive gust of love," Dick Diver adopts the profession, the ethics, the language, the mannerisms, of the scientist, the nineteenth and twentieth century's form of the "spoiled priest" as Fitzgerald called Dick. And in a curious way so did Fitzgerald, whose omnicient narrator in *Tender Is the Night*, given to case histories, general formulae and a nervously held distance of judgment, is like nothing so much as an analyst himself.

But no more than the monastery and religious vows protected Radcliffe's Schedoni or Lewis' Ambrosio or Hogg's Robert Wringhim, do the laboratory and scientific ethics protect Shelley's Frankenstein or Stevenson's Jekyll or Fitzgerald's Dick Diver from the madness that creeps into the eyes from the hungering heart. The Gothic tradition on this subject as far back as Faustus warns that all solitudes, whether religious or scientific, chosen or enforced, are the habitation of madness, and all the products of abstract study, whether benevolent, selfish, or in the service of "truth," are simply mirrors of the student's own fearfully mixed being. When Doctor Diver, escaping from the corruption of Warren money, moves into his own private laboratory, when Victor Frankenstein, in flight from the narrow conventionalism of family and teachers, moves out of the university to his private rooms, when the respectable Henry Jekyll, following his truth, becomes "too fanciful" for the staid Doctor Lanyon and purchases a "sinister block of building . . . with a blind forehead of discolored wall," the Gothic reader knows the scientist is giving pernicious form to his doubleness. The scientist who thinks he is leaving the chaos, stupidity and irrationality of social life for the clean hard ground of scientific truth will discover that he has in fact left the sanity of varied balance for the madness of the detached extreme.

In Diver's case the situation is made still more tragic by the fact, dispassionately, even cruelly repeated several times by the narrator, that Diver has no genius, no profound if destructive scientific truth to elucidate; and so the attempt to divorce his scientific from his husbandly self only reveals an essential sterility and mediocrity in both roles when they are looked at hard and separately. The Gothic scientist is mad but fruitful; this one, in his arid schizophrenia, produces only the lesson that he already wrote about in his youthful pamphlet "A Psychology for Psychiatrists."

In Dick Diver Fitzgerald has created a man who, as the crack-up becomes apparent in himself, must also stop giving himself. This means "freeing" Nicole, or rather, since the condition for freedom is that she transfer herself, like Gatsby's Daisy, from the dreamer to a simpler, stronger man, freeing himself from Nicole. The first step in this process is Rosemary, who was in Book One's "plot" playing the child Nicole to Dick's Warren. In Book Three the operative phrase is not the plot but "the plan." As Dick "shows off" one last time before a Rosemary whom he no longer needs or loves, because she is no longer a "girl," Nicole feels a liberating disgust with him which he sees but does not attempt to counter or heal. The sensitive child-wife feels "that a plan underlay his current actions" (p. 373). And in half-conscious obedience to that plan she and Tommy Barban become lovers. When Dick and Nicole confront each other afterwards and she lets him know for sure that "he no longer controlled her," the narrator says that Nicole has "cut the cord forever," an ambiguous notion which leaves unclear which one is the child. But a great sigh goes up from hero and narrator: "Doctor Diver was at liberty." The two men meet to formalize the transfer of Nicole, who is without doubt still "the girl child" as much as Walpole's Isabella was when Alfonso gave her over to the house of Manfred. Included in that transfer, perforce, are Dick's own daughter and son, for whom also the giving is over: "He was glad he had given so much to the little girl—about the boy he was more uncertain—always he had been uneasy about what he had to give to the ever-climbing, ever-clinging, breast-searching young" (p. 402). The cord is cut all around; the freeing of Nicole is not a cure, it is at best a birth, and Dick Diver has played all the parts in that drama, father, mother, doctor, and priest; in the final scene Fitzgerald has him raise his right hand and bless the beach with a papal cross "from the high terrace" (p. 406).

It is hard to say whether he closes the curtain as a success or a failure. The latter, one must say, if *Tender Is the Night* is read as the social history of a man who set out to make an intellectual career apart from the "world of women" and was dragged into it in spite of himself. But a success, possibly, if Diver's purpose was, as he discovered in the end, the dream-nightmare that moves many fathers, mad scientists, and gothic writers, and that was expressed by William Faulkner perhaps for Diver and Fitzgerald as well as for himself when the great Southern Gothicist mused on the creation and the fate of his Caddy, who also ended up tragically with a military man: "So I, who had never had a sister and was fated to lose my daughter in infancy, set out to make myself a beautiful and tragic little girl."

Princeton University

---

[1]"The Crack-Up," *The Crack-Up,* ed. Edmund Wilson (New York: New Directions, 1945), p. 73.

[2]*The Illusions of a Nation: Myth and History in the Novels of F. Scott Fitzgerald,* University of Illinois Press, Urbana: 1972. Robert Sklar (*F. Scott Fitzgerald: The Last Laocöon,* New York: Oxford University Press, 1967) also holds the view that essentially the seven years between *The Great Gatsby* and *Tender Is the Night* were an odyssey from myth to history, influenced particularly by Fitzgerald's reading of Spengler. But Sklar's work seems to me even more important for its emphasis on influences reaching Fitzgerald from myth-sources, of Cabell's *Jurgen* and Twain's *The Mysterious Stranger,* of Anglo-Catholic mysticism and Keats' Lamia-visions, and above all of the early imprint of H. G. Wells (one thinks especially of the "clinic" of Doctor Moreau).

[3]*Tender Is the Night* (New York: Scribners, 1934), p. 388. All quotations are to this first edition.

[4]To recall at this point Fitzgerald's nervous recognition in "The Crack-Up" that one of the signs of crack-up is to be unable to control that shift into identity with "the objects of my horror or compassion" is to recognize another dimension to that curious female-maleness of Fitzgerald's protagonists to which Leslie Fiedler has called attention (*Love and Death in the American Novel,* New York: Dell, 1960, p. 312). For it is not simply, as Fiedler implies, that whoever plays the "innocent" in American fiction has a female-Clarissa role, but more terribly that whoever is innocent is also not-innocent, also has complicity. In the earlier form of the novel, "The Type," the attacked innocent was a male, Francis, whom Fitzgerald thought to make a matricide. Transposing that male into Rosemary certainly reemphasizes the innocence, but as

Rosemary draws closer to Nicole in the minds of both the innocent Dick and the narrator, and both men draw closer in the reader's mind to the ravaged father, Warren, it is clear that the complicity in the woman which is the object of both horror and compassion is not erased, only buried more deeply, by the shift of sex.

NEILA SESHACHARI

The Great Gatsby: Apogee of Fitzgerald's Mythopoeia

The Great Gatsby marks the apogee of Fitzgerald's craft of fiction, especially in its richness of mythopoeic implications and use of mythic symbols. In this novel Fitzgerald successfully blends local, national, historical, and primitive myths, as a result of which the significance of the novel seems to "enlarge in ever-widening ripples," not only in terms of the personal, historical, and metaphysical as Richard Lehan suggests,[1] but even in terms of the mythistoric leading to myth. *The Great Gatsby* is remarkable for the multi-level mythic interpretation that it suggests. The mythic quality of *The Great Gatsby,* therefore, manifests itself at various levels to different critics. For instance, *The Great Gatsby* variously suggests itself as the perfect expression of the ephemeral Jazz Age; as the enactment of the history of the New World[2]; as the embodiment of the American Dream[3]; as a damaging criticism of that Dream[4]; and as a novel where the hero is so impersonalized as to be a mythic character.[5] *The Great Gatsby* is all these and more, for it is truly polysemous in mythic overtones. Critics, who are all agreed that in this novel Fitzgerald gives a scathing criticism of the myth of the American Dream, have spoken of the American Dream and Gatsby's personal dream as if they were synonymous—as if that were the prime reason why *The Great Gatsby* offers, in effect, a criticism of the American Dream. A closer inquiry into the fundamental difference between the American Dream and Gatsby's personal quest might point to the suggestion that *The Great Gatsby,* which is a damaging commentary on the former, may in fact be an affirmation of the latter. Also, Gatsby may appear to be a mythic character not only because he is impersonalized and appears to be the romantic impulse[6] crystallized in the term American Dream, but also because Gatsby's story offers a complete parallel to the embryonic path of the mythic hero, so that Gatsby, in his death and apotheosis, seems a minor avatar of the truly great mythic heroes of the stature of Theseus, Jason, Karna, and others.

A close study of *The Great Gatsby* will reveal that there are basic generic differences between the traditional American Dream and Gatsby's own personal quest. The American Dream has been an affirmation of the romantic possibilities of the human imagination and a belief in man's inherent greatness. Gatsby's personal philosophy synchronizes with this outlook. However, apart from this common faith, the actual direction that Gatsby's personal dream took does not follow the pattern of the American Dream. The American Dream, historically, has been the outcome of the Renaissance spirit and the later era of economic development and opportunism. The actual opportunity that the new continent offered the seekers of an essentially human dream shaped the forms of that quest. Thus, in 20th-century America, the goals of success are youth and wealth; as Edwin Fussel has pointed out, one aspect of the American Dream is the mythistoric quest of Ponce de Leon, whereas the other is plainly, wealth.[7] Thus at the core, the American Dream may be said to be self-centered. A votary of the American Dream is given to thinking in terms of the glorification of the self; he strives to establish his personal identity and amasses immense wealth before he allows either the gospel or the Internal Revenue Service to channel his thoughts to philanthropy. The hero's yearning after the most beautiful girl in the world is one of the symptoms of his ego-satisfaction. The girl is simply an adjunct or addition to the hero's manifest wealth. She is a visual symbol of his greatness, as Daisy is to Tom Buchanan. It matters not whether there is true love between the two—in fact, true love would imply a recapitulation of ego-seeking values. True love implies an acknowledgment of the worth of the beloved and sharing of glory. In admitting a dependence on the object of love, it diminishes, to that extent, the belief in the absolute power of the self. The American male has not been inclined to share the glory of his conquests with the woman. In the unfolding of the Promethean imagination on the new continent, woman has not shared the victory or the glory of the adventurer. The Women's Liberation Movement is the modern-day protest of this state. The American Dream, thus, is founded on the concept of the expansion of the male self based on a romantic belief in the glory of the self. Gatsby's personal quest appears to be an extension of the American Dream because in the pursuit of his personal dream he was compelled to resort to the material acquisition demanded by the American society in which he lived and of which he was a part. But in reality Gatsby's dream transcends the accepted modes of the American Dream to envelop man's primordial concepts. For Gatsby's quest is not youth and wealth which are the symptomatic goals of the American Dream; Gatsby's personal quest centers wholly on his acquisition of the object of his love—woman—which is really the quest of the mythic ideal.

Woman, in her mythic concept, is the ultimate quest of the hero. She is the symbol of all that is knowable and worthy of being conquered or won. As Joseph Campbell asserts:

> Woman, in the picture language of mythology, represents the totality of what can be known. The hero is the one who comes to know. As he progresses in the slow initiation which is life, the form of the goddess undergoes for him a series of transfigurations: she can never be greater than himself, though she can always promise more than he is yet capable of comprehending. She lures, she guides, she bids him burst his fetters. And if he can match her import, the two, the knower and the known, will be released from every limitation. Woman is the guide to the sublime acme of sensuous adventure. By deficient eyes she is reduced to inferior states; by the evil eye of ignorance she is spellbound to banality and ugliness. But she is redeemed by the eyes of understanding. The hero who can take her as she is, without undue commotion but with the kindness and assurance she requires, is potentially the king, the incarnate god, of her created world.[8]

This symbol of woman standing for world conquest and ultimate glory is operative in fairy tales and folk tales where the union of the hero with his beloved and the assertion of ". . . and they lived happily ever after" imply that the hero has reached his zenith. The hero's union with his beloved implies here, a fulfillment of the purpose of life. Gatsby's quest for Daisy is thus the quest of the mythic ideal and not of the values of the American Dream.

Gatsby's one consuming passion to which all others are either subordinate or nonexistent is his hope of winning Daisy. His acquisition of wealth, his nebulous parties, his mysterious activities are all secondary to his purpose which is to win back his woman. Getting into her "class" of society and accumulating enough wealth to be worthy of her are self-purificatory rites that he has to undergo before he can be worthy of her. His sense of worship—wonderment, anxiety, nervousness—are all obvious when he arranges to meet her at Nick Carraway's home for tea. The entire chapter in which he meets Daisy for the first time since their separation five years previously exudes Gatsby's sense of worship of Daisy. The preparation for the worship is itself very elaborate. Two whole days before their meeting—in fact, on the day it is arranged—Gatsby's home is lit from tower to cellar in an unreal blaze. It isn't the occasion of another party, and when Nick comments to Gatsby that his house looks like the World's Fair, Gatsby answers absently, "I have been glancing into some of the rooms."[9] The self-assured son of God is visibly nervous even in preparation for the visit of his goddess. In his anxiety to have everything right for his beloved, Gatsby has Nick's lawn mowed and flowers provided abundantly. Gatsby's offer of monetary reward to Nick strangely smacks of the offerings made by a devotee to the high priest in a formal worship ceremony. On the appointed day, minutes before Daisy's arrival, Gatsby, "in a white flannel suit, silver shirt, and gold colored tie," makes his nervous appearance. From then on, until Daisy actually arrives and the evening wears on, Gatsby is in a state of nervous tension and panic combined into one. When he disappears from Nick's living room and makes his formal entry befitting the occasion, he looks "pale as death," his eyes are "distraught," and he is generally "trembling" (pp. 104-105). In his anxiety he thinks there has been some terrible mistake somewhere. It is only after Nick discreetly gives them half an hour alone with each other and comes back after making all sorts of noises, that he notices "They were sitting at either end of the couch, looking at each other as if some question had been asked, or was in the air, and every vestige of embarrassment was gone. Daisy's face was smeared with tears. . . . But there was a change in Gatsby that was simply confounding. He literally glowed; without a word or gesture of exultation a new well-being radiated from him and filled the little room" (pp. 107-108). This comment is Nick's observation and approval of Gatsby's successful worship. Later, as Gatsby takes Daisy and Nick round his home, Nick notices that "He hadn't once ceased looking at Daisy, and . . . he revalued everything in his house according to the measure of response it drew from her well-loved eyes. Sometimes, too, *he stared around at his possessions in a dazed way, as though in her actual and astounding presence none of it was any longer real"* (pp. 110-111. Italics mine). Since Gatsby's wealth was acquired with the explicit aim of winning Daisy back and not for its own value, it is natural that his possessions suddenly seem to lose their glamor when he repossesses her. Gatsby's sense of worship of Daisy is seen even when he displays his shirts to her. The reason such a display does not seem vulgar is precisely that there is so much sanctity and ritual involved in the act—the reader intuitively comprehends the seriousness of the situation and holds his breath in awe. The ritual of display has its effect; suddenly, with strained sound Daisy bends her head into the shirts and begins to sob stormily. "They're such beautiful shirts," she sobs, her voice muffled in the thick folds. "It makes me sad because I've never seen such—such beautiful shirts before" (p. 112). At this moment, what Lionel Trilling said of Gatsby himself becomes surprisingly true of even a worship scene such as this: Its "credibility becomes trivial before the larger significance"[10] it implies. This significance, in one vital sense, is the mythic, which Fitzgerald's conceptual imagination seems to have grasped, albeit unconsciously.

Fitzgerald's success in imparting mythic significance to his writings comes from his spotlighting scenes, events, and furnishings that are strongly mythic in their overtones. Gatsby's yacht, for example, functions as a vital mythic symbol. Daisy goes into raptures when she first sees a picture of young Gatsby in yachting costume. Gatsby's career begins when he sees Dan Cody's yacht drop anchor and pulls up in a borrowed rowboat to tell Cody that the wind might catch him and break him up in half an hour. In the mythological formula that outlines the basic life of the hero, the skiff or boat forms, as Joseph Campbell has noted, a very major symbol. With the aid of this, the hero is able to cross the turbulent waters (which is yet another symbol) that endanger his life. The boat or yacht is the symbol of the special talent or virtue that the hero possesses, by which he is ferried across the waters of the world. "And by a like miracle, so will each whose work is the difficult, dangerous task of self-discovery and self-development be portered across the ocean of life."[11]

"To young Gatz, resting on his oars and looking up at the railed deck, that yacht [belonging to Dan Cody] represented all the beauty and glamor in the world. . . . And when the *Tuolomee* left for the West Indies and the Barbary Coast Gatsby left too" (p. 120). We are told that the arrangement lasted *five* years, during which time the boat went *three times* around the Continent. As Norma Goodrich points out, "Numbers in mythology have essence."[12] Mythologically, five denotes the four quarters, North, South, East, West, and the Center of the Earth. The number three is symbolic of both Christian and Hindu Trinity, "the three persons of Language," or the Egyptian Triad. At the end of his mystical journey Gatsby is "left with his singularly appropriate education"; "the vague contour" of Jay Gatsby fills out "to the substantiality of a man" (p. 121). Thus the picture of Gatsby in his yacht, going three times round the world in five annual revolutions of the earth around the sun, channeling his energies to win his woman may be construed as a symbolic one.

These two symbols—the yacht and the girl—meant a great deal to Fitzgerald himself. In "My Lost City," he writes:

> There was first the ferry boat moving softly from the Jersey shore at dawn—the moment crystallized into my first symbol of New York. Five years later when I was fifteen I went into the city from school to see Ina Claire in *The Quaker Girl* and Gertrude Bryan in *Little Boy Blue.* Confused by my hopeless and melancholy love for them both, I was unable to choose between them—so they blurred into one lovely entity, the girl. She was my second symbol of New York. The ferry boat stood for triumph, the girl for romance.[13]

It is significant that these two symbols recur again and again in his novels beginning with *This Side of Paradise.* In this first novel, Amory Blaine is aware that he was "made for glory," for triumph. When the story begins, Amory is Narcissus—but he is not Narcissus sitting on the banks of a brook brooding admiringly over his image. Rather, he is Narcissus in the ferry boat, paying too much attention to his own image in the water to heed where the ferry is drifting. But even Narcissus knows he is on a mission—some mission—even if it can be described only as a mission of glory, triumph, and romance. Although Amory wants to be a hero, in his scheme of values girls are still secondary. Amory's quest is the quest of the dreamer for the mythic grail. The questor is too naive and his initiation is tantamount to an initiation *manqué*. The protagonist of *The Great Gatsby* is a maturer one and is truly a hero. He is the one who overcomes the confines of his birth and his obstacles through his personal triumph (yacht), wins his goddess (or conquers the world), and is purified in the water of life. Through his valor and achievement, he attains apotheosis.

The water symbol is very extensively used in *The Great Gatsby*. Through a linking of the bay that connects West Egg and East Egg, Gatsby's swimming pool and the yacht that takes him thrice around the waters of the world, his aquaplane, and the final rain that gently purifies everything at the time of Gatsby's funeral, Fitzgerald treats the water symbol as a *leit motif*. Water or rain seems to play a baptismal part in all the crucial events in Gatsby's life. His meeting with Dan Cody takes place over the vast waters of Lake Superior from where he is launched in a "skiff" round the waters of the world. Nick Carraway's first glimpse of Gatsby is that of his standing on the shore of the bay stretching his arms in near mystic contemplation towards the dark waters separating him from Daisy. After five years Gatsby and Daisy are reunited in pouring rain. Also, significantly, Nick picks up Gatsby's body from the waters of his swimming pool. A steady, sombre rain beats down on the day of Gatsby's funeral. At the cemetery, someone murmurs "Blessed are the dead that the rain falls on," and the owl-eyed man says "Amen to that." Water, as a purifier, is a mythic symbol. The Vedas, for instance, refer frequently to water as a life-giving symbol. The *Rig Veda,* in a creation legend, states how the Vedic god Indra had to strike down the cosmic serpent Vritra in order to release life-giving waters and bring the world into manifestation.[14] The Christian baptism is a rejuvenation through immersion in life-giving or life-purifying waters. Gatsby's death in his swimming pool thus symbolically becomes the scene of his rebirth and apotheosis. Gatsby's death, as Wilfred Louis Guerin has remarked, is a "death by water-rebirth myth."[15] It is meet that the rain should fall at the time of Gatsby's funeral. The rain is a fertility symbol—it rejuvenates the hero and completes his apotheosis. When he emerges from his final test, Gatsby truly rises to the stature of a mythic hero.

In what is probably the most exhaustive study on the subject, Joseph Campbell describes "the standard path of the mythological adventure of the hero" as a "magnification of the formula represented in the rites of passage: separation—initiation—return" which he calls "the nuclear unit of the monomyth."[16] Campbell describes the basic formula of the monomyth in the following terms:

> The mythological hero, setting forth from his commonday hut or castle, is lured, carried away, or else voluntarily proceeds, to the threshold of

> adventure. There he encounters a shadow presence that guards the passage. The hero may defeat or conciliate this power and go alive into the kingdom of the dark (brother-battle, dragon-battle; offering, charm), or be slain by the opponent and descend in death (dismemberment, crucifixion). Beyond the threshold, the hero journeys through a world of unfamiliar yet strangely intimate forces, some of which severely threaten him (tests), some of which give magical aid (helpers). When he arrives at the nadir of the mythological round, he undergoes a supreme ordeal and gains his reward. The triumph may be represented as the hero's sexual union with the goddess-mother of the world (sacred marriage), his recognition by the father-creator (father atonement), his own divinization (apotheosis), or again—if the powers have remained unfriendly to him—his theft of the boon he came to gain (bride-theft, fire-theft); intrinsically it is an expansion of consciousness and therewith of being (illumination, transfiguration, freedom). The final work is that of the return. If the powers have blessed the hero, he now sets forth under their protection (emissary); if not, he flees and is pursued (transformation flight, obstacle flight). At the return threshold the transcendental powers must remain behind; the hero re-emerges from the kingdom of dead (return, resurrection). The boon that he brings restores the world (elixir).[17]

The embryonic pattern of the life of the hero is thus broad and adaptable, and individual myths usually elaborate on some of these features. As Campbell admits, "The changes rung on the simple scale of the monomyth defy description."[18]

The predominant events of Gatsby's life follow the basic concepts of this monomyth. Gatsby, like the mythic hero, is a man whose origins are steeped in mystery. He is, simultaneously, the son of nobody and of God. He is the nowhere hero. As Nick appropriately points out, "The truth was that Jay Gatsby of West Egg, Long Island, sprang from his Platonic conception of himself. He was the son of God—a phrase which, if it means anything, means just that—and he must be about His Father's business, the service of a vast, vulgar, and meretricious beauty. So he invented just the sort of Jay Gatsby that a seventeen year-old boy would be likely to invent, and to this conception he was faithful to the end" (p. 118).

James Gatz's transformation into Jay Gatsby marks the call to adventure that every hero must answer. Gatsby's apprenticeship with Dan Cody may be termed the symbolic equivalent of the "descent into the underworld," or "withdrawal from the world" for meditation that marks the spiritual myths. The purpose of these is to equip the hero for the tasks ahead. Gatsby's voyage with Cody is simultaneously his voyage into self and into the world. It marks the hero's setting forth on his adventures. As Campell has pointed out, "The adventure is always and everywhere a passage beyond the veil of the known into the unknown."[19] The first adventure of the mythic journey is usually with some protective or guardian figure—the fairy-godmother of fairy tales, or some wizard, hermit, etc. who gives the hero some advice and possibly amulets or charmed possessions with which to protect himself in extreme danger. The higher or macrocosmic mythologies assign this role to some sort of father figure—a teacher, saint, or ferryman conducting the souls in the underworld. Dan Cody is suggestive of such a ferryman. The most important lesson that the hero learns in the first adventure is the notion of self-annihilation or "self-achieved submission." The reason for this would be that "No creature can attain a higher grade of nature without ceasing to exist."[20] Or, to put in other words, "We must lose ourselves to find ourselves in the overall pattern of the cosmos."[21] After his apprenticeship with his guardian figure Dan Cody is over, Jay Gatsby, now a young lieutenant in the army, meets Daisy, his goddess, when stationed in Louisville. Their wonder romance culminates one October evening into what could appropriately be termed a "mystical marriage" with her. That evening, as they were walking, "Out of the corner of his eye Gatsby saw that the blocks of the sidewalks really formed a ladder and mounted to a secret place above the trees—he could climb to it, if he climbed alone, and once there he could suck on the pap of life, gulp down the incomparable milk of wonder" (p. 134). At that moment "He knew that when he kissed this girl, and forever wed his unutterable visions to her perishable breath, his mind would never romp again like the mind of God. So he waited, listening for a moment longer to the tuning-fork that had been struck upon a star. Then he kissed her. At his lips' touch she blossomed for him like a flower and the incarnation was complete" (p. 134). This event marks the hero's initial conquest of the woman and symbolically of the world.

The mythic hero's conquest of the world remains a temporary one if the forces have not yet blessed the hero, and there is often a theft of the boon, "bride-theft" or "fire-theft" etc. In Gatsby's case, the ogre who snatches his bride away is Tom Buchanan. Nick describes Tom as a domineering, aggressive tyrant who has supercilious manners and a powerful, cruel body (p. 8). His voice, in sharp contrast to Daisy's gold-filled, melodious, hypnotic one, is "a gruff husky tenor" and adds to the impression of "fractiousness" that he exudes. He is totally egotistical. He is the ogre who abducts Gatsby's goddess and keeps her in imprisonment. Not until the hero has successfully fought this ogre can he win his bride back.

The entire summer interlude of *The Great Gatsby,* in a sense, depicts the war of the hero for his lost bride or lost love. Tristram P. Coffin, in an article called "Gatsby's Fairy Lover," sees *The Great Gatsby* as an odd mixture of the Celtic fairy tale of *La Belle Dame Sans Merci* and a märchen that is classified as Aarne-Thompson #561.[22] If *The Great Gatsby* is to be interpreted in terms of a märchen type, then perhaps Aarne-Thompson #400 would suit the story better. Gatsby is really in search of his lost wife (or lost love) because he has been eternally wedded to Daisy in mystical rites and comes to claim what he believes to be, not somebody else's, but his own. All the events of the summer culminate in the New York hotel scene where Gatsby "wins" his final battle with Tom and gets back his bride. The open encounter between Daisy and Tom vindicates Gatsby's victory, even though it turns out to be a short-lived one, and Gatsby is dead soon after.

In the embryonic pattern of the mythological hero, the final stage of the hero's journey is his apotheosis; this apotheosis, however, is often reached through the preliminary stage of "crucifixion." Even Jesus, the mythic hero *par excellence,* was crucified as a common criminal. To suggest that Gatsby is similarly killed is not necessarily to imply that he is a prototype of the Jesus-hero of spiritual myths, but to suggest that Gatsby's mortal end falls within the pattern of the mythic heroes. The "extinction" of the hero in death in such cases is only a prelude to the final resurrection or apotheosis. The final pages of *The Great Gatsby* impart to the reader a philosophical sense of tragedy of a mythic ideal—the American Dream—rather than a sense of Gatsby's personal tragedy. It is a tragedy of society, of its shallowness, of its false values, and of its blindness. Gatsby, even in death, is untainted. As a matter of fact, Gatsby's stature may be said to rise in his death. Nick Carraway, who is like the antenna of a moral order of universe, is awed by Gatsby's stature in death, and in Nick's mind and values, there is a reaffirmation of Gatsby's real worth. This is the apotheosis and resurrection of the mythic hero. Through his resurrection, the mythic hero enlarges the vision of the common man, "For the hero figure is," as Emma Jung points out, "one of those eternal archetypal images which slumber in the depths of every soul and which determine human life and destiny in unsuspected measure."[23] In this sense, Gatsby, the mythic hero, operates not only at the macrocosmic level but through the linking of the imagination of the common man, at even the microcosmic level.

Jay Gatsby is a mythic figure because he operates simultaneously at the macrocosmic and the microcosmic levels, without being personally affected by his role. For instance, *The Great Gatsby* is a critique of the American Dream and a criticism of its material values, but this criticism somehow never touches Gatsby's own personality. He is untouched by the implications of the novel. In a corrupt, materialistic world, Gatsby's pursuit remains idealistic and untainted; amongst a class of shallow liars, he turns out to be the one with unswerving values; Gatsby's own wealth and display of it remains totally dedicated to the service of his romantic ideal. And therefore, when the summer interlude ends on the bizarre picture of Gatsby's dead body floating in his swimming pool, even the tragedy does not seem to touch Gatsby's person. It is a tragic commentary on every other character in the novel (except Nick's) and on the American Dream itself, but not on Gatsby. Gatsby curiously appears to vindicate his position. The clue to this final impression that the novel leaves may lie in the fact that "whenever the mythological mood pervades, tragedy is impossible."[24] The death of a mythic hero is a tragedy only for the people; it is always a triumph or ultimate victory for the hero himself. For the hero, who in his life presented a dual perspective (as Gatsby did), in his death is a synthesizing image. So in Gatsby's death are reconciled all the conflicts and tensions of national and human vision, as well as Gatsby's own tensions.

Weber State College

---

[1]Richard Lehan, *F. Scott Fitzgerald and the Craft of Fiction* (Carbondale: Southern Illinois University Press, 1966), p. 118.

[2]Edwin Fussel, "Fitzgerald's Brave New World," *The Great Gatsby: A Study,* ed. Frederick J. Hoffman (New York: Scribner's, 1962), pp. 244-262.

[3]Frederick J. Hoffman, ed., "Introduction," *The Great Gatsby: A Study,* p. 8.

[4]Marius Bewley, "Scott Fitzgerald's Criticism of America," *The Great Gatsby: A Study,* p. 263.

[5]Marius Bewley, *The Great Gatsby: A Study,* p. 272.

[6]Frederick J. Hoffman, *The Great Gatsby: A Study,* p. 11.

[7]"Fitzgerald's Brave New World," *The Great Gatsby: A Study,* pp. 245-246.

[8]*The Hero with a Thousand Faces,* Bolingen Series XVII (New York: Pantheon Books, 1949), p. 116.

[9]F. Scott Fitzgerald, *The Great Gatsby* (New York: Scribner's, 1925), p. 98. All further references to this novel will be indicated in parentheses in the body of the article.

[10]"F. Scott Fitzgerald," *F. Scott Fitzgerald: The Man and His Work,* ed. Alfred Kazin (Cleveland: The World Publishing Company, 1951), pp. 201-202.

[11]*The Hero with a Thousand Faces,* pp. 22-23.

[12]Norma Lorre Goodrich, *Myths of the Hero* (New York: The Orion Press, 1962), p. XX.

[13]*The Crack-Up,* ed. Edmund Wilson (New York: New Directions, 1945), p. 23.

[14]Dorothy Norman, *The Hero: Myth/Image/Symbol* (New York: World, 1969), p. 14.

[15]"Christian Myth and Naturalistic Deity: *The Great Gatsby,*" *Renascence,* V (1962), 85.

[16]*The Hero with a Thousand Faces,* p. 30. Campbell uses the word monomyth from James Joyce, *Finnegans Wake* (New York: Viking Press, 1939), p. 581.

[17]*The Hero with a Thousand Faces,* pp. 245-46.

[18]*The Hero with a Thousand Faces,* p. 246.

[19]*The Hero with a Thousand Faces,* p. 82.

[20]Ananda K. Coomaraswamy, "Akimcanna: Self-Naughting," *New Indian Antiquary,* III (Bombay, 1940), 6, note 14. Quoted by Joseph Campbell, *The Hero with a Thousand Faces,* p. 92.

[21]David Adams Leeming, *Mythology: The Voyage of the Hero* (New York: Lippincott, 1973), p. 6.

[22]"Gatsby's Fairy Lover," *Midwest Folklore,* X (1960), 79-85.

[23]Emma Jung and Marie-Louis Van Franz, *The Grail Legend,* trans. Andrea Dykes (New York: Putnam, 1970), p. 46.

[24]*The Hero with a Thousand Faces,* p. 69.

Enroute from the coast – Here for a few days on business – How are you and the family old sport?

"THE BEAUTIFUL AND DAMNED" DOES NOT LOOK ALL OF THAT

F. Scott Fitzgerald, his wife and their 2-year-old daughter, "Scotty," at their summer home on Long Island. Mrs. Fitzgerald is the heroine of her husband's successful novel, "The Beautiful and Damned."

—Fotograma

Gerlach

The signature of Gerlach was cropped from the illustration on p. 34 of the 1975 *Annual* (" 'How Are You and the Family Old Sport?' — Gerlach and Gatsby"). Here is the complete illustration.

CHRISTIANE JOHNSON

The Great Gatsby: The Final Vision

The last page of F. Scott Fitzgerald's *The Great Gatsby* is a vision. In this passage, the novel is given a dimension that has been latent all along. Here, from the temporal and the inessential, we pass on to the timeless and the essential, in a typically Fitzgeraldian manner: nothing is fixed, everything is fluid, moving, changing. And imperceptibly we are carried from the palaces of Long Island into the eternal flow of time.

In his original manuscript, Fitzgerald had put the first long paragraph of this last page at the end of the first chapter of his novel: it accompanied the gesture that Gatsby made toward Daisy's dock lit by its green light. But the novelist soon realized that, at that place and moment of the narrative, the evocation of the past, of the primitive island, betrayed both too much and too little: it lost its power of evocation and became forgotten in the course of the novel. On the contrary, as a conclusion, it gives the novel a mythical dimension, often pointed out by critics, which is so characteristic of American literature:

Gatsby is much more than a Midwesterner come East; the story of hi dream together with his "heightened sensitivity to the promises of life" are those of America itself, and his tremendous and misled hop becomes that of mankind. Fitzgerald has prepared us for that dimension all through the novel, particularly in the passages of an elegia nature in which Nick, the narrator, meditated on Gatsby, and which because of their very tone, were meant to receive our spontaneous an irrational response. This page is the outcome of those passages.

The vision starts from reality: the narrator, ready to leave for th Middle West, his home, throws a last glance on Long Island where h has spent a momentous summer. Gatsby's house, which he has jus called "that huge incoherent failure of a house" (217), is closed, like al the other palaces, because it is autumn. All lights are out, even though not so long ago, the fantastic lighting of Gatsby's house made it loo like "the World's Fair" (98). The only feature alive is the ferryboa crossing Long Island Sound, that ferryboat which, for Fitzgerald i "My Lost City,"[2] represented the triumphal entrance into New York since it allowed him to apprehend the city in all its glory, New York, fo him the city of all mysteries and of all promises; but here the ferryboa is only a "shadowy moving glow," already losing itself in the vision Replacing the artificial lighting, is the light of the moon, primitive an elementary, which seems to have nothing in common with that moo that shone over Gatsby's parties, "produced like the supper, no doubt out of a caterer's basket" (52). Nick, who earlier compared himself wit Kant (106), is capable of seeing beyond reality, of grasping the essenc beyond existence. This is why the houses, with all the pretention an ostentation they imply, now become "inessential," and give way to th vision. The fluidity of the successive transformations is expresse through the terms: "began to melt away," "gradually I became aware" for the full extent of the vision does not come at once.

The vision begins with a return to the origins of the America nation, to a primitive past, imagined as pastoral and idyllic, for whic Americans have nostalgically been yearning since the remote beginning. Long Island becomes "the old island . . . that flowered," and it i called "a fresh, green breast," and these few words are sufficient t suggest the essence of that pastoral past; but the maternal image "breast," betrays an even deeper longing in man, the desire to be unite again to nature as mother (the buried cause of America's attraction t its pastoral past). Nick, who is from the rural Middle West, is liable t be particularly aware of that nostalgia (and he gives hints of his insigh when he remarks on the pastoral character of Fifth Avenue i ummer).

Then follows a vast period which takes us beyond reality, beyond pace, beyond time. Reality is there only in the negative: "vanished rees," implying, although in a very minor key, the ruthless destruction f those primitive trees, so much more essential than the present ouses. And now the sentence erases limitations: it deals at once with a ertain man, with man, with the continent, with "the greatest of human reams." Dreams, the enchanted moment, aesthetic contemplation, onder: all this belongs to the field of the irrational, for the sentence oes not express a rational, intellectual reaction, but a purely emotion-l and instinctive response to a moment of perfect harmony between spiration and reality, in which man was "compelled into an aesthetic ontemplation, he neither understood nor desired." The reader is ompelled, too, through the power of words, of sounds, of repetitions, ut mainly of the epic rhythm: he is made to share that moment. But at e same time, the ephemeral quality of the scene gives it its poignancy: e adjective "last" is repeated twice; "man must have held his breath" ontrasts, with its connotations of short duration, of precarious alance, with the solidity of "this continent." Regret and nostalgia are voked at the very climax of the vision, the phrases "transitory nchanted moment" and "for the last time in history" suggesting that, its very perfection, the vision carries its unavoidable destruction. he only thing left at the end is the unsubstantial "capacity for onder."

We are now, so it seems, far from Gatsby and his story. But all along, e are constantly, even if imperceptibly and almost unconsciously, rought back to his particular case by verbal suggestions, associations nd echoes. Speaking of the old island, the narrator says that it *lowered* once for Dutch sailors' eyes"; thus Daisy, when Gatsby issed her for the first time, "blossomed for him like a flower" (134). he maternal image of the "green breast" recalls another maternal nage, just before Gatsby incarnates his dream in Daisy: "he could ick on the pap of life, gulp down the incomparable milk of wonder" 34), in which love for a woman, motherly love and love for nature as other become one. And of course the "green breast" is also evocative f Daisy's "green light." The word "pandered," with its connotations of licit love, while it announces how the first settlers would exploit the rgin land that was revealed to them, also ties the dream to the eceitful attraction of the girl who is both too fragile and too corrupt to arry it. In the next paragraph, more explicitly, "the greatest of all uman dreams" becomes "his dream," and "Gatsby's wonder" echoes an's "capacity for wonder." "This blue lawn" calls back the "blue gardens" of the third chapter, in which the famous parties took place. And "he could hardly fail to grasp it" takes us back to the end of the first chapter, when Gatsby, stretching out his arms towards Daisy's dock, had so intrigued Nick. Thus the whole novel—and more than the novel—is present in this last page, through suggestions and allusions but everything is transformed, transposed. At the same time, the choice of words entertains a confusion which is intended to enlarge Gatsby's dream and to merge it with the dream of a whole nation. Through a very Fitzgeraldian dialectics, the very mention of Gatsby, the man suggests the deceiving, adulterated quality of his dream and of the broader dream as well; just as the verb "pandered," in the context of the "fresh, green breast of the new world," is bound to evoke the Fall from the Garden of Eden. But all this is allusive to the extreme, a minimum of words carrying a maximum of meaning.

The deliberate confusion is carried further through the constant passing from present to past, then to future, and later the expression of all three at the same time. The "new world," which, for the first settlers the Dutch sailors, represented the future, is now for Nick "the old unknown world." The present, pregnant with the future, has become itself the past. It has been necessary for the narrator to be of the present in order to know and express what the Dutch sailors could not know that their dream vision was the greatest one in the history of mankind but also the last one, that the enchanted moment was only passing transitory. What was for them a marvellous future is for us only a past just as Gatsby's dream "was already behind him" when he thought he had attained it with Daisy. And Gatsby and the Dutch sailors became identified with the same words, "dream" and "wonder," applying to both. The very parallelism of grammatical constructions underline this identification: "man *must have held* his breath," and "his [Gatsby's] dream *must have seemed* so close"; in those constructions, the present is relived in its compulsiveness at the same time as it is experienced as past. In a subtler manner, the sentence "he could hardly fail to grasp it," if it recalls, as we said, Gatsby's gesture at the end of the first chapter, also announces "stretch out our arms further," expressed in the future in the next paragraph. Therefore this page is more than timeless: it partakes of past, present and future at once, and shows how it is their interplay that causes timelessness.

If Gatsby's dream is "already behind him," it is because it is connected with past hope, the past hope of a whole nation, as is, once more, suggested by "the dark fields of the republic." The word "republic," with its implications of aspirations and ideals, prolongs the fresco which started with the Dutch sailors and the discovery of the continent, and contributes further to place the novel in a historical context much wider than the 1920's. Those fields which "rolled on" are the Middle West and the West, the Frontier, still unknown to the first settlers, but which was to feed the dream here first revealed to them and which would continue to exist long after them. "Fields" and "republic" also evoke Jefferson's democratic ideal and dream of keeping the country rural. Furthermore, the word "fields" recalls battlefields, the battlefields of the Civil War and of the American Revolution, fields on which the *Republic* fought for its very survival.

In Fitzgerald's first draft, this passage was very personalized: it was Nick who "could feel . . . beyond that [the city] the dark fields of the republic rolling on under the night." But here, the novelist moved the emphasis from the narrator's personal immediate experience to a contemplation in which the persons of Nick and of Gatsby himself have become accessory. The comforting Eden-like and maternal vision of the beginning is gone, leaving only obscurity; even the elementary light of the moon has disappeared. And the paragraph ends on that notion of darkness on which the novelist insists: "vast obscurity," "dark fields," "under the night". The scene takes us "back in that vast obscurity," which suggests confrontation with the primeval darkness that is not without anguish: the anguish of primitive man cut off from maternal earth, the anguish at the thought of the future, the metaphysical anguish of man faced with the darkness of destiny.

At this point, Gatsby's dream becomes completely transcended: from "I" and "he," the narrator passes on to "we," through a process of assimilation: "*Gatsby* believed in the green light, the orgastic future that year by year recedes before us." We have now become Gatsby, but at the same time Gatsby is us, Gatsby is every man. And the green light is much more than the light "at the end of Daisy's dock;" it is now called "the orgastic future." We know Fitzgerald meant "orgastic," which, he said, "is the adjective for 'orgasm' and it expresses exactly the intended ecstasy. It is not a bit dirty"[3]. The fact that the one term is most likely to suggest the other underlines the ambivalence of Gatsby's dream which partakes both of the kind of ecstasy Fitzgerald had in mind and of the orgies into which Gatsby's parties degenerated. And what is implied here is that no dream is exempt from this ambivalence.

In the first paragraph, the dream was associated with the "fresh, green breast of the new world"; in the preceding sentence, it was "already behind him," lost in "the dark fields of the republic"; and now it becomes the ungraspable future that "recedes before us." It is at the same time behind and before, the very contradiction is expressed by th terms "future" and "recedes," the first leading forward, and the secon expressing a movement backward. The fusion of past, present an future is complete, and the three grammatical tenses are used, striking ly, in the same sentence: "It eluded us then, but that's no matter– tomorrow we will run faster . . . ," after the back and forth movemen that continually led from the one to the other (the present here being timeless present).

Let us notice the choice of physical gestures in the whole passage trying to grasp, running forward, stretching out arms; they are a gestures of a quest, an unceasing quest toward a goal that is neve reached. The human condition is to aspire, and the quest counts mor than the goal which remains unattainable. With Gatsby, the reason i clear: the future to which he is aspiring is a false future, it is a future tha attempts to repeat the past, it is both before and behind.

But the movement of the third and fourth paragraphs, by carrying u toward the last sentence and the final image, seems to suggest that a men are likewise endlessly aspiring toward the past. The movement c that ending is swifter, the sentences are shorter, more syncopated, as i to render those constant and vain attempts at reaching a receding goa The numerous nouns and adjectives of the beginning, which contribut ed to evoke the vision, are now being replaced by a great number c verbs, in order to express movement. And the reader is led irresistibl to the final image of the current, the flow of life on which men are onl frail boats. The alliterative b's give that last sentence a decisive an final quality. All limitations, in time as well as in space, hav disappeared. Just as Gatsby's hope was both before and behind him we don't know whether the current is carrying us forward or backwarc Man is at the same time acting and acted upon: "we beat on," but w are "borne back." And the last word is "past." Man is endlessly aspirin toward the past, toward a lost paradise. His continual quest for th future can only lead him into the past. But there is grandeur in hi constant quest in spite of his helplessness.

In this whole passage, Fitzgerald carries his reader, not through an logical reasoning, since he is in a field where logic simply does nc apply, but through the power of words and the primordial an mythical images they suggest. He succeeds, in an extremely poetica page, where serenity prevails, in evoking the whole human conditior And this seems to us its greatest value: the breadth of its vision lendin it an archetypal quality.

Université de Paris VI

[1]F. Scott Fitzgerald, *The Great Gatsby* (New York: Scribners, 1925), p. 2. All references are to this edition.

[2]F. Scott Fitzgerald, "My Lost City," *The Crack-Up,* ed. Edmund Wilson (New York: New Directions, 1945).

[3]*The Letters of F. Scott Fitzgerald,* ed. Andrew Turnbull (New York: Scribners, 1963).

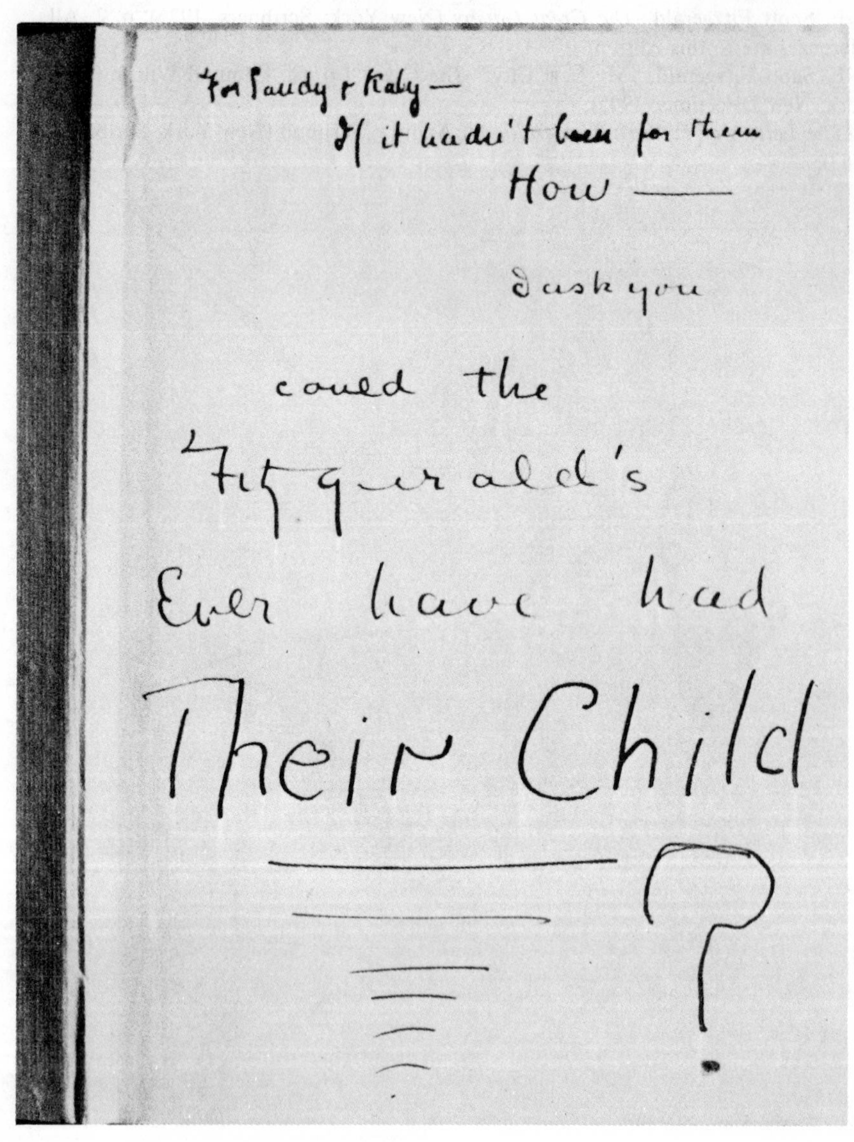
For Sandy & Katy—
If it hadn't been for them
How ——

I ask you

could the
Fitzgerald's
Ever have had
Their Child
?

The Beautiful and Damned. Courtesy of Mrs. C. O. Kalman.

LLOYD HACKL

FITZGERALD IN ST. PAUL: AN ORAL HISTORY PORTRAIT

" 'Andrew, I wish you'd dispel this idea Mizener and other people that have written about Scott keep talking about—[Scott as] the little boy from the other side of the tracks.' I said, 'It's perfectly ridiculous and it's not true.' But Andrew didn't dispel that idea either."

This conversation with Andrew Turnbull, then working on his biography of F. Scott Fitzgerald, was recalled by Mrs. C. O. (Xandra) Kalman, a lifelong friend of Fitzgerald, during an hour-and-a-half recorded interview which is part of a project being conducted by the Minnesota Historical Society. The oral history project consists of interviews with St. Paul contemporaries of Fitzgerald. Tapes and transcriptions will be housed at the Historical Society Building in St. Paul.

Time has been kind to many of the Fitzgerald contemporaries, for many are still alive and reside in and around St. Paul, though some still spend the colder months away from the ice-palaced winters of Minnesota in pursuit of sunshine elsewhere. Interviewees range from intimate friends such as Mrs. Kalman and Norris Jackson to the girl who ran the switchboard at the St. Paul Commodore Hotel where Zelda and Scott Fitzgerald stayed briefly in October of 1921.

Although time has in many instances been an ally to the Fitzgerald researcher, it also presents problems, for even the most recent memories are thirty years old, some confidantes reaching back almost seventy years to recall stories about Scott Fitzgerald. Too, almost everyone has read biographies and/or other writings about Fitzgerald, so that it's sometimes difficult for the interviewer to distinguish between "pure" memories and memories embellished with retelling, or even memories imagined. Another difficulty encountered by would-be interviewers is that Fitzgerald confidantes have become almost inaccessible, partly for survival—so many requests are made of them, and partly, I've been told, because some researchers have published stories about Fitzgerald which were given to them in confidence. The aegis of the Minnesota Historical Society has, fortunately, persuaded some to consent to participate in this project.

Sometimes personal reasons have kept memorabilia from discovery, as in the instance of one person who until now kept silent about a letter from Fitzgerald to her mother because, she felt, her "mother's correspondence was private business." The delightful letter, dated 15 September 1913, is framed in black and contains a two-page note of mock-mourning over Fitzgerald's being unable to accept an "invite." Written to Elizabeth Clarkson, the "Litz" of the *Ledger,* the letter concludes with a poem:

My mind is all a-tumble
And the letter seems a jumble
For the words they seem to mumble
And my pen's about to stumble
And the papers made to fumble
So I sign myself your humble

Servant

Francis Scott Fitzgerald

During her mid-August 1975 interview, Mrs. Kalman asserted, "In those days it was a very tight-knit society. There were the ones that belonged and the ones that didn't, and the Fitzgeralds certainly belonged. Molly was at every debutante ball. She went everywhere.

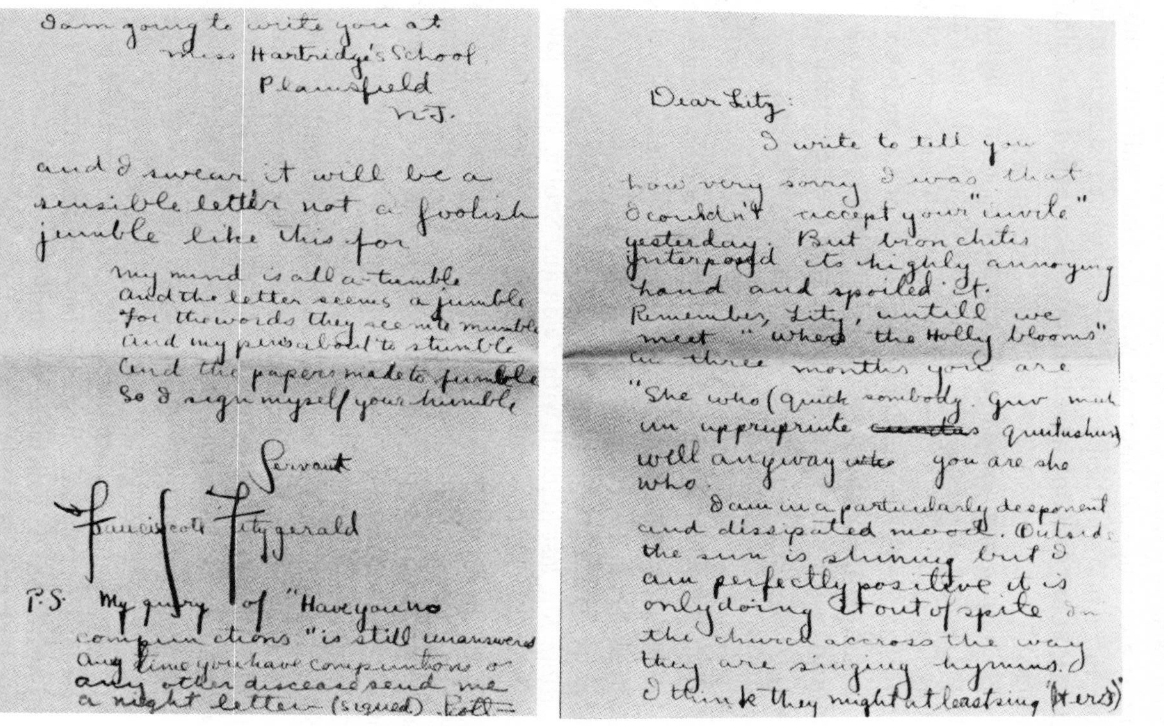

Dear Lity:

I write to tell you how very sorry I was that I couldn't accept your "invite" yesterday. But bronchitis interposed its highly annoying hand and spoiled it. Remember, Lity, untill we meet "where the Holly blooms" in three months you are "She who (Quick somebody. Give me an appropriate [struck out] quotation) well anyway you are she who.

I am in a particularly despondent and dissipated mood. Outside the sun is shining but I am perfectly positive it is only doing it out of spite. In the church accross the way they are singing hymns. I think they might at least sing "Hers"

I am going to write you at
Miss Hartridge's School,
Plainsfield
N.J.

and I swear it will be a sensible letter not a foolish jumble like this for

My mind is all a-tumble
And the letter seems a jumble
For the words they seem to mumble
And my pen's about to stumble
And the paper's made to fumble
So I sign myself your humble

Servant
Francis Scott Fitzgerald

P.S. My query of "Have you no compunctions" is still unanswered. Any time you have compunctions or any other disease send me a night letter—(signed) Scott—

To Elizabeth Clarkson Wann, September 1913. Courtesy of Mrs. Robert Biner.

There's been so much written on the other side. That Scott was sort of the little boy looking in. He went to all of the parties, he went to the dancing school—which was very exclusive—only the best families." On a subsequent visit, untaped, Mrs. Kalman reaffirmed this belief, citing Fitzgerald's participation in parties while a student in the East, stating that he "wouldn't have been invited to them if he wouldn't have belonged."

Mrs. Kalman reminisced about Fitzgerald's parents, the times spent with the Fitzgeralds in St. Paul, Dellwood, New York, and Paris—the Kalmans went to Europe every spring for ten years in the 1920s. She regrets that researchers didn't make more use of her late husband who, she says, "analyzed people more," remembered more than she (Fitzgerald readers will recall that Oscar Kalman was in the Paris cab with Zelda Fitzgerald when she had her first breakdown.) Mrs. Kalman grew up in St. Paul with Fitzgerald, spent practically every day with them during the Fitzgeralds' St. Paul-Dellwood stay (1921-22), and visited and corresponded with the Fitzgeralds before, during, and after the breakdowns. Mrs. Kalman remembers Fitzgerald surprising them on a New York street and having lunch with her husband during his infamous Dartmouth weekend. She says he "looked all right" on that occasion. She last lunched with Zelda and Scottie Fitzgerald in New York in the 1940s and still corresponds with Scottie Smith.

Her memories of Fitzgerald's parents focus mainly on his mother: "Mrs. Fitzgerald was a very intelligent person . . . a great reader . . . she was very absent-minded. We'd meet her on the street. She might have one brown shoe and one black shoe on and a perfectly goofy hat of a vintage of twenty years before. She'd always be coming from the library, her arms full of books." Of Fitzgerald's father, her remarks were brief, "He tried different things. . . . He was a failure. Molly's money supported the family."

Of her relationship with Zelda Fitzgerald, Mrs. Kalman said, "For some strange reason I was one of the few women that Zelda got close to. . . . We were together practically every day [in St. Paul]." Testaments to this intimacy are the many letters she received from Zelda Fitzgerald (the originals now at Princeton) and several oil paintings (see illustration) and sketches she mailed to her.

Recalling that Sinclair Lewis and Donald Ogden Stewart (then working for the telephone company) lived a block down Summit Avenue in 1921, Mrs. Kalman remarked that one could see why Zelda Fitzgerald found men more interesting, more stimulating mentally than women.

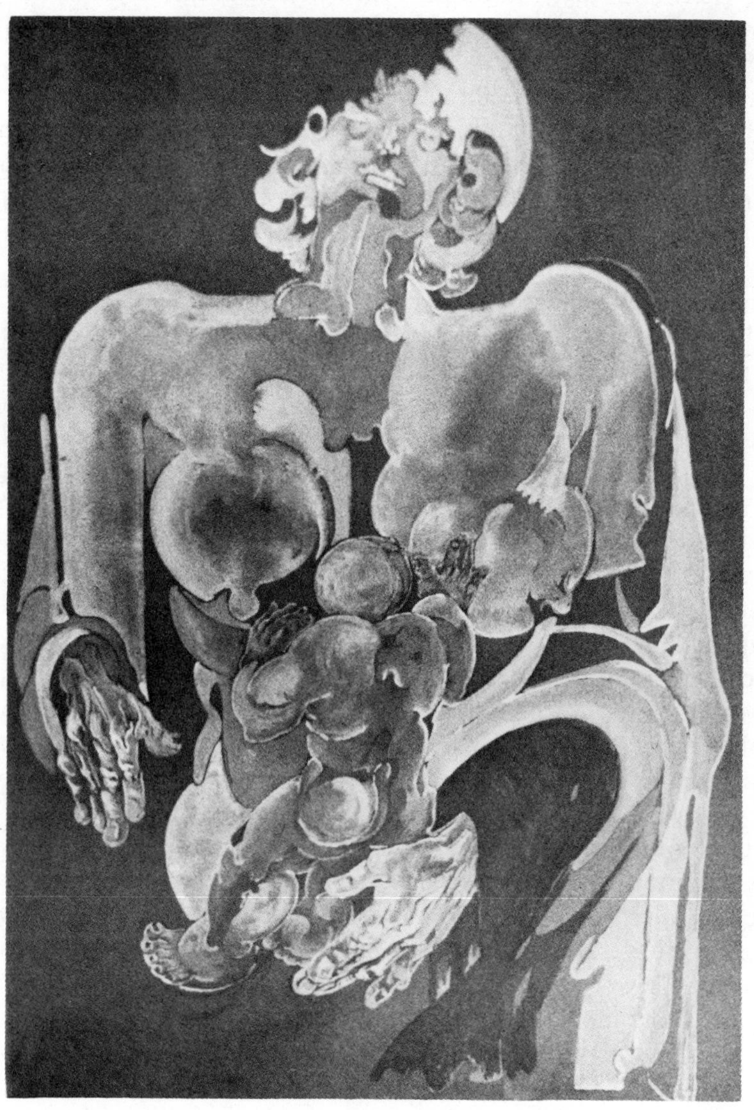

Untitled gouache by Zelda Fitzgerald. Courtesy of Mrs. C. O. Kalman.

"They [St. Paulites] soon learned that she wasn't a belle-butterfly, that she was an extremely intelligent person." In support of her intelligence, Mrs. Kalman recalled that at the end of every day during their Dellwood stay, Fitzgerald, "then writing religiously," would go over with her everything he'd written that day, incorporating her suggestions.

During a September visit to her home, Mrs. Kalman spoke to me of Zelda Fitzgerald's "naturalness," stating that she had no affectations . . . no exaggerated southern drawl that with some seems more pronounced the longer they've been out of the South. She said, "They were both frank and very natural," though on another occasion Mrs. Kalman remarked that one "never felt quite 'home' with Zelda"—meaning quite at the center of her identity.

She remembers Fitzgerald popping in and out of the delivery room where Zelda Fitzgerald was giving birth to Scottie, jotting things down in a little notebook he always carried with him. "When I asked him what he'd hurriedly scrawled during Zelda's labor, he replied, 'Help!' and 'Jesus Christ!' When I asked why he wrote it down he said, 'I might use it some time.' "

Of the 1920s, she said, "Everybody was having affairs. . . . flirtations mostly."

Her tone grew affectionate when speaking of Scott and Zelda Fitzgerald, "I think of two very attractive, charming people that were devoted to each other. . . . His devotion to Zelda was something unbelievable . . . during all those awful years and everything. I don't think it ever failed." Then she turned cooler as she affirmed, "I mean, I'm as sure as I am that I'm sitting here that his loyalty to her topped everything. . . . He never would have married that Sheilah Graham—or anyone as long as Zelda was alive."

In addition to what has been recounted here, Mrs. Kalman, a gracious, alert, intelligent woman, read from letters she'd received from the Fitzgeralds, and recalled many incidents and events already recorded elsewhere, but perhaps the most touching moments on the tape are those moments when she crawls back into the memories and, through her, the voices drift across the years to us, as, recalling a dinner at a Paris hotel when, with Zelda Fitzgerald on the wagon in training for her ballet and Fitzgerald ordering drink after drink, she intones Zelda Fitzgerald's plaintive "Oh, Goofo, don't drink so much."

"It is a sad saga," she mourns, remembering the last Fitzgerald years, but the light in her eyes grows bright with other memories of Fitzgerald and her voice soft as she recalls "He had such a darling side. . . . He always had time for everyone."

Lakewood Community College

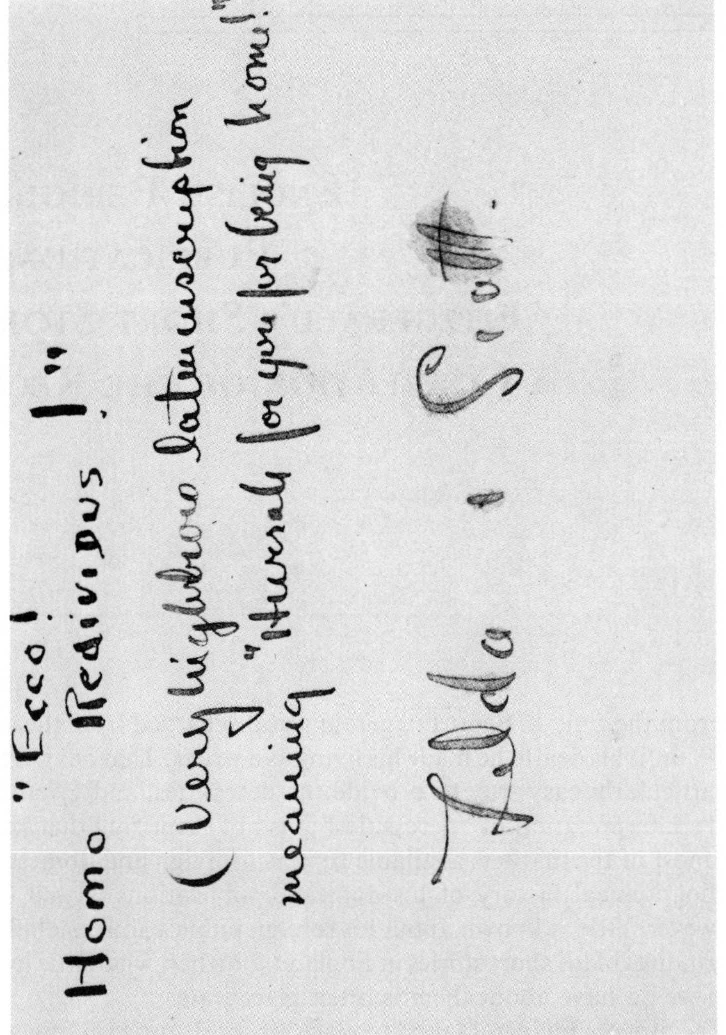

"Ecco!
Homo Redivivus!"
(Very highbrow latin inscription
meaning "Hurrah for you for being home!")

Zelda + Scott.

Courtesy of Lloyd C. Hackl.

THOMAS E. DANIELS

English Periodical Publications of Fitzgerald's Short Stories: A Correction of the Record

From the time F. Scott Fitzgerald was discharged from the army in 1919, until his death, he made his living as a writer. That has never been a particularly easy way to provide the necessities, and given Fitzgerald's interpretation of "necessities" it is not surprising that he wrote for most of the markets available to him—foreign and domestic. The bibliographical history of his domestic publications is well known. However, little is known about his foreign publications, including the reprintings of his short stories in England. Further, what little information we do have about them is often inaccurate.

The process Fitzgerald used to place his short stories in England was similar to that he used in the United States. That is, either his agent, Harold Ober, dealt directly with various English journals in attempts to place individual stories; or Scribners dealt with Curtis Brown, an international publishing bureau, in an effort to find a publisher for the collected volumes of short stories which Scribners had brought out in the United States.[1]

There have been a number of bibliographical studies published recently on Fitzgerald's material, the two most important being Jackson Bryer's, *The Critical Reputation of F. Scott Fitzgerald;*[2] and Matthew J. Bruccoli's, *F. Scott Fitzgerald: A Descriptive Bibliography.*[3] Bryer does not include Fitzgerald's foreign publications but Bruccoli's bibliography attempts to list all of the first appearances of Fitzgerald's stories in English periodicals. He states, "the first English publication of stories [in magazines and newspapers] is noted, but none of these English appearances has been seen by the compiler."[4] The cautionary note is well advised, since there are many errors in the entries. Bruccoli relied primarily on Fitzgerald's *Ledger* and on his letters to Ober for his information concerning the stories sold to English periodicals. This is unfortunate because Fitzgerald made many "minor" errors in recording his sales. The *Fitzgerald Bibliography* lists twenty-four stories which appeared in England in periodical form. Of those, I have been able to locate and read twenty-one and have discovered that ten of the twenty-four have incorrect dates of publication listed in the *Fitzgerald Bibliography.* One of those ten has an incorrect date listed, but I have not been able to find it to correct the entry. One of the twenty-one I have seen has an incorrect title listed. There also may be errors of entry for the two stories which I have not yet been able to find and about which I have no information.

The following entries are accurate in the *Fitzgerald Bibliography;* I have seen the texts and double-checked them:[5] "Topsy Turvey," ("Head and Shoulders," in America), *Yellow Magazine* (24 March 1922), 688-697; "Myra Meets His Family," *Sovereign* (July 1921), 214-226; "The Offshore Pirate," *Sovereign* (February 1922), 304-315; "Two For a Cent," *Argosy* (April 1933), 54-60; "Dream Girl of Spring," ("Winter Dreams," in America), *The Royal Magazine* (February 1923), 538-545, 631-636; "Magnetism," *Grand Magazine* (August 1928), 710-722; "Flight and Pursuit," *Britannia and Eve* (June 1932), 34-37, 106-108; "The Fiend," *London Evening Standard* (29 March 1935), 26-27; "Shaggy's Morning," *London Daily Express* (1 June 1935); "Except to Bill," ("Zone of Accident" in America), *Woman's Journal* (April 1936), 20-23, 91-93; "Goodbye to Provence," ("Image on the Heart" in America), *Woman's Journal* (November 1936), 26-29, 85, 87-89; and "Last Kiss," *London Evening Standard* (1 August 1949), 8-9.

The ten stories for which the *Fitzgerald Bibliography* lists incorrect dates are: "The Camel's Back," *Pearson's* (February 1923), 157-164. The *Fitzgerald Bibliography* follows Fitzgerald's *Ledger* and records

July 1921 as the publication date.

"Gretchen's Forty Winks," *Home Magazine* (March 1924). The *Fitzgerald Bibliography* follows Fitzgerald's *Ledger* and records March 1924 as the publication date. It does not appear in that issue and I have been unable to locate it.

"The Third Casket," *Pearson's* (November 1924), 440-448. The *Fitzgerald Bibliography* follows Fitzgerald's *Ledger* and records December 1924 as the publication date.

"Rags Martin-Jones and the Pr–nce of W–les," *Woman's Pictorial* (18 October 1924), 6-8, 27-30. The *Fitzgerald Bibliography* follows Fitzgerald's *Ledger* and records December 1924 as the publication date; a question mark follows the date, however.

"The Sensible Thing," *Woman's Pictorial* (22 November 1924), 13-17. The *Fitzgerald Bibliography* follows Fitzgerald's *Ledger* and records December 1924 as the publication date; again, the date is questioned.

"Love in the Night," *Woman's Pictorial* (9 May 1925), 6-9, 23-25. The *Fitzgerald Bibliography* follows Fitzgerald's *Ledger* and records December 1925 as the publication date.

"One of My Oldest Friends," *Red Magazine* (4 June 1926), 363-372. The *Fitzgerald Bibliography* follows Fitzgerald's *Ledger* and records July 1926 as the publication date.

"A Penny Spent," *Modern Woman* (September 1926), 7-10, 48, 50, 53-54. The *Fitzgerald Bibliography* follows Fitzgerald's *Ledger* and records July 1926 as the publication date.

"Presumption," *Woman's Pictorial* (30 November 1926), 24-27, 34, 36, 39, 40, 43. The *Fitzgerald Bibliography* follows Fitzgerald's *Ledger* and records June 1926 as the publication date.

"The Adolescent Marriage," *Woman's Pictorial* (October 1927), 4-8, 47-48. The *Fitzgerald Bibliography* follows Fitzgerald's *Ledger* and records July 1926 as the publication date.

The one error in the title of a story can also be attributed to reliance on the *Ledger*. The *Fitzgerald Bibliography* lists the story published in America as "The Adolescent Marriage" as being published under the same title in England. However, the English title in the *Woman's Pictorial* is "The Youthful Marriage." As previously mentioned, the date of English publication of this particular story is also in error in the *Fitzgerald Bibliography*.

In addition to the above, there are two English publications listed in the *Ledger*, and therefore listed in the *Fitzgerald Bibliography*, which I have not been able to find nor have any information about: "Bernice

Bobs Her Hair," *Pan* (?) or *20 Story* (?), (August 1921); "A New Leaf," *Homemaking* (August 1933).

Fitzgerald lists in the *Ledger* "A New Leaf" as being published by "Amalgamated Press (*Home Mag.*) 1931." The Fitzgerald/Ober correspondence lists August 1933 as the publication date. This story does appear in the *Ledger* record for 1933, but the entry does not specify August. The title also appears in the *Ledger* record for 1931, though that entry does not include the title of the journal. The other two stories which I have not been able to locate have the same publication dates listed in the *Ledger* as the *Fitzgerald Bibliography;* I assume, therefore, that the *Ledger* is the only source of information about them. The entry in both the *Ledger* and the *Fitzgerald Bibliography* for "Bernice Bobs Her Hair" lists "*Pan* (?) or *20 Story* (?) August 1921" as the journal[s] and date of publication. Obviously, Fitzgerald couldn't remember which journal published the story. However, it does not appear in the August 1921 issue of *Pan,* nor does it appear anywhere in the July through December volume of that journal. Therefore, it is either in the magainze *20 Story* or Fitzgerald was quite wrong concerning the date of publication in *Pan.* I have not been able to find the 1921 issues of *20 Story* and so cannot make a judgment.

There are good reasons why a scholar as thorough as Bruccoli would have difficulty obtaining absolutely accurate information about these English publications without doing direct research. The British do not have an equivalent to our *Reader's Guide to Periodical Literature.* Their *Subject Index to Periodicals,* which covers materials from 1915 to 1962, does not include fiction or verse, and the *British Humanities Index* begins its coverage in 1963. Also the *International Index* does not include any of the journals in which Fitzgerald published in England. A search through his correspondence with Ober is helpful, but those letters do not usually contain the detailed information which is needed for a full bibliographical entry, and often the prospective date of publication mentioned does not turn out to be the actual date; indeed, in some instances Fitzgerald's stories were bought by journals but never published. This, of course, causes confusion for the bibliographer.[6] However, it must be remembered that in the *Ledger* Fitzgerald was primarily interested in recording the sales of items, not bibliographical entries. Therefore, the only way one can check on Fitzgerald's records is go directly to the periodicals he identifies in his *Ledger* and see if the stories are in fact there. If not, it then becomes a matter of checking through "likely" issues of journals. Insofar as possible, this is the process I followed in gathering the data for this paper.

It is likely that Fitzgerald sold no more stories to English periodicals during the period covered by his *Ledger*—1919-1936—since no such sales are listed there, and Fitzgerald was very fastidious about recording the sales of stories. About the only way we can check this assumption out, however, is to go directly to those journals which would have been most likely to buy his material. *Woman's Pictorial* published five of his stories from 1924-1926, but a careful check of the magazine throughout the entire decade did not turn up any other publication by him. Interestingly, all of the entries in the *Ledger* and in the *Fitzgerald Bibliography* for the *Woman's Pictorial* have incorrect dates, but all the stories were published by the magazine during that general period of years.

One major reason I was not able to find three English publications of the twenty-four listed in the *Fitzgerald Bibliography* is that the British Museum Library, certainly the major collector of British popular journals in the world, lost a portion of its collection during WWII. For example, the collected file of *Yellow Magazine,* which according to the *Ledger* published "Topsy Turvey" in March 1922, is listed in the *British Union Catalogue* as being held only in the British Museum Library. However, the British Museum Library has only Volume I of that magazine (January through December 1921). The rest of the file is listed as "bombed out." The only response I got as to why the full file is still claimed in the *British Union Catalogue* and in the British Museum Library "Catalogue," is that the Museum Library expects to replace all that material which was lost and does not want to go through the process of re-cataloging when that day arrives. In the meantime, it does cause some confusion. However, I finally found this story at the Bodleian Library.

This correction of the bibliographical record may not be final since I have not found all those stories which first appeared in English journals to which Fitzgerald's *Ledger* refers. Bruccoli wisely points out that "a bibliography is outdated the day it is published," and I am continuing the search. I hope that in the near future the other three stories will be located so the record concerning them can also be corrected, if indeed that proves to be necessary.

University of Wisconsin—Green Bay

[1]The British publishing house, William Collins Sons and Company Limited, published *This Side of Paradise, The Beautiful and Damned, Flappers and Philosophers* and *Tales of the Jazz Age*. However, they refused the play *The Vegetable,* and *The Great Gatsby*. The contract for *This Side of Paradise* stipulated that Collins would have the option to publish the next two novels, and they did exercise that option for *The Beautiful and Damned,* but, as mentioned, turned down *Gatsby,* their reason being "The atmosphere of the book is extraordinary foreign to the English reader, and he simply would not believe in it. . . ." The Curtis Brown agency received that word on 15 June 1925, but by 9 September of the same year Scribners signed a contract with another English publisher, Chatto and Windus, for *Gatsby's* publication; obviously, Curtis Brown had little difficulty placing the novel even though Fitzgerald's works were not selling well in England. L. Pollinger who was originally with Curtis Brown Limited, later became Fitzgerald's agent in England.

[2]Jackson R. Bryer, *The Critical Reputation of F. Scott Fitzgerald: A Bibliographical Study*, (Hamden, Conn.: Archon Books, 1967).

[3]Matthew J. Bruccoli, *F. Scott Fitzgerald: A Descriptive Bibliography* (Pittsburgh: University of Pittsburgh Press, 1972). Material dealing with Fitzgerald's "appearances in magazines and newspapers," and therefore, the section with which this paper is concerned, is "C," pp. 205-252. All subsequent references to the *Fitzgerald Bibliography* are to Bruccoli's compilation.

[4]*Ibid.*, p. 205.

[5]The stories are arranged in the order in which they appeared in the United States. They did not appear in that same order in England.

[6]See Jenifer McCabe Atkinson, "Lost and Unpublished Stories by F. Scott Fitzgerald," *Fitzgerald/Hemingway Annual 1971,* pp. 32-63.

KENNETH S. KNODT

THE GATHERING DARKNESS
A STUDY OF THE EFFECT
OF TECHNOLOGY I
The Great Gatsb

It has become almost a commonplace among critics to cite th pastoral elements in *The Great Gatsby,* whether noting the rift betwee East and West with the more pastoral West offering solace ar morality (exemplified by Nick's return to his more secure and mo moral world) or seeing the pastoral elements suffusing the enti novel.[1] Critics have also noted the importance of the machines in th novel, particularly the car, but they view the emphasis on machin rather narrowly. For example, Laurence MacPhee notes in his articl "*The Great Gatsby*'s 'Romance of Motoring,' " that "Fitzgera employs the automobile as a part of a pattern of images embodying th disorder of the Twenties."[2] Only Leo Marx in his classic study *Th Machine in the Garden* has touched upon the importance of techno ogy to the destruction of pastoral values. As Marx notes when includes Faulkner, Frost, Hemingway, and West with Fitzgerald *The Great Gatsby,*

> Again and again they invoke the images of a green landscape—a terrain either wild or, if cultivated, rural—as a symbolic repository of meaning and value. But at the same time they acknowledge the power of a counterforce, a machine or some other symbol of the forces which have stripped the old ideal of most, if not all of its meaning.[3]

Further, Marx feels that "In *The Great Gatsby* . . . the machine represents the forces working against the dream of pastoral fulfillment."[4] Marx uses only Gatsby's car to support his point, but a close reading of the novel reveals an abundance of machine images in conflict with the pastoral experience.

It is my intention to look at the tremendous impact of technology upon both landscape and characters in the novel, and to show how the "gathering darkness" of technology leads to the destruction of a simpler, easier, pastoral world. Consider the technology in the novel: there are automobiles, of course; trains; telephones; motorboats; motorcycles; a telegram; a foghorn; a juice extractor; electric lights; telephone or telegraph wires; cameras; hand guns and, even more to the point of a technological age, *machine* guns; an elevator; even a mechanical ash tray! Throughout the novel there are numerous instances of technology's intrusion on the land, and while the unspoiled land conveys goodness, the symbols of technology are connected with destruction and evil.

From the opening of *The Great Gatsby,* Nick represents the pastoral world. He sees himself as a "pathfinder, an original settler"[5] and moves to West Egg because he can't accommodate himself to the city in summer. When he and Daisy talk at dinner, he feels "uncivilized" and asks, "'Can't you talk about crops or something?'" (15). But Nick is swept up in sordid events which begin with a machine—Nick's initiation into the world of the Buchanans starts with an automobile ride after which "the history of the summer really begins" (7), and the train trip with Tom into New York ends with Nick's attendance at Tom and Myrtle's chaotic party.

Daisy, too, represents some kind of pastoral ideal as her name relates to nature, and she is described in pastoral terms. In her Louisville meeting with Gatsby she "blossomed . . . like a flower" (134), but even there in her innocent world technology was present, for she "had a little white roadster, and all day long the telephone rang in her house" (90). And it is technology (the "death car") and Daisy's inability to handle the mechanical which ends the pastoral relationship of Daisy and Gatsby.

The negative references to the automobile are numerous: not only are there four separate accidents caused by the car, but the car is seen as a way of interpreting emotions. Jordan conceptualizes her affair with Nick in a car metaphor which parallels the Daisy-Gatsby relationship: " 'You said a bad driver was only safe until she met another bad driver? Well, I met another bad driver, didn't I?' " (214). The car has such a pervasive influence on Nick that he is, consciously or unconsciously, continually interpreting events through the car metaphor. For example, when Daisy asks Nick if Chicago misses her, he replies that ' "The whole town is desolate. All the cars have the left rear wheel painted black as a mourning wreath' " (12). Later, when Nick sees Gatsby standing on his car, he notes, "He was balancing himself on the dashboard of his car with that resourcefulness of movement that is so peculiarly American" (76), a precarious balance symbolic of technology about to destroy the world of Gatsby's innocence. Nick and Gatsby's drive into New York across the Queensboro Bridge takes on greater significance than just an outing, perhaps even implying a voyage into hell ("Anything can happen now that we've slid over this bridge" (83), says Nick). The relationship between Gatsby's grand car and the hearse which crosses the bridge with them is symbolic for a pall is put over Gatsby's car, and because of this, Gatsby's destruction is prefigured.

Cars even take on their own personalities, replacing human emotions: Nick's taxi "groaned" (98), and when Gatsby doesn't have one of his customary Saturday night parties, cars, not people, "turned expectantly" (135) into Gatsby's drive. Finally, when Nick is about to leave the East, he remarks that cars are still coming to Gatsby's mansion—a kind of mechanical homage to Gatsby's life-style.

Garages built to service these cars mar the landscape. Wilson's garage is so desolate that Nick cannot, at first, accept it: "this shadow of a garage must be a blind" (29). Tom, thinking of George Wilson, the lackluster owner of the garage, and searching for a way to mock the photography of Mr. McKee (who has photographed his wife one hundred twenty-seven times), purposely inverts the qualities of McKee's pastoral "studies"—" 'Montauk Point—The Gulls,' " and " 'Montauk Point—The Sea' "—by proposing his own study, " 'George B. Wilson at the Gasoline Pump' " (38, 40). The prime symbol of the machine age, the car, supercedes the pastoral vision.

Suggesting a world becoming darkened by technology, Nick envisions his future on his thirtieth birthday in a motor road metaphor: "Before me stretched the portentous, menacing road of a new decade"

(163). The road which runs by Wilson's gas station and into the valley of ashes connects Myrtle Wilson with the machinery of technology. The connection of the two shows a direct contrast between a prime symbol of the pastoral and a clear symbol of technology: "Then the valley of ashes opened out on both sides of us, and I had a glimpse of Mrs. Wilson straining at the garage pump with panting vitality as we went by" (81). Myrtle, the only true flesh and blood person in the novel, is described as a kind of earth mother:

> She was in the middle thirties, and faintly stout, but she carried her flesh sensuously as some women can. Her face, above a spotted dress of dark blue crêpe-de-chine, contained no facet or gleam of beauty, but there was an immediately perceptible vitality about her as if the nerves of her body were continually smouldering. (30)

Her name also relates her to the pastoral. According to the *Palmer Fieldbook of Natural History,* the myrtle tree is

> Found near waterways or along lake shores or streams or in swamps, in Nova Scotia and Minnesota[!]. Also found wild in Europe and Asia. Has many common names including sweet myrtle. . . . Thrives best in moist soil but may be grown in shallow water. Fruit when mature is dry and bears few seeds.[6]

Fitting the definition, Myrtle lives near water ("bounded on one side by a small foul river" [28]), but this water which is part of her natural setting has been spoiled by the technology which has polluted the river. The waste land of the valley of ashes is continually seen in terms of distorted pastoral—it is the nineteenth-century picture of rural America inverted by the technology which has destroyed this land: "a fantastic farm where ashes grow like wheat into ridges and hills and grotesque gardens" (27). The nineteenth-century garden has become the twentieth-century *grotesque* garden. It is in this world that Myrtle is being held prisoner by a man who makes his living from patching up the wrecks of technology. Not only does technology destroy this representative of the pastoral, of real life, but it also completely severs Myrtle's dignity:

> . . . she rushed out into the dusk. . . . The "death car" as the newspapers called it, didn't stop; it came out of the gathering darkness, wavered tragically for a moment, and then disappeared around the next bend. . . .

> when they had torn open her shirtwaist . . . they saw that her left breast was swinging loose like a flap. . . . (165)

It seems significant that the only other mention of a breast is Nick's description of Long Island "that flowered once for Dutch sailors' eyes—a fresh, green breast of the new world" (217). The severing of Myrtle's breast by the machine shows the destruction of Myrtle's life force and of the vitality the Dutch sailors saw two hundred years before. Technology has ruined the pastoral image of America.

The waste land of the valley of ashes is also linked to the original "machine in the garden," the railroad. "About half way between West Egg and New York the motor road hastily joins the railroad and runs beside it for a quarter of a mile, so as to shrink away from a certain desolate area of land. This is a valley of ashes" (27). The word "hastily" reminds us that the motor road is the newcomer and suggests that it is only carrying on the tradition of the railroad in destroying the pastoral. And in this scene the immoral and destructive technology purposely shrinks away from contact with the hellish land it helped create. Gatsby may be identified with his car to many, but to his father he is most closely associated with the railroad. Mr. Gatz tells Nick that " 'If he'd of lived, he'd of been a great man. A man like James J. Hill [the railroad tycoon who founded the Great Northern Railway Company]. He'd of helped build up the country' " (202). The railroad, presumably the means by which Nick originally left the garden of the West to come East, is, at the end of the novel, tied in with fond memories of his past college days; it is, however, in coming back West that Nick is thrilled. Any glamour attached to the train is soon directed to the land itself. The beauty of this passage is caught up in the appeal of the landscape:

> When we pulled out into the winter night and the real snow, our snow, began to stretch out beside us and twinkle against the windows, and the dim lights of small Wisconsin stations moved by, a sharp wild brace came suddenly into the air. We drew in deep breaths of it as we walked back from dinner through the cold vestibules, unutterably aware of our identity with this country for one strange hour, before we melted indistinguishably into it again. (211-212)

Contrasted with this are the passages involving the train in the East, for in every instance it is seen in hellish, destructive, or confining terms. It is the train which brings people close to the valley of ashes for a look at the modern world: "when the drawbridge is up to let barges through, the passengers on waiting trains can stare at the dismal scene for as long as half an hour" (28). It is the train that first brings Nick into the valley of ashes, his introduction beginning when Tom, who has ridden out with him, "literally forced me from the car" (28). And it is also the train that allows Tom to set up his affairs with Myrtle. Tom's command to Myrtle to take the train ironically links Myrtle with Daisy, since Tom originally made an impression on Daisy and her Louisville world when he came down from Chicago with a hundred people in four private railroad cars. While Daisy's child is an angelic reflection of herself, Myrtle, fitting the description of the myrtle tree, "bears few seeds" and is childless. Instead, ironically connected with Myrtle is an image of a child in the grotesque garden, sowing the only kinds of seeds that will root there: "a gray, scrawny Italian child was setting torpedoes in a row along the railroad track" (31). On the day Myrtle is killed, the warmest day of the summer, Nick takes a train out to East Egg. The conductor emphasizes how hot it is by repeating the word five times. It is a hellish situation, so hot that "The straw seats of the car hovered on the edge of combustion" (136). The train, intensifying the heat, makes people unpleasant to each other. When Nick returns a woman's dropped purse, he is suspected of being a thief. Later, when Nick feels especially close to Gatsby, whose car has just been the death car, he doesn't want to leave, but feels the press of business, so he expresses his need to run in a technological image: " 'Twelve minutes to my train' " (184). Then, when Nick passes the ashheaps on this ride into town, he "crossed deliberately to the other side of the car" (187). Nick again has been transported into an unpleasant world by the machine.

Perhaps as important as the car and the railroad to the age of technology and its ensuing destructiveness is the telephone. Though telephones were in widespread usage by the turn of the century, by the 1920's, as Daniel Boorstin suggests, the entire country seemed to have telephones, and instant communication was possible with almost anyone.[7] The telephone in *The Great Gatsby* is dehumanizing, a device that breaks up relationships, ends love affairs, and allows the conduct of Gatsby's shady dealings. At numerous places the phone interrupts ongoing conversation and relationships. After each phone call, an altered, usually less pleasant relationship ensues. At the Buchanans, a telephone rings "startlingly" and the conversation becomes "broken fragments" which "vanished into air" (19). The telephone has such prominence that Nick even thinks of it as a "fifth guest" (20). Myrtle, in New York, sitting on Tom's lap, knows no better way to enjoy herself than to telephone several of her friends. The telephone is so important to Gatsby's way of doing business, that in one scene when Nick and Gatsby are talking, the phone interrupts them twice. Later, when Nick, Gatsby, and Meyer Wolfshiem are having lunch, Gatsby bolts from the conversation to make a call to Nick's surprise; however, Wolfshiem, unflustered, takes it as a matter of course, realizing that the telephone is the normal way of conducting negotiations.

The telephone is even part of the reinterpretation of reality. When Nick arrives at the Buchanans on the hottest day of the summer, he first describes a telephone call—emphasizing its relative importance—rather than the characters. The call becomes distorted in Nick's mind and prefigures Gatsby's death: " 'The master's body!' roared the butler into the mouthpiece. 'I'm sorry, madame, but we can't furnish it—it's far too hot to touch this noon!' What he really said was: 'Yes . I'll see' " (137). The telephone is also connected abstractly with destructiveness. Tom, a despoiler of considerable force, uses all the instruments of technology: he has used the railroad to win Daisy and meet Myrtle; he uses a car as a device to interest George Wilson so he can see Myrtle; he uses the telephone to carry on his relationship with Myrtle. And when Gatsby, Tom, Nick, and Jordan go to a New York hotel on this hot day, their stuffy hotel room moves Daisy to say, " 'Well, we'd better telephone for an axe—' " (151). As if it had a life of its own, the telephone book falls off its nail and crashes onto the floor.

Finally, the telephone allows a person to distance himself from close, personal human relationships, emphasized when Nick breaks off his affair with Jordan over the phone. Immediately after this call Nick tries to contact Gatsby, but each time Gatsby's line is busy, being kept open for a wire from Detroit. It's initially on the phone that Nick tries to contact Wolfshiem to get him to come to the funeral, but he is unable toget through. The only way Nick is able to get an answer is through direct human contact—he goes to New York to see Wolfshiem, and only then is he able to get Wolfshiem's reply. Nick, being drawn into Gatsby's world, soon receives a phone call from a Chicago gangster who initially mistakes Nick for Gatsby. But relationships over the phone form quickly and end quickly: "then a quick squawk as the connection was broken" (200). The last reference to the telephone in the novel is the call Klipspringer makes refusing to come to Gatsby's funeral for the shallowest of reasons: " 'there's a sort of picnic or something' " (203). The telephone is one of those cold instruments of technology which permits people to act in ways they might not have acted in a more personal, less technological world.

Technology destroys Myrtle (the car) and also destroys Gatsby (the gun). Guns, mentioned throughout the novel, aren't a modern invention, but the gun most directly attached to Gatsby—the machine gun—was a development of World War One. Alexander Tamke in his article "The 'Gat' in *Gatsby*" explores the signficance of guns and the term "gat."[8] Gatsby's accomplishments as the leader of a machine-gun battalion are twice mentioned. Also, his association with Wolfshiem reminds us of one of the hazards of the gangster profession which Rosy Rosenthal, shot three times in the stomach, discovered. Even reporters are seen by Nick in gangster terms. When one was on a "fishing expedition" (my phrase) for news about Gatsby, Nick sees the reporter as taking a "random shot" (117) at him. But the final shot of the novel is not random as Wilson kills Gatsby with a gun. It is a fitting end that a man so allied to technology is also destroyed by technology. Tom, a man not to be bullied by other men, shows the power of technology when he explains to Nick how Wilson got him to reveal Gatsby's identity as the owner of the death car: " 'He was crazy enough to kill me if I hadn't told him who owned the car. His hand was on a revolver in his pocket every minute he was in the house' " (215).

Other machines figure prominently in the novel. The juice machine that Gatsby's servants use parallels the life of the party: on weekends fresh groups of people come to Gatsby's world, while on Mondays Gatsby's gardeners need to begin "repairing the ravages of the night before" (47); and similarly, the juice extractor mechanically sucks the life out of the fruit:

> Every Friday five crates of oranges and lemons arrived from a fruiterer in New York—every Monday these same oranges and lemons left his back door in a pyramid of pulpless halves. There was a machine in the kitchen which could extract the juice of two hundred oranges in half an hour if a little button was pressed two hundred times by a butler's thumb. (47)

At another party in the New York apartment, Myrtle dreams of all those material things she'd like, but she links the objects strangely, suggesting the deathlike quality of the mechanical contrivances. She wanted " 'one of those cute little ash-trays where you touch a spring, and a wreath with a black silk bow for mother's grave that'll last all summer' " (44). After the death of Myrtle, Nick finds that he can't sleep, and technology seems to echo Nick's internal disorder, reminding him of death and suffering: "I couldn't sleep all night; a fog-horn was groaning incessantly on the Sound, and I tossed half-sick between grotesque reality and savage, frightening dreams" (176).

At no point in the novel does technology really benefit any of the characters. It extracts Nick and Gatsby from their more comfortable, secure worlds. It serves as a status symbol. It is a means of transacting wider, but not deeper, relationships. And it is ultimately responsible for killing two characters and seriously upsetting several other characters' lives. Technology, therefore, is destroying the previous Edenic garden, and its "gathering darkness" is what Fitzgerald sees upon the American horizon.

La Sàlle College

---

[1]See David Stouck, "White Sheep on Fifth Avenue: *The Great Gatsby* as Pastoral," *Genre,* 4 (1971), 335-47, and David F. Trask, "A Note on Fitzgerald's *The Great Gatsby," University Review,* 33 (Spring 1967), 197-202.

[2]Laurence E. MacPhee, "*The Great Gatsby's* 'Romance of Motoring': Nick Carraway and Jordan Baker," *Modern Fiction Studies,* 18 (Summer 1972), 207.

[3]Leo Marx, *The Machine in the Garden: Technology and the Pastoral Ideal in America* (London: Oxford Univ. Press, 1964), pp. 362-363.

[4]*Ibid.,* p. 358.

[5]F. Scott Fitzgerald, *The Great Gatsby* (New York: Scribners, 1925), p. 4. All further references will be cited in the text.

[6]Lawrence E. Palmer, *Fieldbook of Natural History* (New York: McGraw-Hill, 1949), p. 125.

[7]Daniel J. Boorstin, *The Americans, The Democratic Experience* (New York: Random House, 1973), p. 391.

[8]Alexander Tamke, "The 'Gat' in *Gatsby*: Neglected Aspect of a Novel," *Modern Fiction Studies,* 14 (1968), 443-445.

Ernest Hemingway

I think 293-294 need cutting but perhaps not to be cut altogether.

Why not end the book with that wonderful paragraph on P. 241. It is the most eloquent in the book & could end it rather gently & well.

A beautiful book it is!

Kiss my ass
EH

Courtesy of The Hemingway Collection, John F. Kennedy Library.

CHARLES MANN

F. Scott Fitzgerald's Critique of *A Farewell to Arms*

Fitzgerald's comments on Ernest Hemingway's work are well known. They survive in letters and in the memoirs of those who knew the two men. Indeed, there now exists a very small body of criticism which plainly shows that Hemingway had few readers who followed his work as closely and as sharply as Fitzgerald. That Fitzgerald constantly championed Hemingway's work is part of the legend. Anyone who met Fitzgerald in the twenties or later in the thirties appears to have been immediately made aware of Fitzgerald's enthusiasm for Hemingway.

But that is not the whole story. Fitzgerald, while full of praise in discussing Hemingway's work with others, would generally meet him head on when asked to give a critique. Further, his admiration was qualified; there was much he did not like in *The Sun Also Rises,* and perhaps more he did not like in *A Farewell to Arms.*

In 1970 Philip Young and I published in the *Fitzgerald/Hemingway Annual* an extended critique by Fitzgerald of *The Sun Also Rises,* written in the form of a letter. Nestling somewhere in the vault where the papers were, or hidden in a warehouse in upper Manhattan that sadly we did not visit, was another sheaf of penciled notes, which Fitzgerald had made upon reading a typescript of *A Farewell to Arms.* Somehow they escaped us; I offer them here as one more bit of documentation of an extraordinary literary relationship. In this new commentary Fitzgerald's words are delivered with slap and sting. They are direct and beseeching in nature. Having slammed *The Sun Also Rises* for its deadening (and later deleted) opening pages three years before, Fitzgerald in this novel takes after the famed Hemingway dialogue, and blazes away at Catherine Barkeley. Twice she is spoken of as "too glib." She is Eleanora Duse disguised as a Red Cross nurse. Her persona as a brave expectant mother is doubly underlined as an *old situation.* Chapter XXI of the book, with its crucial spare dialogue in which Catherine and Frederic Henry come to terms with her pregnancy, is the central target. In a superb insight into Hemingway's work, Fitzgerald matches Catherine's speech against the brilliance and pain expressed in the words of the bitterly disillusioned woman in "Hills Like White Elephants" whose lover hopes that she will agree to an abortion. In that story, Hemingway was "really listening to *women.*" In this novel, Fitzgerald accuses Hemingway of "only listening to yourself, to your own mind beating out facily a sort of sense that isn't really interesting . . . nor really much except a sort of literary exercise." Fitzgerald urged that the chapter be "*thoroughly* cut, even re-written." The force of this criticism comes over doubly if one takes the trouble to read "Hills Like White Elephants" and Chapter XXI together. Catherine's tremulous bravery and self-effacing understatement does not ring "new." At this point, Fitzgerald tried to lessen the strength of this particular hit, and in a parenthesis noted, "(Our poor old friendship probably won't survive this but there you are—better me than some nobody in the Literary Review that doesn't care about you & your future.)"

What Hemingway could have done about Fitzgerald's complaints at the time they were made is problematical. As the typescript Fitzgerald read contains the ending as it appeared in the first edition, it is evident that he was reading a late draft.[1] At such a late stage Hemingway presumably was not willing to accept the kind of drastic changes Fitzgerald was suggesting.

Which brings us to the other passage in these notes worth emphasizing. This relates in part to Hemingway's well-known difficulties in fashioning an ending to *A Farewell to Arms,* and to Fitzgerald's appreciation of his friend's gifts as a stylist. In 1934, Fitzgerald was plagued with the problem of ending *Tender Is the Night,* and in a long response to Hemingway's complaints about *that* novel, he traced his own choice of a down-beat closing to Hemingway's contention that "the true line of a work of fiction was to take the reader up to a high pitch but then let him down or ease him off."[2] While thanking Hemingway for this bit of "burglary," and noting that he also owed something to an idea of Conrad's, concerning lingering after-effects, Fitzgerald mentioned the alternate endings for *A Farewell to Arms.* An earlier draft of the novel which Fitzgerald had seen had had an ending resembling "an old fashioned Alger-book summary." He went on to say, "You may remember my suggestion to take a burst of eloquence from anywhere in the book that you could find it and tag off with that."[3]

The "burst of eloquence" Fitzgerald had in mind is clear enough from these notes, and anyone who has read much about Fitzgerald in 1929 might easily have guessed it anyway. Morley Callaghan recounts for us an incident in Fitzgerald's apartment which indicates that Fitzgerald's admiration for the passage went far beyond its possible utility as an ending for the novel:

> Suddenly he asked if we had read *A Farewell to Arms.* Only some parts of it? Hurrying to his study he returned with a manuscript copy, and glowing with enthusiasm, he fumbled through the pages till he found the part he wanted. "Just listen to this," he said. He read that passage, "—if people bring so much courage to this world the world has to kill them to break them—" He read it with emotion. When he finished he asked quietly, "Isn't it beautiful?"[4]

Fitzgerald wanted more reaction to the passage than Callaghan was prepared to give, and after some internal deliberation, closed the typescript and went on to other things. That Hemingway's near Biblical words made a strong impression upon him is plain enough in these notes, but there is a very human and touching statement on the typescript itself. Fitzgerald marked it in only one place, and then presumably erased his note, but it can still be made out easily. On the margin of page 241 he wrote, "This is one of the most beautiful pages in all English literature." He erased these words, and in his notes said much more temperately, "P. 241 is one of the best pages you have ever written I think." But the erased sentence records the emotion with which he first read the words.

Thus Fitzgerald's disenchantment with the dialogue, and his deep admiration for the poetic quality of the novel are main concerns of his notes. The other suggestions are less important; he finds some of the comedy dull, some of it good; he enjoins Hemingway not to let the war get out of sight, he worries about censorship, and characteristically warns Hemingway twice about leaving himself open to the professional reviewers. Indeed, what Fitzgerald has to say *is* professional, and to the point, and in a measure these notes contradict Hemingway's recollections recorded in several letters written many years later to Arthur Mizener wherein Fitzgerald's ideas for improving *A Farewell to Arms* are summed up as being ludicrously off-base, particularly one suggestion that the U.S. Marines be brought in to rescue Frederic and Catherine at the end.[5]

To avoid over-emphasis, it must be kept in mind that Hemingway made perhaps only one of the changes suggested. Twice elsewhere in his career, we know that he took Fitzgerald's advice, and that once he bitterly regretted it. The loss of the opening anecdote to "Fifty Grand" bothered him a great deal, and the discarded pages from the story were found in his papers with the note "Story mutilated by Scott Fitzgerald" at their head.[6] Hemingway did omit the opening pages of *The Sun Also Rises* but makes little mention of it beyond a letter to Fitzgerald in which he says he cut all that Cohn stuff. With the thought of previous cuts haunting him, Hemingway may have been less willing to alter *A Farewell to Arms.* However, a cut was made. As Sheldon Grebstein points out in his review of the manuscripts of *A Farewell to Arms,* one of the very few changes made in the novel was the omission of a passage which Fitzgerald briefly mentioned in his notes as needing cutting but perhaps not needing to be cut altogether. Grebstein notes that the passage is "a more extended and detailed version of the protagonist's bitter observations on cosmic injustice and predictability, which are retained elsewhere in the novel."[7]

The above change appears to be the only solid difference in the text attributable to Fitzgerald's notes. However, there is some tangible evidence that the suggestions were considered. In the typescript there is a large X drawn across the pages from 114 to 121. These concern the meeting with the American singers, upon which Fitzgerald fired a salvo. Despite the crossing out, this scene, albeit "gassy" and "slow," remained.

Otherwise the notes are valuable as one more instance of Fitzgerald's honesty and critical skill. Always the craftsman, he wasted little time in gushing praise but came down hard on chapter and verse. There were ways in which matters might be improved, and he was not afraid to say so. This frankness in criticism sometimes burned his friends severely but he offered it nonetheless. Ernest Hemingway etched his reaction in ink at the end, and one wonders whether he was responding with an embarrassed "thanks-for-nothing" mood to the last line, "A beautiful book it is!" or expressing his irritation at Fitzgerald's working over of much of what Hemingway found satisfying in the first place. However, the two men were fairly thick-skinned in their literary exchanges, and no punches were pulled. For those who feel that Hemingway received the worst of it here, he himself was none too gentle in assessing *Tender Is the Night* in a letter written to Fitzgerald in 1934. In replying Fitzgerald responded happily to Hemingway's "old charming frankness" and opened up his own defense with the phrase, "next to go to the mat with you on a few technical points."[8] They had been together on that mat many times before.

These notes were first described in an unpublished document, "The Ernest Hemingway Papers in the John F. Kennedy Library," prepared by Miss Jo August, the Curator of the Papers. This is a guide to material prepared for use and microfilmed, which at this date includes only material related to the novels. Miss August's description appears as follows:

> Fitzgerald's Notes. Pencil notes by F. Scott Fitzgerald on FTA. W/EH annotation at end. 9pp. Verso: p. 9.

Attention was first publically called to Fitzgerald's notes in a press release from the John F. Kennedy Library, dated 23 January 1975, and brief quotations from them appeared in an article by Robert Reinhold, "Hemingway Papers Open for Study in a Setting that Belies Their Utility," in the *New York Times,* 31 January 1975, pp. 35, 66.[9] They are here fully reproduced, and with Fitzgerald's sometimes erratic spelling and punctuation retained. His spelling in this instance was rather good, and the manuscript is clearly written.[10] There is some evidence of revision, and several passages are apparently afterthoughts, the two sections marked "Later" and "Still later" certainly being so. It also appears that the long passage beginning, "I mean—you're seeing him in a sophisticated way . . ." is an addition, as it quite fills the space before "122 ect" and is continued into the margins of the sheet. Hemingway's comment was added in ink and circled.

The appended commentary includes explanatory matter and identifies the passages in the book to which Fitzgerald refers. His own page numbers correspond to the typescript now in the Hemingway Papers, identified in Miss August's list as "no. 65-7." This also appears as Young/Mann 5b in *The Hemingway Manuscripts: An Inventory* (University Park: Pennsylvania State University Press, 1969), p. 11.

Pennsylvania State University

---

[1]There is a distressing typo in the last paragraph of the typescript reading, "It was like sawing goodbye to a statue."

[2]Andrew Turnbull, *The Letters of F. Scott Fitzgerald* (New York: Scribners, 1963), pp. 308-309.

[3]Philip Young cannot account for the fact that Fitzgerald's notes are missing from our inventory, but recalls seeing the "burst of eloquence" among a few other discarded endings to the book.

[4]Morley Callaghan, *That Summer in Paris* (New York: Coward-McCann, 1963), pp. 151-152.

[5]See *Hemingway at Auction,* 1930-1973, comp. M. J. Bruccoli and C. E. Frazer Clark, Jr. (Detroit, Gale Research, 1973), pp. 167, 175 for excerpts from the letters which were dated January 4, 1951, and January 23, 1953.

[6]See Philip Young and Charles Mann, *The Hemingway Manuscripts: An Inventory,* (University Park: Pennsylvania State University Press, 1969) for a reproduction of Hemingway's note, facing p. 19.

[7]Sheldon Grebstein, *Hemingway's Craft* (Carbondale & Edwardsville: Southern Illinois University Press, 1973), pp. 214-215. The passage originally followed the opening sentence of Chapter XL, "We had a fine life."

[8]Turnbull, p. 308.

[9]Since the completion of my article, Michael S. Reynolds has put the Hemingway Papers to good use in his *Hemingway's First War The Making of A Farewell to Arms,* (Princeton: Princeton University Press, 1976), in which he refers to Fitzgerald's comments a number of times.

[10]For a text which displays the capricious nature of Fitzgerald's spelling to the fullest, see Philip Young and Charles Mann, "Fitzgerald's Sun Also Rises: Notes and Comment," *Fitzgerald/Hemingway Annual,* 1970, pp. 1-13.

F. Scott Fitzgerald's Memo on the Typescript of A Farewell to Arms

For permission to print F. Scott Fitzgerald's memo on Ernest Hemingway's *A Farewell to Arms*, we thank Mary Hemingway and Scottie Fitzgerald Smith.

I wish to acknowledge the kind treatment received from the staff of the John F. Kennedy Library which is presently located at the Federal Records Center, Waltham, Massachusetts. I am particularly grateful to Hemingway Papers Curator Jo August, who first called my attention to the notes, and who aided me with a key reference when I badly needed it. As always I am grateful to Mary Hemingway, who permitted me to be the first scholar to use her husband's papers in the Kennedy Library; and to Philip Young, who took me on as his first collaborator. Fitzgerald's memo may not be reprinted without the formal permission of Harold Ober Associates.

114-121 is slow + needs cutting[1]—it hasn't the incisiveness of other short portraits in this book or in yr. other books. The characters too numerous + too much nailed down by gags. *Please* cut! There's absolutely no psycholical justification in introducing those singers—its not even bizarre — if he got stewed with them + in consequence thrown from hospital it would be O.K. At least reduce it to a sharp + self sufficient vignette. It's just rather gassy as it is, I think.

For example—your Englishman on the fishing trip in T.S.A.R. contributes to the tautness of waiting for Brett. You seem to have written this to try to "round out the picture of Milan during the war" during a less inspired moment.

(Arn't the Croats Orthodox Greeks?[2] or some Byzantine Christian Sect—Surely they're not predominantly Mohamedens + you can't say their not Christians

P. 124 *et sequitur*[3]
This is definately *dull*—it's all right to say it was meant all the time + that a novel can't have the finesse of a short story but this has got to. This scene as it is seems to me a shame.

Later I was astonished to find it was only about 750 wds. which only goes to show the pace you set yourself up to that point. Its dull because the war goes further + further out of sight every minute. "That's the way it was" is no answer—this triumphant proof that races were fixed!—I should put it as *400* word beginning to Chap XXI

Still later Read by itself it has points, but coming on it in the novel still believe its dull + slow

---

Seems to me a last echo of the war very faint when Catherine is dyin, and he's drinking beer in the Café.

Look over Switzerland stuff for cutting

P. 130[4]—

This is a comedy scene that really becomes offensive for you've traine everyone to read every word—now you make them read the wor cooked (+ fucked would be as bad) *one dozen times.* It has ceased t become amusing by the 5th, for they're too packed, + yet the scene ha possibilities. Reduced to five or six *cooked* it might have rythm like th word "wops"[5] in one of your early sketches. You're a little hypnotize by yourself here.

133-138[6]

This could stand a good cutting. Sometimes these conversations with her take on a naive quality that wouldn't please you in anyone else's work. Have you read Noel Coward?

Some of its wonderful—about brave man 1000 deaths ect. Couldn't you cut a little?

(ie. 2nd page numbered 129)

129[7] (NW) Now here's a great scene—

your comedy used as part of you + not as mere roll-up-my-sleeves- + pull-off a-tour-de-force as on pages 114-121

134[8]

Remember the brave expectant illegitimate mother is an <u>old situation</u> + has been exploited by all sorts of people you won't lower yourself to

ad—so be sure every line rings *new* + has some claim to being incar-
ated + inspired truth or you'll have the boys apon you with scorn.

---

the way—that buying the pistol is a *wonderful* scene.[9]

Catherine is too glib,[10] talks too much physically. In cutting their nversations cut some of her speeches rather than his. She is too glib—I mean—you're seeing him in a sophisticated way as now you see urself then—but you're *still* seeing her as you did in 1917 thru nineteen old eyes. In consequence unless you make her a bit fatuous occasion-y the contrast jars—either the writer is a simple fellow or she's Eleanora ise disguised as a Red Cross nurse. In one moment you expect her to ophecy the 2nd battle of the Marne—as you probably did then. Where's at desperate, half-childish dont-make-me think V.A.D.[11] feeling you oke to me about? It's there—here—but cut *to* it! Don't try to make r make sense—She probably didn't!

122 ect.[12]

"Cat in the rain" + in the story about "That's all we do isn't it, go + new drinks ect," You were really listening to women—here you're ly listening to yourself, to your own mind beating out facily a sort of nse that isn't really interesting, Ernest, nor really much except a sort literary exercise—it seems to me that this ought to be *thoroughly* cut, en re-written.

(Our poor old friendship probably won't survive this but there you e—better me than some nobody in the Literary Review that doesn't re about you + your future.)

The book, by the way is between 80,000 + 100,000 wds—not 160,000 you thought

P. 241[13] is one of the best pages you've ever written, I think

209- + 219[14] I think if you use the word cocksuckers here the book ll be suppressed + confiscated within two days of publication.

All this retreat is marvellous the confusion ect.
The scene from 218[15] on is the best in recent fiction

I think 293-294 need cutting but perhaps not to be cut altogether.

Why not end the book with that wonderful paragraph on P. 241. It is the most eloquent in the book + could end it rather gently + well.

A beautiful book it is!

Commentary on Fitzgerald's Memo

I have matched the corresponding page numbers for Fitzgerald's references to the first edition of *A Farewell to Arms* (N.Y.: Scribners, 1929), identified in the footnotes as *FTA*.

1 "114-121 is slow & needs cutting—"
This passage has an X drawn across it in the typescript, but was retained as part of Chapter XIX, from the meeting with "Old Meyers and his wife" getting out of a carriage (*FTA,* p. 126) through the discussion Frederic has with Ettore and the singers about medals (*FTA,* p. 129). The crossing out of the pages seems to imply that Hemingway gave Fitzgerald's suggestion some thought but perhaps this advice came too late to act upon.

2 "(Arn't the Croats Orthodox Greeks?"
A reading of the typescript turns up no passage which seems to apply here except for a line in Chapter XXVI (*FTA,* p. 189) where the priest says to Frederic Henry, "The Austrians are Christians—except for the Bosnians." Fitzgerald may have transposed Bosnians into Croats when jotting down his query. Bosnia today is still made up of three religious groups living together: the Croatian Catholic, the Serbian Orthodox, and the Muslims. The Muslim religion is a survival of the period when the area was ruled by the Turks, and many Bosnians turned Muslim. I am indebted to Thomas Magner, Professor of Slavic Languages at Pennsylvania State University, for this information.

3 "P. 124 et sequitur"
This refers to the opening page of Chapter XX (*FTA*, p. 136) which is about Frederic and Catherine's bittersweet day at the race track. The comments from "Later" to the reference to cutting "Switzerland stuff," which comes much later in the novel, appear to be subsequently added afterthoughts and indeed are so noted by Fitzgerald.

4 "P. 130" is the opening for Chapter XXI (*FTA*, pp. 142-143) and contains a characteristic word play passage of a British major summing up the state of the war.

5 The reference "wops" refers to the "Chapter IX" vignette in the Paris 1924, *in our time*, later printed in slightly different form as "Chapter VIII," *In Our Time* (N.Y.: Boni & Liveright, 1925).

6 "133-138"
This passage is also in Chapter XXI and begins with "I'm late darling" at the top of page 146 and continues to the end of the Chapter at page 151. It contains Catherine's crucial announcement that she is going to have a baby.

7 "*129* (NW)"
Fitzgerald is referring to Chapter XXII (*FTA*, pp. 152-155), wherein there is much by-play on Miss Van Campen's discovery of eleven empty bottles of brandy in Frederic's hospital room. The typescript is erratically paged, 1-138, 129-141, 152-154, 145-170, [170-181], 182-322, which accounts for the change in page references in Fitzgerald's notes.

8 "134"
Catherine announces, "I'm going to have a baby darling" (*FTA*, p. 147).

9 "By the way—"
The buying of the pistol occurs in Chapter XXIII at pp. 158-159.

10 "Catherine is too glib."
From context this would seem to include all of Chapter XXI, pp. 133-141.

11 "V.A.D."
Volunteer Aid Detachment.

12 "122 ect"
This refers to the last part of Chapter XIX, particularly to Frederic and Catherine's "talking softly on the balcony" at page 134 and following, where Catherine fears the rain because sometimes she sees herself dead in it. The story "Cat in the Rain" appears in the 1925 edition of *In Our Time,* as does "Hills Like White Elephants" with its bitter conversation between a young couple on a station platform in Spain. The young man tries to persuade his girl to have an abortion, and her disillusionment is total. As Fitzgerald so pungently recognized, the story is much more effective when considered in context with the plight of Frederic and Catherine.

13 "P. 241"
The passage, famous enough by now, even if criticized by some as a set piece or too biblical, opens, "that night at the hotel . . ." (*FTA,* p. 266). Fitzgerald wrote on the margin of page 241, "This is one of the most beautiful pages in all English literature." The words were erased but are easily readable.

14 "P. 209— & 219"
The words were deleted and replaced with dashes at pages 228 and 238.

15 "from 218 on."
This is from the point when Frederic Henry strikes a carabiniere who pulls him from the line of men in retreat (*FTA,* p. 237).

16 "I think 293-294 need cutting . . ."
This passage of 44 lines was cut as noted in the introduction to this article. For its content, see Sheldon Grebstein, *Hemingway's Craft* (Carbondale & Edwardsville: Southern Illinois University Press, 1973), pp. 214-215.

The book, by the way is between 80,000 + 100,000 wds — not 160,000 as you thought

P.241 is one of the best pages you've ever written, I think

P.209 + 219 I think if you use the word cocksuckers here the book will be supressed + confiscated within two days of publication.

All this retreat is marvellous the confusion etc.

The scene from 218 on is the best in recent fiction

Courtesy of the Hemingway Collection, John F. Kennedy Library.

JEROME MECKIER

Hemingway Reads Huxley: An Occasion for Some Observations on the Twenties and the Apostolate of the Lost Generation

In 1921 Hemingway became another of the many Americans then in Paris, and during the next five years he diligently taught himself to be a writer. The story of this period is set down in *A Moveable Feast,* one chapter of which, appropriately entitled "Une Génération Perdue," contains Hemingway's only extended reference to Aldous Huxley:

> To keep my mind off writing sometimes after I had worked I would read writers who were writing then, such as Aldous Huxley, D. H. Lawrence or any who had books published that I could get from Sylvia Beach's library or find along the quais.
>
> "Huxley is a dead man," Miss Stein said. "Why do you want to read a dead man? Can't you see he is dead?"
>
> I could not see, then, that he was a dead man and I said that his books amused me and kept me from thinking.[1]

No matter how uncomplimentary the reference sounds, Huxley must have impressed the young Hemingway if he was willing to incur Miss Stein's displeasure by reading the *enfant terrible* of English litereature, the cynic in ragtime, who was Hemingway's senior by five years and an expatriate of sorts in the south of France, where he found the warmth of the Mediterranean superior to the splendors of Paris. Miss Stein's premature obituary and Hemingway's refusal to participate in Huxley's interment—at first glance it is merely a minor incident in a famous American writer's Parisian interlude. Yet it invites speculation as to which of Huxley's works Hemingway read and what influence they had on him during this extremely formative period.

I wish to suggest that Huxley's influence was considerable. Already the author of six books by the time Hemingway arrived in Paris, the English satirist was inventing the mood for the twenties well before the decade began. Parodic, irreverent, and anti-Romantic, his volumes of poetry, three major collections by 1920, two of them during the traumatic war, may have been responsible for Hemingway's abortive attempts at a cynical, satirical poetry, in which case the deadness Miss Stein complained of, namely Huxley's mixture of malicious brightness with urbane *ennui* and cultured despair, probably struck Hemingway as something novel, vibrant, and alive, which indeed it was. Huxley's penchant for parody, a predominant mode throughout his poetry and early fiction, could have inspired Hemingway's sophomoric assault on Sherwood Anderson. Moreover, this time more fruitfully, Huxley's experiments with counterpoint may have influenced the structural arrangement of *A Farewell to Arms* and *The Sun Also Rises.* Finally and most importantly, one must mention Huxley's gallery of defeated youths and Circe-like, insatiable, but essentially unloving females. To these undone youths and deceiving *femme fatales* several of Hemingway's most notable heroes and heroines trace their ancestry. The vanquished youths in Huxley stand for the collapse of traditional ideals in the face of uncooperative modern realities. The heartless sirens who allure these youths only to arouse, frustrate, and sometimes actually debase them, symbolize the unresponsiveness of modern life to idealistic expectations, usually Romantic and literary in origin. The disenchanted youth and the girl who enchants merely to disappoint (or who cannot help being a disappointment) develop for Huxley into a modern myth: youth, or unfounded, egotistic idealism, is invariably impaired, perhaps even destroyed, by an ultimately meretricious postwar reality generally personified by a bewitching female. Huxley carefully extends his myth, giving it metaphysical dimension, until the male-female dichotomy is a paradigm for the fundamentally contrapuntal nature of modern life, until romantic love and the contratemps of lust signify an unending tension between the pattern-forming mind and the disorganization of matter, between ideals and reality, art and life, expectation and fulfillment. Originating in Huxley, this central myth for the twenties recurs with variations in Hemingway, Fitzgerald, and Waugh, and is rejected by Lawrence when the questing female, Connie Chatterley, brings Mellors back to life. The characters comprising it—a disillusioned, frustrated male, who is a lapsed idealist, and a loveless woman, who satisfies neither herself nor her lovers—can be recognized as sterile types whose kindred nevertheless proliferate in novels of or about the first truly modern decade.

It would be convenient to have a precise list of the Huxley books Hemingway read. Even without such a record, however, one can still assert that Hemingway thought about Huxley in the early twenties more frequently than he cared to admit some forty years later. By then their careers had developed differently, and critics no longer eagerly linked them as "Apostles of the Lost Generation."[2] Curiously, it was during Hemingway's stay in Paris that he enjoyed his closest contact with the modern British novel. From Sylvia Beach's library and the quai bookstalls he received an education independent of, perhaps contrary to, anything Paris offered, despite the celebrated friendships with Pound, Miss Stein, and Fitzgerald. Hemingway's Parisian years can be seen as his only major period of Anglophilia. In the short, rather spirited literary discussion at 27 rue de Fleurus, Miss Stein, having buried Huxley, dismisses Lawrence as a "pathetic and preposterous" failure, an author who "writes like a sick man,"[3] but Hemingway, politely independent, defends his decision to include both British novelists on his syllabus for the aspiring writer.

For the Huxley scholar there are several advantages to a brief Huxley-Hemingway comparison: he can re-affirm that Huxley's cynicism, his tone of amused despair at the tragic farce of modern life, had a tremendous hold on his contemporaries, American as well as British, a hold surpassed only by Eliot's image of modern life as a waste land; he can show that Huxley's experiments with counterpoint were not ignored by succeeding writers, for whom they were as consequential as Joyce's plunge into the stream of consciousness. For readers interested in the twenties, the comparison re-enforces the impression that novelists of that decade, whether separated by the Atlantic or rubbing shoulders in Paris, were more of an intellectual fraternity than any comparable group of British and American writers has been since. Finally, the spectacle of Hemingway making several false starts, first as poet, then as parodic novelist, before finding the right path proves that one author must often shed some of the influence another major writer has had on him before he can capitalize on the remaining, deeper affinities. Scholarly discussions of literary influence amount ultimately to conjecture. Crucial differences tend to be ignored, and the ignorance is not always inadvertent. Nevertheless, for the critic of American literature, speculation about the effects the reading of Huxley had on Hemingway adds another chapter to what is already known about Hemingway's emergence from the final phase of his apprenticeship.

I

Though never robust, Huxley was hardly a "dead man" when the twenties commenced. True, the London Life Association turned down his request for a policy in 1920, classifying him as "a Bad Life," a poor risk.[4] But Huxley's enervation was the result of constant over-exertion to make a living as a writer. In the decade between 1916 and 1926, the last half of which can be termed Hemingway's Parisian apprenticeship, he published thirteen books. Miss Stein's derogatory judgment was clearly not clinical. It probably means that for her Huxley's early satires appeared to rest on no discernible moral code. For all their cynical cleverness and technical felicity, they seemed to have no fresh, positive values to propose. Such an evaluation was, of course, as premature as a literal death certificate and, even in 1921, quite erroneous; it ignored the already evident Pascalian side of the ostensibly Peacockian, occasionally Swiftian satirist.

Hemingway also initially ignored the early signs of Huxley's Pascalian side. These were elements Hemingway chose not to imitate until 1926 when, as will be shown, Calamy, the incipient mystic in *Those Barren Leaves* (1925), and Jake Barnes in *The Sun Also Rises* are closer than they seem. It was the so-called 'dead' side of Huxley, his irreverent exposition of the deadness of modern life, the uselessness of once valued ideals, that appealed immediately to Hemingway. Under Huxley's influence he tried, briefly and with only modest success, to become a satirist, first a satiric poet and then a satiric novelist. Clearly, Huxley's mordant estimate of post-war life was one that Hemingway found congenial, but he had to learn to make a corroborating assessment in a more serious voice and terser style of his own, one that borrowed Huxley's Pyrrhonist mood but not his self-consciously clever, thoroughly English tone.

Several of Hemingway's poems issued by the Contact Publishing Company in Paris in 1923 seem to be an attempt to emulate Huxley's early verse, most of which, even the poems often misread as serious poetry, is actually irreverent, parodic, and extensively satiric. Hemingway's verses have little in common with those of Pound, his other Parisian mentor, nor do they imitate Eliot. The voice that speaks in "Roosevelt" and "Oklahoma" is that of a disillusioned, cynical young man enjoying his cleverness, the same sort of stance the mischievous but world-weary persona adopts more engagingly in many of Huxley's better poems. The initially ambiguous thesis of Hemingway's "Champs D'Honneur," for example, is that soldiers never die well. The poet then proves his case by remorselessly listing the gruesome and unsavory deaths enlisted men can meet. Similar but better disturbing poems abound in Huxley, such as "Topiary" in *The Defeat of Youth* (1918), where only the theory of God as a Topiarist, a perverse gardener, can explain the ugliness of so many human forms, the diseases and deformities man's flesh is heir to. "Montparnasse" perfectly captures Huxley's tone of urbane *ennui* with its lament that "There are never any suicides . . . among people one knows." This poem resembles in manner and tone a poem such as "Verrey's" in *Leda* (1920), where Huxley naughtily and with more sprightliness compares the celebrations of the bright young nightclubbers in their subterranean vault to a "funereal agape" for Epicurus. These revels are merely death disguised as frenetic life. As a poet, Hemingway is no match for Huxley. His range is narrower; his lines, somewhat mechanical, are neither as nasty nor as lively; but he responds eagerly to Huxley's sense of life's meaningless perversities and his iconoclastic irreverence, bred of disillusionment and boredom. He can appreciate these qualities even as his somewhat leaden verses fail to imitate them successfully.

II

More amusing than Miss Stein's coroner's report is Hemingway's rejoinder that he read Huxley, the century's most cerebral novelist, to keep from thinking. This declaration may be tongue-in-cheek. The point of the jest would be Hemingway's conviction, much of it retrospective, that ideas *per se* must be kept out of novels, whereas Huxley insisted that they were the very stuff of fiction, both more interesting and defensible as subjects than the less searching, less philosophical concerns of the so-called "congenital" novelists, the born storytellers. Huxley was always greatly interested in ideas, his own and his characters'. His peculiar talent, he maintained, was to reveal "attitudes toward life," to study the behavior of his characters in light of their explanations of "man's relation to the world."[5] With Huxley, Hemingway might argue, one did not have to think; it was all done for the reader by the novelist and the hypertrophic intellects of his *dramatis personae.* Actually, Hemingway seems to have read Huxley, Lawrence, and others largely for diversion: "When I was writing," he notes, "it was necessary for me to read after I had written. If you kept thinking about it, you would lose the thing that you were writing before you could go on with it the next day."[6] But he could not, nor could any writer or critic, remain impervious to what he read, unaffected by it as an artist. So it is no surprise that *The Torrents of Spring* (1926), an atypical Hemingway work, has been called a "satirical novel,"[7] probably written in imitation of Huxley's specialty, the satirical novel of ideas. This judgment can stand even if the similarity between *Torrents* and, for example, *Crome Yellow* is in the attempt, not the result.

Hemingway and Faulkner were both drawn to Huxley's format for the satirical novel of ideas. In a period when the sense of agreement community brings dramatically disappeared, it seemed perfect for ridiculing other authors, subverting outmoded ideas, and challenging absurd new ones. But neither *Torrents* nor Faulkner's *Mosquitoes* (1927) could manage the difficulty of reconciling excellent fooling with a gift for serious thought, even if Hemingway and Faulkner later surpassed Huxley in a variety of other respects. The satirical novel of ideas, as developed by Huxley from its rather simplistic Peacockian days, has found few subsequent practitioners because, as with Joyce's triumphant use of stream of consciousness, it is not only difficult to write the form well but almost impossible to take it further than Huxley did. He was able to make the structure and design of his discussion novels an extension of the themes they contained.[8] His novels of ideas were *real* novels, indisputably works of a significant literary artist. And his attacks on contemporary eccentricities of thought and behavior became a merciless exposition of the wearisome conditions of humanity. Significantly, Hemingway and Faulkner both imitated Huxley before *Point Counter Point* (1928) appeared and, in effect, closed out the form.

Following Huxley's lead, Hemingway tried to carve a niche for himself by carving up writers from the previous generation, Sherwood Anderson in particular. Huxley's *Crome Yellow* mocked the intellectual pretensions of its characters, often pitting one character's ideas against another's until both were undercut by the contrast. Hemingway implies that Anderson and his characters, Yogi Johnson and Scripps O'Neil especially, have no recognizable ideas at all, nothing that can be articulated or defined, no matter how pretentious the novel's chapter titles become (i.e. "The Struggle for Life," "Men in War and the Death of Society"). Hence neither the English intelligentsia nor the 'real' people of America, neither privileged thinkers nor the democratic proletariat, seem to have anything worthwhile to offer their respective novelists. The calm, peaceful decadence suggested by the title of Huxley's first novel is belied by the often bizarre intellectual fermentations it contains, as though Crome were really an asylum, while the furor of Hemingway's title, an allusion to his characters' allegedly profound emotions, quickly becomes mere flaccidity. If the second decade of the present century was a time of purposeless frenzy set against a background of collapsed values, then literary parody—the depiction of certain kinds of literature, perhaps literature *per se,* as a false and played-out game—is an appropriate tactic. It is a way of underlining the loss of values, of actually collapsing them and their now inoperative formats before the reader's eyes, while clearing the ground for one's own work. The caving in of values, literary and philosophical, is accentuated by the parodist's ability to collapse the forms, modes, and specific works that once contained them.

The key to both first novels is definitely parody. *Crome Yellow* is largely the story of Denis Stone's multiple disappointments. The facile Romanticism of this would-be Georgian poet is rudely rebuffed by the world of experience. When Denis, in full retreat by novel's end from the scenes of his discomfiture, terminates his development by refusing to grow up, Huxley parodies the *Bildungsroman.* Yet Denis' is a plausible decision since traditional guidelines for emotional and intellectual advance prove inoperable. Furthermore, none of the alleged adults in the novel, despite the conversational brilliance they often display, is appealingly mature. The theories and crotchets of Huxley's constant talkers enable him to satirize the mentality of his age, fashion a mock *Decameron,* and ridicule the country-house novel. Given the modern world and the quality of its minds, there can be no meaningful retreat from the care-plagued metropolis, no utopian Abbeys of Thélème. *The Torrents of Spring* travesties the anti-intellectualism of American realism and points out the unnaturalness of its naturalism. Both novels satirize literary and philosophical attitudes toward life and are therefore novels of ideas. The characters in both are caricatures, grotesques who reduce to nonsense the excesses they attack. The eccentric intellectual formulations of Huxley's thinkers imprison each theorist in his own private world as thoroughly as Beckett traps his in womb-like rooms and trash cans. Anderson is blamed first for making his characters' drives and internal stresses uncontrollable, and then for investing these ungovernable, inarticulated forces with a specious profundity. Thus both novelists belittle literature as the creator and preserver of values, and both lament a loss of communicability.

To bait the naturalists further, Hemingway virtually eliminates cause and effect. As in Beckett, nothing in *The Torrents of Spring* seems to follow inevitably from anything else. Using Johnson and O'Neil, Hemingway makes the common, average, and everyday—all of them fetishes for naturalist and realist alike—simultaneously so banal and unintelligible that they almost cease to be an interesting literary subject. Huxley's characters are modeled on several of the more intelligent artists and thinkers of the period, but his analysis of their eccentric ideas and behavior precludes man's intellectual development: growth, maturity, and even evolution become chimerical. By scoffing at some of the techniques of Joyce, Anderson, and Miss Stein while also decrying themes and ideas borrowed from Lawrence and Dos Passos, Hemingway challenges the quality, vitality, and direction of literary life in Europe and America. At some points Hemingway amalgamates his targets, striking Anderson, Lawrence, and naturalism at once. The grotesque Indians Yogi Johnson meets by the clubful are not merely unlike Cooper's and Twain's. They are also a parody of Lawrence's fascination with Aztecs and Red Indians in *Aaron's Rod* (1922) and *The Plumed Serpent* (1926). If there is nothing meaningful to be learned from the lives of ciphers like Johnson and O'Neil, even less can be gleaned from those darlings of the naturalists, simple primitives. Indeed their simplicity is irrecoverable, so Hemingway endows them with a social club to undercut their alleged propensity for significant violence with an absurd, Waughesque sophistication. This ultimately makes them as anomalous as John Savage, another but later parody of the Lawrencian ideal, in Huxley's *Brave New World.*

Huxley's *Crome Yellow* compromises the world of ideas, the realm which he himself initially inhabits as satirical novelist of ideas and later, more straightforwardly, as a thinker and sage with positive proposals to supplement his satire. His strategy in the early novels is to discriminate his own satiric conceptions of modern life from the absurd notions of his eccentrics and the untenable, Romantic ideals his more admirable younger characters cannot live up to. Hemingway compromises the so-called realistic world of everyday experience, of action, adventure, and feeling, the realm he eventually was to make his own. The nonsense of psuedo-realists and bogus naturalists must be swept away in the interests of his own allegiance to fidelity. As parodists, Huxley makes a path for his own ideas and Hemingway clears one for his version of reality. Different though their theories of the novel may be, both novelists are parodists *par excellence,* their goal being not merely to defrock absurdity but to cleanse a mode or a genre for further use.

Admittedly, the antics of brilliant but warped eccentrics are more amusing than the intellectual fumblings and emotional gropings of unintelligent grotesques. Huxley was more fortunate in his choice of targets. Today, *Crome Yellow* remains colorful and exuberant, while *The Torrents of Spring,* a parodic celebration of banality, often seems as dull as its setting, as tasteless as the food in Brown's Beanery. If asked to identify *The Torrents of Spring,* the well-read contemporary critic probably cites the Turgenev novel from which Hemingway, in quest of an ironic allusion, borrowed the title.

Furthermore, Hemingway never acquired the rare ability to make his own points strongly enough through parody. Huxley was always able to make a statement peculiarly his own in order to give his work a life independent of its target. *Crome Yellow* remains re-readable even if one has never heard that it is a parody of Garsington society, embellished with caricatures of Lady Ottoline, Bertrand Russell, Arnold Bennett, and a host of other luminaries who retreated there to escape London and news of the war and share impressions and ideas as if they were participants in a modern *Decameron.* Fortunately for Huxley, the persons he caricatures have remained famous. Garsington and its goings-on have become legendary. Yet Huxley's targets are often obscure. This is not the case when he lampoons Russell's blueprint for an excessively rational state, dismisses Bennett's prolificness in terms of Barbecue-Smith's formulae for automatic writing, and expresses contempt for Stone's Georgian literary mannerisms. But he also devotes an entire chapter to a parody of a deservedly forgotten sermon by the Rev. E. H. Horne (ch. 9) and burlesques the fortune-telling sequence from *Jane Eyre.*[9] No matter how topical the satire becomes, however, the incidents remain plausibly ludicrous in themselves, part of the novel's plot and relevant to its Huxleyan themes. As the characters fail to communicate and remain, as Denis' theory explains, a hopeless collection of uncrossing parallel lines, *Crome Yellow* permits Huxley to comment on the human condition. By contrast, Hemingway's targets seem less accessible today. The writers he parodies, with the obvious exception of Lawrence, are less widely read than they once were. As a result, *The Torrents of Spring,* which primarily attacks the vagaries and vapidity of Anderson's fictional concerns and the inadequate literary movements they spring from, is almost incomprehensible, merely an atrocious novel, if one has not recently read *Dark Laughter* and *Winesburg, Ohio.*[10]

III

Carlos Baker's sections on "Counterpoint" and "Circe and Company" in *Hemingway: The Writer as Artist* never mention Huxley, but one feels that they should. *Point Counter Point,* Huxley's finest novel, employs a multiplicity of plots which comment on each other satirically through skillful juxtapositioning. This strategy must have influenced the contrapuntal treatment of love and war in *A Farewell to Arms,* even if Hemingway's novel as a whole is less experimental, less complex structurally. Only one year after Huxley's masterpiece sold over 10,000 copies, a good figure for 1928, Hemingway's novel told a love story and a war story by turns, taking each through complementary stages of development, letting each strand of the plot modify the other. Indeed, the bitter satire on the stupidity of war emerges most insistently from the counterpoint of love scenes and war scenes. This enables Hemingway to do parts of the battle sequences with a reportorial objectivity denied the satirist but essential for the realist. However grim, resigned, and ironical this realist may be, he also senses the excitement of war and the opportunities for camaraderie and heroism. Counterpoint, so crucial to the satire, also ensures that some objectivity survives, even though Frederic Henry, who actually tells the story, speaks mainly of the incompetence and catastrophes responsible for the total defeat of his youthful idealism. For the first time among the instances discussed so far, the influence of Huxley on Hemingway is indisputably beneficial. Hemingway combines what he borrows from the English satirist's cynical mood and contrapuntal manner with a style and experiences of his own. Much of Huxley's dissatisfaction in the early works can be traced to a general depression resulting from the first war of world-wide proportions. By linking the cynicism he found so congenial in Huxley with the disappointments he had experienced first-hand, Hemingway was able to attribute Huxley's mood and the attraction it held for him to a common cause. This allowed him to clarify his own recent history and crystallize the process behind the decade's widespread malaise. What Hemingway made explicit now seems obvious to literary historians, and surely it was no surprise to Huxley or contemporary readers familiar with the war poets and lines 19-30 of *The Waste Land.* But in 1929, when Hemingway's novel appeared along with Aldington's *Death of a Hero,* Remarque's *All Quiet on the Western Front,* and Graves' *Goodbye to All That,* the mood generated in large part by the war had been widely explored and exploited by novelists like Huxley well before any novel graphically presented one of its major causes. For Hemingway, and perhaps for Aldington and Graves as well, the cynical tone of defeated idealism, popularized by a sensitive moral seismograph, namely Huxley the non-combatant, became a means long after it had already been an end or result.

The two novels, of course, are very different. *Point Counter Point,* with its savage satire, its bestial characters and crescendo of deaths, is bleaker than anything in Hemingway, though also intentionally more comical; and there are many parts of *A Farewell to Arms,* particularly its tenderer moments, which Huxley would have found it difficult to write. But the overall techniques are similar, and so is the assumption that in an age suddenly without absolutes the artist can only make his points and evolve his values through a complex of carefully staged contrasts: the norms that do emerge—Henry's unilateral surrender, a flight that traditionally might have been described as cowardly desertion, and Rampion's advocacy of a wise, Grecian balance, an unrestricted wholeness that takes some liberties with conventional notions of passion and restraint—find their vouchsafement mainly in their superiority to alternatives that are less attractively portrayed. Hence the tremendous value of counterpoint in a rudderless age. Where the stream-of-consciousness novelist reacts to the loss of universals by retreating inward, making each individual's psychology a worthwhile study in itself, a microcosm, the contrapuntalist preserves the novel's capacity for variety, panorama, and overview. While capturing the chaos of conflicting ideas, he forestalls complete despair by allowing his personal prescription, generally entrusted to an articulate standardbearer, to emerge from a welter of competing opinions and unworkable life-styles.

This is even truer of Hemingway's earlier novel, *The Sun Also Rises,* which, as Baker realizes, is an extremely proficient contrapuntal work,[11] probably Hemingway's most satisfactory use of this highly original structural technique. Title and mood, regularly associated with *Ecclesiastes,* may be equally indebted to Huxley's "Soles Occidere et Redire Possunt" in *Leda* (1920). The poem is a parodic elegy for an intelligent young man whose disillusionment and death in the Great War put a premature end to his mental growth. This is a disaster that the would-be elegist cannot disguise or palliate. Counterpoint develops in *The Sun Also Rises* because, as Baker argues, the norm is carried in tandem by Jake Barnes, Bill Gorton, and Pedro Romero in contrast to the abnormal vanities of the neurotics in the Ashley-Campbell-Cohn triangle. Although never fascinated with the novel of ideas to the extent Huxley was, Hemingway distinguishes healthy from unhealthy attitudes toward the apparent futility of modern life by contrasting these two groups. Something quite similar happens in *Point Counter Point* when Huxley surrounds the Rampions with a series of couples who distort and pervert the sane wholeness they represent. Hemingway is strictly for counterpoint through character contrast, and even here there are just two major classifications despite subtle differences between the members of each group. One finds little interest in multiplicity of plot, few violent alternations of manner and mood, and none of the other complicated devices Quarles' notebook considers essential if fiction is to imitate the shape of post-war life, if it is to capture the absurdity and yet the haunting intricacies of the human fugue. But in Hemingway the characters' attitudes, their philosophies, all of which express possible relationships between man and the world of the twenties, are successfully embodied dramatically. They are seldom discussed. Such is not always the case in Huxley, where the more oratorical protagonists occasionally risk becoming mere mouthpieces for ideas, and lively, lengthy discussions by the characters themselves often furnish the main drama.

The two groups of major characters in *The Sun Also Rises* and, more important, their outlooks are very sharply paralleled, that is, contrasted and compared in a contrapuntal manner reminiscent of Huxley. This happens, for example, with their conflicting views on the value of love. Jake's perspective is quite different from Romero's yet ultimately closer to his than to Brett's, and certainly healthier than hers. Still, Hemingway could not have derived his approach to love nor could he have learned his contrapuntal technique from *Point Counter Point* because his novel preceded Huxley's by two years. The answer lies in *Those Barren Leaves* (1925), which appeared in time to influence *The Sun Also Rises.*

Huxley's third novel is essentially a contrast of the different paths chosen by its major characters: the super-cynic Chelifer takes what he considers the realist's only alternative to escapism and plunges despairingly into the rubbish heap of modern life; Calamy, a detached, potential contemplative tactfully withdraws to a mountain top and waits. In Huxley's book as in Hemingway's, a sifting of healthy male attitudes from their sickly variants is a primary concern, and the question of what constitutes a viable life-style predominates. Though Calamy isolates himself by novel's end, cuts himself free from society as firmly as Jake is shut off from Brett, he appears more fortunate than Cardan, Mr. Falx, and especially Chelifer, none of whom can evolve in new directions. Similarly, Jake's position, wound and all, seems preferable to Campbell's or Cohn's, both of whom are really more impotent because they are totally bankrupt philosophically.

More germane to the opposing triads of *The Sun Also Rises* is Huxley's section entitled "The Loves of the Parallels" (Part Three); it depicts the inadequacy of love as an ideal or absolute in the post-war world. A series of unpalatable love affairs are contrasted thematically and schematically when each pair of lovers occupies a terrace, one above the other, of the Cybo Malaspina. Part Three of the novel depreciates most of its major figures (Chelifer, Mary Thriplow, Cardan, Mrs. Aldwinkle), who are neurotic, eccentric, opportunistic, or hopelessly cynical. But it improves one's estimate of Calamy, who shed the hypocritical Miss Thriplow, like Brett a user of men, to become progressively more disinterested in the sense recommended by the mystics he has begun reading. Viewed with Huxley's novel in mind, Jake's inability to love, like Calamy's refusal to go on doing so, is a ticket-of-leave from a Circe-like world that unfailingly disappoints and debases one's romantic ideals.

Given such conditions, lovers and cynics (merely inverted idealists) fail resoundingly. Only the disinterested have any capacity for a meaningful endurance that can await new developments or lead to new values. Chelifer's cynicism proves little protection: he is devoured by Mrs. Aldwinkle, an aging siren made desperate by her sense of time's flight. Mary Thriplow, who also must have lovers to satisfy her ego, vampirishly uses them to provide the materials for episodes in her novels. Brett's tragedy is not that the only male in the novel who might have satisfied her is physically unable. Love itself, too tired an ideal, cannot satisfy any longer. Her contention that she and Jake could have had a wonderful time under different circumstances amounts to self-delusion. This attempt to conceal the post-war collapse of meaning renders her nymphomania a perversely quixotic, romantic search for an unattainable ideal. It also makes her a refutation of Lawrence's questing female. Brett is primarily a Circe, a *femme fatale.* Like many of Huxley's alarming females, the fading Mrs. Aldwinkle among them, she personifies the modern world's false allure. But she is also its victim, an Ursula for whom there can be no Birkin because Jake, whose physical disability is the sign of his permanently impaired idealism, resembles Calamy in that he must have something other than love.

Along with Irene and Lord Hovenden, two innocent sillies who nevertheless find themselves genuinely in love in the traditional sense, Calamy emerges as one of the novel's few tributes to normalcy. He seeks a higher kind of love, a union with Ultimate Reality. Embarked on an intensely personal quest, fully prepared to evolve his own code and keep his own counsel, he is the new man, Huxley's revised hero, and a new ideal. He replaces the cynical Pyrrhonist, Chelifer, who is the *alter ego* for the pre-1925 Huxley, the writer whose unrelieved cynicism and aptitude for parody impressed Hemingway the would-be poet and satirical novelist. Jake, no matter how outlandish the claim seems, is probably Hemingway's version of Calamy. More than a war wound separates Brett from Jake and Jake from society. Even with his injury Jake, who cannot make love, is saner and more virile than Cohn, who can, just as Calamy, who simply takes flight, appears to be the only character in *Those Barren Leaves* with direction and purpose. The two are scarcely soulmates, but both are strongly anti-Lawrencian in conception. Their mutual disenchantment with modern life and love invites comparison, as does their resolve to endure. The detachment both deem it wise to cultivate until some original means of rapport with the world can be found is another characteristic they share. Hemingway's wounded hero, the sidelined Spartan, and Huxley's tired lover, an aspiring ascetic, have more in common than one might have supposed. *Those Barren Leaves* and *The Sun Also Rises,* novels seldom mentioned in the same sentence, display a few surprising similarities, the one between opposing triads and "The Loves of the Parallels," two exercises in the examination of an idea (such as love) in terms of variations on a theme, paramount among them.

Baker insists that *The Sun Also Rises* is not primarily a romantic study of sexual and spiritual frustration, though such a description would fit Hemingway's novel and *Those Barren Leaves* as well as *Point Counter Point.* Instead, he argues, it is a qualitative analysis of varying degrees of physical and spiritual manhood.[12] Such an interpretation is implicitly contrapuntal and thoroughly applicable to *Those Barren Leaves:* it envisions the novel as a series of variations, at least one of which emerges as the norm or main melody, with the others grouped round it as unsatisfactory approximations that are either slightly off-key or else outright perversions. This is the method used to separate Calamy from the other males; it is also the basis for the contrast-comparisons in "The Loves of the Parallels" and, more extensively, the counterpoint of plots, moods, characters and themes, throughout *Point Counter Point.*[13] One should not overlook the possibility that Faulkner, having outgrown *Mosquitoes,* is nonetheless indebted to Huxleyan counterpoint for the narrative techniques of *The Sound and the Fury* and *Absalom, Absalom*! But on Hemingway the influence of Huxley's mood and methods is more evident. Huxley's first three novels and *Point Counter Point,* his fourth, combine with *The Sun Also Rises, A Farewell to Arms,* and Fitzgerald's *The Great Gatsby* to make the best Baedecker one has to "Une Generation Perdue."

Since Jake and Calamy both draw back from the dance, neither ends as a *bona fide* member of the lost generation. Though Hemingway had little sympathy for Huxley's Pascalian side, he sensed in Calamy, the incipient mystic, an analogue for Jake's withdrawal to a position as detached observer. By the end of *Those Barren Leaves* and *The Sun Also Rises,* the hero in each case has effectively disassociated himself from the neurotic or eccentric preoccupations of the rest of the unsettled cast. This holds true even though Jake travels to the Hotel Montana in Madrid to collect Brett. Like their respective authors, Calamy and Jake find the antics of the twenties amusing, yet they are also saddened, sick at heart, and isolated by choice. Both await some sign that can lead them toward new commitment. For the losses suffered by the lost generation, its awareness of vanquished expectations and collapsing ideals, Huxley and Hemingway express genuine regret. But the responses most of their characters make to new and bewildering situations leave them sceptical. Often these responses—unheroic, neurotic behavior in Hemingway, eccentric ideas and ridiculous theories of conduct in Huxley—provoke outright contempt. Underlying the decade's frenetics, its celebrated capacity to roar, both writers sense a desperation equivalent to their own.

For practically the last time, Huxley and Hemingway resemble one another quite closely in 1925-6 as their different yet similar heroes nurse some disappointments and contemplate their next moves. Hemingway adopts a personal code of courage, self-dependence, and stoicism that often seems no more advanced than Jake's. Intense discipline, a strong sense of personal integrity and, above all, devotion to duty are Hemingway hallmarks. The last of his heroes, Thomas Hudson, speaks for all of them in *Islands in the Stream* (1970) when he grimly observes: "Love you lose. Honor has been gone for a long time. Duty you do." Huxley embraces Vedanta's belief that the Atman or divine particle in each man is his real self. Because Atman is essentially the same as Brahman or God or the Divine Ground, the attentive individual can overcome his ego, activate this real self, and achieve mystical unity not only with the One but with all of creation. This perennial philosophy Calamy, looking within himself, can already tentatively formulate.

IV

Strictly speaking, neither writer's recommendation was brand new. Although Huxley's was Eastern, imported, and would seem exotic to many, there were plenty of similarities between Western and Oriental religious thought. Calamy is busily unearthing a common denominator in the teachings of thinkers as diverse as Lao-Tzu, Buddha, and Christ. Each writer could thus claim that his future course was to be traditional as well as novel, both timeless and timely. The notion of an apostolate for the twenties still applies. But in the closing years of the decade the cynical bearers of sad tidings now have some recourse to offer. Each could insist that he was propogating an updated reapplication of possibilities not discredited by that deterioriation of values which led to the War and was in turn aggravated by it.

Both prescriptions seem rather demanding, too much so for either to enjoy universal implementation. As Huxley's own struggles with meditation soon convinced him, there are few potential mystics in any society, and they are almost always totally without influence. Hollywood to the contrary, there are even fewer Hemingway heroes, although a conception of such a hero, relentlessly bastardized by all forms of pop entertainment, becomes a part of every individual's fantasy life years before he learns of *The Upanishads* or *The Tibetan Book of the Dead.* Unlike the genuine article, the popular rendition of the Hemingway hero generally inhabits a transparently meaningful world, an assumption that would fall flat for Jake Barnes and Frederic Henry. Of the two alternatives, Huxley's now seems the more optimistic and open-ended. Everyone can apparently progress at least a short distance along the path Calamy, Beavis, Sebastian Barnack and perhaps Huxley himself chose to travel. Whether he appreciates the fact or not, each individual harbors Atman within him and is therefore equipped for spiritual development. By contrast,

Hemingway's path is more of a holding action than a progress, tight-lipped endurance rather than growth. Though all allegedly have a spiritual principle within, it is by no means certain that one in a thousand has Jake's fortitude or Robert Jordan's nerve.

Despite a superficial resemblance of titles, the last completed works we have from each writer, *Island* (1962) and *Islands in the Stream* (1970) substantiate this impression of Huxley's continuing viability. In *Islands in the Stream* Thomas Hudson, ordinarily a painter, is drawn back into the he-man world of action and adventure. He dies in harness at sea as he and his crew pursue survivors of a German submarine in waters off the coast of Cuba. Hudson becomes an older, wiser, Robert Jordan, laying his life on the line in yet another of the world's trouble spots. Hemingway's ideals, it seems, are best exhibited not by artists or thinkers, no matter how intense their self-discipline, but by activists who are rigorously tested in times of danger, ordeal, and stress. For the Hemingway hero to thrive, the world must be falling apart. Violence is absolutely essential. Huxley's ideals require privacy, stability, and peace. Hemingway's are thus somewhat fatalistic, or at least inherently anti-utopian, while Huxley's, purportedly an answer to turmoil and unrest, are easily impeded by any manifestation of the very conditions they are meant to resolve. For Huxley's new thoughts World War II was a challenge and a disaster. In 1936, Anthony Beavis of *Eyeless in Gaza* seems on the brink of spiritual awareness, but Huxley, though safe in America, seems to have spent the war years in a state of constant depression.[14] To Hudson as for Hemingway, the war brings a kind of apotheosis. The move from a painter's easel to an improvised Q-boat is a course directly opposite to the one the Huxley hero must take. For him the world of politics and warfare constitute a spiritual trap. Even the artistic impulse and the sexual urge, both of which Hemingway respects, ultimately appear in the later Huxley as external signs of the more important internal religious drive. In *Ape and Essence,* for example, Dr. Poole, though trapped in dystopia, moves from a discovery of sex to an equally stimulating discovery of Shelley; and beyond both there is a spiritual awakening that Huxley's closing pages can only hint at.

The enlightened Palanese in *Island,* profiting from the texts Calamy cites and combining Eastern spirituality with Western know-how, fashion the perfect society from blueprints which Huxley, a well-read intellectual co-ordinating ideas collected over a lifetime, optimistically supplies. This is the utopia Jordan's small crusade and Hudson's escapade probably never will produce. Yet this perfect state cannot outlast the novel. Pala is swallowed by the forces of Colonel Dipa, a fascist dictator of the sort Hudson and Jordan would gladly have fought. The sort of event that brings Hudson out of retirement is precisely what dooms Huxley's spiritually aware society. Before its demise, Pala proves its efficacy by converting Will Farnaby, a cynical Westerner who reminds one of Francis Chelifer. By a leap of imagination Huxley creates a situation in which the ideal state can help to save the individual by showing him its vision of personal and corporate perfection. Hemingway's final novel pictures the individual still trying to save society. This apparently unending process the Palanese, internally at peace, refuse to master. Without Calamy's brand of awareness, without guru-figures like Mr. Propter and Bruno Rontini or planners like Dr. Andrew MacPhail, utopia may be impossible. Without the expertise of men like Jordan and Hudson, no utopia can survive. And there, unfortunately, the matter rests, since these two kinds of knowledge, Pala's and Jordan's, are intrinsically incompatible. In 1926 Jake and Calamy seem related, but Hemingway and Huxley gradually become mutually exclusive.

What *Islands in the Stream* and *Island* ultimately have in common is a belief that one must learn not only how to live but, more important, how to die. The *ars moriendi,* as demonstrated by Dr. Robert MacPhail's wife, who dies painfully of cancer (ch. 14), is almost blissful in its assumption that one perishes into something: the individual soul is absorbed into a world of clear light. For Thomas Hudson, death is defined with stoical humor as the only thing you never get over. "Death is what is really final."[15] Whether fact or fancy, the circumstances of Lakshmi's expiration bear a closer resemblance to Maria Huxley's and to Aldous' own than Hudson's death, or Jordan's, does to Hemingway's.

Of the two prescriptions for the twenties, then, Huxley's was blatantly religious, much more so than Eliot's, but even Hemingway's initially had a spiritual aura. This became even truer in *For Whom the Bell Tolls* when Robert Jordan was presented as a secular saint and martyr. He helps to explode the old order in hopes of establishing heaven on earth, a "new world,"[16] with the devotees of Marx as its architects and apostles. The initial resemblance between Huxley's ideal and Hemingway's, between Calamy and Jake, was soon obscured when subsequent development took the Huxley hero away from the 'real' world, now seen as Maya or illusion, while the Hemingway hero, freshened, was returned to the arena of public events where he was again able to find the sacred in the profane.

If Hemingway ultimately fails to find a new religion, whereas Huxley does, Huxley can be said to conceive a new romanticism, as does Hemingway. Huxley's interest in Eastern thought gradually permits him to revive, perhaps the word is rehabilitate, facets of the idealistic Romanticism he began by debunking. Reconsidered, some of the better passages in Romantic poetry can be read more credibly in light of the perennial philosophy. With the support East can give West, Shelley's insistence that "The One remains," his notion that this world is an illusion, a stain on "the white radiance of Eternity," becomes tenable once more. The same holds true for Wordsworth's intimations and spots-in-time, his eloquent but groping explorations of the Atman-Brahman relationship he senses within himself on those rare occasions when he becomes "a living soul." For Hemingway the Spanish Civil War rekindles a Romantic belief in the nobility of common men and the inevitability of meaningful democracy through revolution. Jordan confesses that he really believes in Liberty, Equality, and Fraternity, or Life, Liberty and the Pursuit of Happiness,[17] not in Russia and Marx. Fighting for the Spanish Republicans, he is a Prometheus for Pablo's band as he provides them with explosives. Anti-tyranny in an idealistic, Romantic way, he is also Byron and the struggle for Greek independence all over again, even if his final act, a sniper shot at the decent Lieutenant Berrendo, will compromise this stance.

Ironically, the thirties, with its rebirth of political idealism, its deceptively appealing Marxists, Socialists, and International Brigades, all barking ferociously at the bugbear of Fascism, seemed to favor the Hemingway hero. The decade was made to order, a new, invigorating call to arms for the detached Spartan. By contrast, Huxley's contemplatives, such as Beavis in *Eyeless in Gaza* and Huxley himself, were slated to be conscientious objectors, supporters of the Peace Pledge Union, and foes of all false, secular ideologies, Fascism, Marxism, and Nationalism among them. This explains why Hemingway flourished in the late thirties and forties while Huxley lost most of his original audience. *For Whom the Bell Tolls* (1940) became the American writer's most popular novel, quite a contrast in tone to Huxley's dystopia, *Brave New World* (1932), and in direction to the introspective, mystical *Eyeless in Gaza.* Since the 1960's and the fiasco in Viet Nam, however, the trend has gradually gone the other way. Beavis and his successors in Huxley's later novels do not rival the popularity the Hemingway hero still enjoys, but they seem believable once more.

V

Antic Hay (1923) and *The Sun Also Rises* both end with hero and heroine, who are unable to satisfy one another, riding rather aimlessly in a taxi. As Gumbril, Jr. and Myra Viveash crisscross London in search of companions to relieve their boredom, this conveyance becomes the perfect symbol for the pointlessness of modern life, an in-transit existence between a vanished world order and new patterns which have yet to emerge. In fact, *Antic Hay* is packed with images of purposeless motion. The taxi Brett and Jake take in Hemingway's final chapter is probably meant to remind the reader of Huxley's novel. No reliable still-point materializes for lovers in either novel. Like *Antic Hay* and *Those Barren Leaves,* which fail to produce a single convincingly successful marriage or love affair, *The Sun Also Rises* is sceptical about love. In a variety of ways all three novels use the inability or refusal of their characters to love, whether to love at all or to do so rewardingly, as the major sign of a generation's frustrated idealism and general disillusionment.

It is unfair for Mark Spilka's essay on "The Death of Love in *The Sun Also Rises*" to give Hemingway (and Lawrence) all the credit, and Huxley none at all, for analyzing this phenomenon. The idea of a death of love as a metaphor for the death of idealism is central to Huxley's myth for the twenties. Lawrence's competitive myth, as seen in *Lady Chatterley's Lover* and, more starkly, in "The Man Who Died," is actually about the resurrection of the body, the rebirth of love. Hemingway falls somewhere in between. No matter how cynical he becomes, he never ridicules the very process of love-making as viciously as Huxley does. There is no Swiftian emphasis on the grossness and bestiality of the flesh. Nor is there an insistence upon the constant undermining of reason and resolve by passion. Hemingway never equates lovers with "twin cannibals in bedlam" or likens fornicators to a two-backed beast.[18] Where Hemingway is simply disillusioned, Huxley at times is also disgusted. When events of the thirties reactivate Hemingway's sidelined Spartan, filling him with the hope and political idealism that seem possible once more for the crusading activist, Hemingway can readily shift his allegiance. He can substitute an adaptation of Lawrence's positive myth for his earlier, more moderate version of Huxley's negative one. But no matter how hopeful he becomes, he never elevates love to the position of beatific prominence it enjoys in Lawrence. Robert Jordan is the Hemingway hero recalled to action and hence to life and love, as happens to Mellors after his meeting with Connie. Far from undermining resolve, love, Hemingway decides, can sweeten duty, even if duty must always take precedence. Connie brings Mellors back to life, and he causes her physical resurrection. Similarly, Maria breathes some warmth into Jordan's rather grim devotion to human freedom, and he in turn accomplishes her rebirth by enabling her to forget being physically humiliated and then raped by the Falangists. Jordan and Maria restore each other's essential humanity: a demolitions expert and a ravished girl are no more incongruous than a gamekeeper and the Lady from Wragby Hall. Maria and Jordan revive each other's capacity to love, which humanizes their capacity to champion a cause. Mellors and Jordan both possess arcane knowledge which is essential for their respective worlds to be remade. Familiarity with animals, animality, and the natural, physical world of the wood is entirely different from expertise with explosives. Yet both can be life-giving, the former a badly needed counter to the death wish seemingly inherent in industrialized society, and the latter a weapon against whatever political and military forces threaten the life of freedom. The Lawrencian resurrection motif reappears in *For Whom the Bell Tolls* in the dying Jordan's somewhat sentimental belief that he has become immortal. He will remain alive through Maria's surviving love for him. Like Connie, who is temporarily separated from Mellors at the end of *Lady Chatterley's Lover* but probably carries his child, Maria has been impregnated by Jordan's ideals and personality, especially his sense that one must do one's duty. This is the final lesson he teaches her by insisting that she flee to safety with Pablo and Pilar. This final lesson is the equivalent of the epistolary lecture Mellors gives to Connie in Lawrence's final chapter. Mellors and Jordan are mentors as well as lovers. Although Maria has told Jordan that she cannot have children and he has declared that the times are not right for bringing them into the world, Jordan's parting insistence that he goes with her, that "Whichever one there is, is both,"[19] sounds curiously like the conclusion of Mellor's letter, in which the prospective father reminds Connie that "a great deal of us is together, and we can but abide by it."[20]

Eventually, Hemingway and Huxley both make their peace with Lawrence's myth, though neither ever shares his belief that the way to salvation is primarily through a tender, sacred, physical love. Huxley's accomodation is much more cautious, at times almost resentful and begrudging, yet ultimately more optimistic than Hemingway's. As late as *The Genius and the Goddess* (1955), Huxley creates the doomed Katy Maartens, the life-giving goddess of the piece, to enumerate the limitations of Frieda Lawrence, Connie Chatterley, and the questing Lawrencian heroine's philosophy. In *Brave New World* (1932), sex, more than soma, was the opiate of the people. Male and female generally complete one another in Lawrence. Copulative fusion brings heightened self-awareness as well as self-transcendence. Huxley's males and females, as will be shown, are almost always dichotomous. They are virtual schematizations of the counterpoints, the opposing ideas and principles, that make the human condition so dualistic and problematic. The only believable happily married couple anywhere in the early novels is the Rampions. Though modeled on Lawrence, Mark appears to have had no impact on Hemingway, who may have been more impressed with Mellors. Love enjoys some status in Huxley's *Ape and Essence* (1949) and *Island* (1962), where Poole discovers Loola and Will Farnaby is tutored by Susila, but only as a preliminary ideal. Huxley finally concedes that lovemaking affords a way out of the egotistic self. It is therefore vaguely analogous to the mystical, more so for Lawrence, Huxley decides, than for most men. Like Calamy and Jake, the later Huxley still wants something other than physical love, something higher, more mental, and pacific, less degrading. By *For Whom the Bell Tolls,* Hemingway joins Lawrence to vote for love's restoration: the latter equates it with the life force itself, and the former envisions it as a temporary compensation for the rigors the activist regularly endures and the extinction he invariably must face alone.

Of all the writers dealing with the demise of love in World War One, Spilka asserts, Hemingway "caught it whole."[21] If so, he accomplished this remarkable feat with a strong assist from Huxley's better war-time poems and subsequent early fiction. In both places the failure of love is almost always a metaphor for the breakdown of those ideals which were originally predicated on the meaningfulness of life and the fundamental nobility of an undivided, harmonious self. Several of Huxley's best poems explore the inefficacy of love as an absolute, a reason for living. These are major poems, such as the satiric sonnet sequence entitled "The Defeat of Youth," the mock-epic of "Leda," and the parodic elegy called "Soles Occidere et Redire Possunt," which, along with many lesser efforts on similar themes, appeared *during* or shortly after the war. And the inquest was then pursued in such excellent anti-romantic stories as "Happily Ever After" in *Limbo* (1920) and "The Giocanda Smile" in *Mortal Coils* (1922), not to mention the early novels. All of these probe the phenomenon of love and the conventions of Romantic idealism with an incisory scepticism.

VI

In *Those Barren Leaves,* Chelifer, parodic poet and total cynic *par excellence,* becomes the *locus classicus* for the anti-love, anti-Romantic sentiments which saturate the fiction of the twenties. In him the intricate modern syndrome of martial experience, disillusionment, and the consequent deflation of love as a goal or ideal is vividly personified. When his "Autobiography" recounts the events leading up to his 'conversion' to cynicism, Chelifer identifies war as the occasion and names love as the lecturer.[22] From the stresses of the battlefield he turned to Barbara Waters as one might have turned to God in a more religious age, only to find her, like modern life itself, infinitely alluring but essentially vapid, mindless, debasing, and coldly indifferent to his idealistic expectations. For the twenties love failed to prevent war and then to serve as an antidote to its horrors, either because love was itself contaminated by the times or, more likely because it was always an inflated ideal, a bogus absolute. It was promoted to a *code* for living by the Troubadours and then mistakenly elevated as an *alternative to faith* by many of the major poets in the Western tradition. Not until the war was its speciosity finally exposed and magnified. At first the post-war Hemingway has no prominent place for love in his code, and Huxley initially sees it as an impediment to faith, a terrible distraction, by no means an alternative. A former Romantic idealist, Chelifer is another of Huxley's lapsed Shelleyans. He is a disenchanted youth, a portrait of the failed artist as a young cynic. He is a case of arrested development for which the nature of the human condition in modern times is largely to blame. For novels of the twenties, Hemingway's included, Chelifer, along with his important forbears in Huxley's poetry and short fiction, becomes a seminal figure.

Huxley's strongest influence on Hemingway and his most signficant contribution to the first truly modern decade is thus his concept for a new character. But the new type is not the contemplative Calamy, an embryonic positive force who augurs the unpopular direction Huxley's later work was to take. Nor is it Rampion the life-worshipper, that overly talkative product of Huxley's personal regard for his friend Lawrence. Instead, it is Chelifer, the permanently defeated youth, the irreverent, satirical poet whose art, like life itself and his own eccentric life-style, is a constant put-on. Chelifer's thoughts and experience, as contained in the magnificent "Autobiography" he is writing throughout Part 2 of *Those Barren Leaves,* summarizes the dead-end life and art seemed to have reached in the post-war years. Francis becomes an expression of the state of mind of his generation, a poet who is the mind of his age but only in the negative cynical sense the times require. He develops into the laureate of meaninglessness. Huxley's poems and early fiction are packed with idealistic young men, such as Chelifer once was, whose defeat at the hands of un-Romantic realities, undependable love, meretricious females, who symbolize both, or in the Great War signals the collapse of a philosophical mode of perception and a set of ideals. The defeat of a youth, of hope and anticipation, ranspires again and again in Huxley's early works. It is his recurrent metaphor not only for the death of love, but also for the loss of faith and innocence, the end of optimism, and the collapse of traditional Western ideals.

Identified earlier as the new man, the new ideal for Huxley after 1925, and the source for Jake's withdrawal and detachment, Calamy is also a defeated youth, but he is on the path to recovery. Ironically, as Huxley begins to outgrow the cynical Chelifer and move toward Calamy, other novelists appropriate his concept of the defeated youth, recognizing it as one of the most formative ideas of the era. They begin exploiting it for their own purposes. By the time Fitzgerald finishes *The Great Gatsby,* the myth of a youth's defeat, borrowed from Huxley, is also the demise of a national dream. The new character Chelifer represents first appears as "He" in "The Walk," an attack on Wordsworth's "Tintern Abbey" and the best parody in *The Burning Wheel* (1916). So the type is no longer new to Huxley at the time his apotheosis in novels of the twenties begins. Vanquished youths continue to play important parts in his fiction well after 1925, but Huxley is already seeking solutions to youth's defeat when the defeat itself, as he first articulated it, captures the imagination of the decade and obscures the newer man Calamy signifies. When one imagines the ypical Huxley character, he resembles Chelifer, not Calamy, Gumbril, r. and Philip Quarles, not Anthony Beavis. Huxley fictionalized his generation's state of mind so brilliantly that the diagnosis has remained more compelling than the equally ingenious cures suggested. This would be a unique case of an author's influential success getting in the way of his further development were it not for the fact that some of Calamy rubs off on Jake Barnes.

To understand the new character Huxley bequeathed to Hemingway nd the twenties, one must reread "The Defeat of Youth" (1918). From the unhappy protagonist of this underrated poem both Chelifer and Calamy trace their descent. "The Defeat of Youth" terminates parodically with its hero's suicide. It is the only sonnet sequence in literary history to end so catastrophically. Though it has no direct connections with the war, no specific references, this philosophical-satiric poem of ideas speaks of the protagonist's crucial failure to validate his idealistic notions, generally Romantic-Victorian, about women, the world and, possibly most important, his own nature. To this validation process the atmosphere of uncertainty created by the war is only one of many stumbling blocks: the real villain, with the war as its traumatic manifestation, is revealed to be the uncooperative, apparently purposeless nature of things, which has nothing to do with the human mind or its ideals, philosophies, and expectations.

Huxley's poem was both timely and prophetic. By imparting its title to his second major collection of poems, "The Defeat of Youth" coined a mood-setting slogan more descriptive of the post-war decade and the modern period in general than Spengler's *Decline of the West,* which appeared the same year, or Miss Stein's subsequent notion of "Une Generation Perdue." The youth's Shelleyan encounter with a girl who only appears to be his sister soul gradually leads him away from the facile idealism of "Epipsychidion" to a hard, contrapuntal reality in which his romantic conception of love is threatened by illicit desire The love-lust dichotomy, a version of the body-mind dualism pervasive in Huxley's writings, in turn unfolds to suggest the even larger contrapuntal oppositions the poem uncovers between art, especially Romantic art, and the disarray of modern life, between a number of traditional Western ideals, such as belief in the power of love and beauty, and emergent post-war reality.

In Huxley's seminal negative myth for the twenties, youthful expectations are always denied their fulfillment. The disappointed defeated youth, his ideals crudely rebutted by reality, becomes a case of arrested moral and intellectual development. Disillusionment is no longer the salutary experience it was for Scott's Waverly or Dickens Pip. The new loss of innocence is the compulsory abandonment of belief in life's purposefulness. The modern period rejects the benevolent maturation process celebrated in Wordsworth's *Prelude* and copied assiduously by countless nineteenth-century *bildungsromans* In the parodic anti-*bildungsromans* made fashionable by Huxley Chelifer's "Autobiography" prominent among them, many famous protagonists of the twenties cannot, or will not, grow up. Faced with the grim prospect of modern life as a series of Romantic setbacks increasingly negative epiphanies, the twenties hero literally chooses suicide, as does the protagonist in Huxley's "The Defeat of Youth," or figuratively kills himself by prematurely terminating his mental growth: he elects to remain a perpetual adolescent by ignoring the fragility of his ideals (Denis Stone in *Crome Yellow*); or else he is forced to become a hardened cynic and never entertains an ideal unsceptically again (Chelifer in *Those Barren Leaves*). Even Calamy and Jake Barnes fall loosely into this second category. The mystic in embryo and the side-lined Spartan, each diligently cultivating a commendable detachment, are not merely alternatives to, but also variants of, Chelifer's total cynicism about the world's worth.

Developing the myth of youth defeated as *the* theme for the twenties, Huxley fashioned the mood and mold for several of the most memorable male characters in the fiction of that decade. This is surprising in view of the hackneyed contention that Huxley could not create character. Oversensitive, often fated to fail as both lover and artist, the undone youth originates with "He" in "The Walk," is repeated with greater success as the protagonist in "The Defeat of Youth," reappears as Ridley, the parodic Hallam of "Soles Occidere et Redire Possunt," and then recurs throughout Huxley's early novels as Denis Stone, Gumbril, Jr., Francis Chelifer, Walter Bidlake, and numerous others. The list even includes John Savage in *Brave New World.* He is a Romantic juvenile in a world of scientifically created infantiles whose arrested development he finds so repugnant without ever sensing his own. If Deltas and Epsilons have been warped by modern science, John has been equally conditioned by Shakespeare. Mond and his fellow Behaviorists perversely reshape the world and retard human nature to suit their own designs. By trying to interpret this world in outmoded, romantic, Shakespearian terms, with himself at first as Romeo (later Othello) and Lenina as Juliet (later Desdemona), John is playing the same game; but the discrepancy between life and art, which is even starker than that between life and the Pavlovian reduction of it, makes him at least as ludicrous as Mond and completely unsuccessful, even if he is more nobly motivated. Invariably, the real casualties in Huxley's poetry and prose are the Romantic, Western ideals his young men cannot maintain under stress—the purity and nobility of love, the supposed alliance between truth (or knowledge) and beauty, the accessibility of wisdom, and even the validity of positive art itself. Without Chelifer and the protagonist from "The Defeat of Youth," figures as fertile for the twenties as Prufrock was, it is unlikely that Jake Barnes, Frederic Henry, the duet of Nick Carraway and Jay

Gatsby, or Waugh's Paul Pennyfeather and Tony Last, to name only a few, would have appeared so convincingly and in such quick succession. None of these young men really matures fruitfully: Denis leaves Crome in a vehicle he himself likens to a hearse, Gumbril, Jr. flees to the Continent, Calamy forsakes society, Chelifer buries his poetic talents as editor of *The Rabbit Fancier's Gazette,* the Savage hangs himself, the wounded Jake withdraws, Frederic Henry drops out, Robert Cohn is reduced to tears, Gatsby is murdered, Jordan is a casualty in a civil war that failed to forestall a global one, Nick heads back to the mid-West, Paul assumes a new identity, and Tony finds in the Brazilian jungle a death-in-life existence worse than the one he left behind at Hetton. What Bergonzi defines as Waugh's basic myth,[23] his recurrent picture of the English gentleman or gentle man as victim of the modern world's vulgar absurdity, begins in *Decline and Fall* (1928) and continues through *Sword of Honour* (1966), but has its clearly discernible source in Huxley's early work. The mode for the twenties, for such figures as Chelifer, John, Gatsby, and Tony Last, is a contrapuntal mixture. In *Those Barren Leaves,* Huxley calls it *tragic farce:*[14] one's ill-fated attempts to validate ideals or attain one's goals are prevented from achieving tragic stature by the farcical aspects such attempts in a world that is frustratingly meaningless and absurd.

Novels of the twenties, especially *The Sun Also Rises,* also follow Huxley's lead whenever they use a *femme fatale* to personify the modern world's destructive allure, its Circe-like propensity to attract the young Romantic idealist so that it can enchant him and then fail to satisfy. In Huxley, however, the satire works both ways. Unlike Hemingway, who sympathizes completely with Frederic Henry and Jake Barnes, Huxley ridicules the egotism of his youthful protagonists. He treats them as severely as Hemingway handles his cruelest version of them in Robert Cohn. Huxley's young men are satirized because they expect the world to conform to the designs they generate within their own minds. They demand that life substantiate the ideals they have culled from the best literature of the preceding hundred years, especially the poetry of Wordsworth, Shelley, Keats, and Tennyson. There is ultimately little difference in Huxley's novels between these younger men and their seemingly more eccentric, more Peacockian elders, who create private worlds for themselves where they can keep their theories of life intact. These younger men, though nurtured on Romantic poetry rather than Pavlov, are just as conditioned and therefore limited as the brave new worldians. Intellectual though he is, overly cerebral to many, Huxley consistently lambastes his characters for their naive, rationalist assumption that mind controls matter. This is the silliest illusion of all, a sort of ultra-Romanticism, and it is perennial. The abberation was exalted by the Romantics but Huxley demonstrates that it has been shared by other eras and writers as well. Thus he has the Elizabethan founder of Crome, Sir Ferdinando, build his privies in the topmost room of the house. This enables him to sustain his theory of human nature by feeling noble and close to heaven even while emptying his bowels. And Sir Hercules the Dwarf, his eighteenth-century descendant, builds a dwarf-sized world at Crome to protect his ego in a milieu rudely tailored to his limitations. Like the Romantics, Huxley implies, Elizabethans, eighteenth-century Rationalists, twentieth-century Behaviorists, and mankind in general are always quite willing to distort the world until it flatters their interpretations. The belief that man's reason can half perceive and half create because it is easily as versatile as the material world always provokes Huxley's derisive laughter. As Denis Stone laments, "In the world of ideas everything was clear; in life all was obscure, embroiled."[25] In Huxley's opinion, this counterpoint of mind against matter is largely responsible for man's persistent unhappiness. Throughout his work Huxley descredits the glorious overviews of poet and scientist alike. But at the same time, the disillusioned idealist within him, the deprived Romantic, despises the world of matter for its fundamental ugliness beneath the deceptive veneer, for being so uncooperative and malign, so intricate, intriguingly chaotic, and yet thoroughly alien to man's explanations and designs. To humble the idealist's ego and also to express its author's personal dissatisfaction with the nature of things, Huxley's early poetry marshals a veritable regiment of women who stand for the undependable enticements of love and the futility of all love affairs with the modern world. The list includes "She" in "The Walk," the girl in "The Defeat of Youth," and perhaps even the heroine of "Leda," with whom Jove enjoys an all-too-brief union. Frequently without any excess of malice, these women are simply the unreliable vessels into which Huxley's male protagonists pour their own untenably idealistic notions of how love, beauty, and the world of matter ought to perform. More often, these symbolic women prove heartlessly indifferent. In the early novels they become increasingly more ruthless: the flighty Anne Wimbush of *Crome Yellow* leads to the death-in-life figure of Myra Viveash in *Antic Hay,* the insipid, mindlessly vulgar Barbara Waters of *Those Barren Leaves,* the master sadist, Lucy Tantamount in *Point Counter Point,* and Lenina the parodic Juliet from *Brave New World.* Huxley's recurrent negative myth, the collision of idealistic males and vapid or heartless females to signifiy reality's refusal to correspond to the presumptuous designs of the mind, is a sad revelation of life's inability to imitate art. It proves that dualism and dichotomy are the essence of life. This negative myth assails the positive one on which the Modern Age, that is, the period since Descartes, has built its grandest hopes: the belief that man can know and manage the world by the unaided efforts of his reason.[26]

Hemingway, and later Fitzgerald and Waugh, do not take over Huxley's somewhat anti-feminist myth literally, nor do they seem to have understood its full scope. It is philosophical and metaphysical as well as social. But all three borrow from it liberally, albeit with variations, in fashioning comparable defeats for their major protagonists. And it is Huxley's myth that so much of Lawrence strenuously combats and actually tries to reverse. Cohn accurately calls Brett a Circe. The similarity of their roles and the resemblance in their names suggest that Myra Vive*ash,* who makes the males in *Antic Hay* dance with unsatisfied desire, is the prototype for Brett Ashley.[27] Both sirens inspire love in others without ever truly satisfying them or themselves. Although Brett is a nymphomaniac and Myra so emotionally exhausted, so incapable of serious involvement, that she seems liable to expire at any moment, the two are different extremes of the same malady, two burnt-out cases in the modern waste land. They are both victims of the war and become in turn impressive symbols of the discrepancies between romance and reality, promise and fulfillment, which the war so painfully pointed out. The parallel extends even further because Myra's despair can be traced to the battlefield death of Tony Lamb, sacrificially named, the only man she apparently ever loved; and Brett's frustrations are heightened, though not caused entirely, by Jake's war wound. Moreover, Jake claims that Brett married Ashley during the war after "Her own true love had just kicked off with the dysentery."[28]

Incurably listless though she appears, Myra was a fertile enough creation to inspire a line of disaster-producing *femme fatales* that includes Lady Brett, Daisy Buchanan, Brenda Last, Margot Beste-Chetwynde, and Virginia Crouchback-Blackhouse-Troy. When a bomb falls on Uncle Peregrine's London flat toward the end of World War Two and destroys Virginia, Waugh's Everard Spruce, the asinine editor of *Survival,* functions for once as a perceptive critic. He eulogizes Virginia as "the last of twenty years' succession of heroines," the last of those "ghosts of romance who walked between the wars." To have known Virginia, he concludes, is to understand Michael Arlen and Scott Fitzgerald. Spruce reads from *Antic Hay* a paragraph which describes with appreciation the alluring magic of Myra simply crossing a street, and then he expounds on it:

> . . . the passage I read, believe it or not, is Aldous Huxley 1922. Mrs Viveash. Hemingway coarsened the image with his Bret, but the type persisted—in books and in life. Virginia was the last of them—with expiring voices—a whole generation younger. We shall never see anyone like her again in literature or in life and I'm very glad to have known her.[29]

Although Spruce fixes the date of Huxley's novel a year too early and spells Brett with only one *t,* he traces Virginia's genesis correctly, provides her a fitting epitaph, and corroborates my argument. The phrase "ghosts of romance" is particularly apt. But Huxley's males are not as glad to court Myra or Hemingway's to know Brett as Spruce is to have met Virginia. Myra, Brett, Daisy, Brenda, and Margot, along with Lucy Tantamount, form a sextet that seems responsible for ninety per cent of the emotional carnage in novels of the twenties.

Huxley's original impetus was probably no more than a determination to parody Petrarch's veneration for Laura, Dante's vision of Beatrice, and all the more recent repetitions of such scenes in Keats' "Endymion," Shelley's "Epipsychidion," and the famous epiphany of the wading girl which climaxes Stephen Dedalus' search for identity and vocation in chapter four of *Portrait of the Artist as a Young Man.* However, he quickly invested his parodies of these false, unrealistic, romantic sequences with the status of a negative myth which was peculiarly suited to express the young modern's disappointment with a meaningless world of counterpoints and insurmountable contraries. Huxley's negative myth of defeated youths in a Circe-like world caught on because it summarized the feelings of his generation. Hence it reappeared in a variety of forms in the novels of his contemporaries, principally Hemingway, Fitzgerald, and Waugh.

VII

If Hemingway and Huxley were the primary apostles of the lost generation, the writers who brought its condition most accurately into print, they were definitely not strict contemporaries. Vital differences aside, Hemingway sometimes follows from Huxley by a kind of apostolic succession, and important elements in Fitzgerald and Waugh are also the outcome of this transmission. Though these two writers disagree radically about the uses of literature and the nature of good style, Huxley's early work illuminates Hemingway's and *vice versa.* Indeed, Huxley, Hemingway, Fitzgerald, and Waugh, not to mention the effect *The Waste Land* had on *Antic Hay, The Great Gatsby,* and *A Handful of Dust,* supply a fascinating series of complex trans-Atlantic interactions, the Huxleyan impact on Hemingway by no means the least interesting. Studies of the twenties which ignore the Anglo-American interplay do so at their peril.[30] Hemingway may have leafed through Huxley and Lawrence *after* producing his own daily allotment of words, but he remembered what he had read when next he sat down to write. Miss Stein's reservations to the contrary, reading those books from Sylvia Beach's or purchased along the quais paid off handsomely.

University of Kentucky

---

[1]Ernest Hemingway, *A Moveable Feast* (New York: Scribners, 1964), p. 26. Huxley's letters contain only two references to Hemingway, neither of which is substantial. But when asked in a London interview by John Chandos about writers "who will survive, who will be read," Aldous, in the summer of 1961, named Proust, Hemingway, and Faulkner in that order. "I think some of Hemingway's stories are *very* remarkable, his short stories," observed Aldous. It is clear however, that he was remembering works he had not read in a long time. The incident is recorded in Sybille Bedford, *Aldous Huxley: A Biography* (New York: Knopf, Harper and Row, 1974), p. 682.

[2]Herbert J. Muller, *Modern Ficition: A Study in Values* (New York: Funk and Wagnall's, 1937), ch. 21.

[3]*A Moveable Feast,* p. 26.

[4]Bedford, p. 114.

[5]Grover Smith, ed., *Letters of Aldous Huxley* (New York: Harper and Row, 1969), p. 228.

[6]*A Moveable Feast,* p. 25.

[7]Philip Young, "Ernest Hemingway," *The Reader's Encyclopedia of American Literature* (New York: Thomas Y. Crowell, 1962), p. 450.

[8]See Jerome Meckier, *Aldous Huxley: Satire and Structure* (London: Chatto & Windus, 1969).

[9]See ch. 27 of *Crome Yellow* where Mr. Scogan, costumed as "Sesostris, the Sorceress of Ecbatana," prophesies disasters for all his unattractive customers at Crome Fair: "financial losses, death by apoplexy, destruction by air-raids in the next war." But to the attractive girl "dressed in white muslin, garnished with pink ribbons" he predicts a rendezvous next Sunday with a man who will meet her along a certain footpath, ask her "Can you tell me the way to Paradise?" and then lead her to a hazel

copse. Of course he intends to be that Paradise-seeker. Huxley brings out the latent sexuality in ch. 19 of *Jane Eyre,* in which Mr. Rochester, disguised as a fortune-telling gypsy, tries to learn Jane's feelings toward his real self. Moreover, it was Huxley's scene that gave Eliot the idea for Madame Sosostris. Perhaps there is also a connection between the series of vignettes that constitute *The Waste Land* and the deceptively episodic chapters in Huxley's first novel, where the different talkers and events turn out to be variations on several central themes.

[10]Hemingway's other novel for 1926, *The Sun Also Rises,* may have profited from the failure of *The Torrents of Spring* to stand on its own. The secret of the *roman á clef* is one that bears on the necessity for superior parody to hit its mark and yet exist independently. Characters in *The Sun Also Rises,* like those in *Crome Yellow, Antic Hay,* and *Those Barren Leaves* before it, are interesting enough in themselves to make the added dimension they acquire when one learns their real-life models a kind of dessert.

[11]Carlos Baker, *Hemingway: The Writer as Artist* (Princeton: Princeton University Press, 1963), p. 82.

[12]Baker, p. 93.

[13]See Meckier, chs. 1, 3, and 5.

[14]Bedford, pp. 396ff.

[15]Ernest Hemingway, *Islands in the Stream* (New York: Scribners, 1970), p. 449.

[16]Ernest Hemingway, *For Whom the Bell Tolls* (New York: Scribners, 1940), p. 236.

[17]*For Whom the Bell Tolls,* p. 305.

[18]See Aldous Huxley, *Time Must Have a Stop* (London: Chatto & Windus, 1945), p. 23. A comparison of Sebastian Barnack and Mrs. Thwale in 1945 with Jordan and Maria in 1940 would illustrate the essential differences between Huxley's and Hemingway's reservations about love.

[19]*For Whom the Bell Tolls,* p. 463.

[20]D. H. Lawrence, *Lady Chatterley's Lover* (Paris: Privately printed, 1929 [1928]), p. 365. That Hemingway had been impressed by Lawrence's novel as early as 1929 can be seen from a comparison of Frederic Henry's comments in *A Farewell to Arms* with Connie Chatterley's on page 71 of *Lady Chatterley's Lover.* Henry decides that Abstract words such as glory, honor, courage, or hallow were obscene besides the concrete names of villages, the numbers of roads, the names of rivers, the numbers of regiments and the dates" (p. 196). Connie regrets that "all the great words . . . were cancelled for her generation: love, joy, happiness, home, mother, father, husband, all these great, dynamic words were half dead now, and dying from day to day." The two passages on the death of value words and hence of values are quite similar. Connie's lament, which goes on to bemoan the death of love, must have inspired Henry's less eloquent complaint.

[21]Mark Spilka, "The Death of Love in *The Sun Also Rises,*" in Robert P. Weeks, ed., *Hemingway: A Collection of Critical Essays* (Englewood Cliffs, N.J.: Prentice-Hall, 1962), p. 127.

[22]Aldous Huxley, *Those Barren Leaves* (London: Chatto & Windus, 1925), p. 127.

[23]Bernard Bergonzi, *The Situation of the Novel* (London: Macmillan, 1970), p. 105.

[24]*Those Barren Leaves,* p. 53.

[25]Aldous Huxley, *Crome Yellow* (New York: Doran, 1922), p. 40.

[26]See Allen Wheelis, *The End of the Modern Age* (New York: Harper Torchbooks, 1973), p. 3.

[27]Although Fitzgerald names his heroine after a flower, the sense of love and hope

having been reduced to ashes, a sense that the names of Myra and Brett convey, is preserved in the "valley of ashes" separating West Egg and New York.

[28]Ernest Hemingway, *The Sun Also Rises* (New York: Scribners, 1926), p. 39.

[29]Evelyn Waugh, *Sword of Honor* (Boston: Little Brown, 1966), p. 752.

[30]Frederick J. Hoffman's unsurpassed study *The Twenties: American Writing in the Postwar Decade* (New York: Viking Press, 1955) contains only three passing references to Huxley. Similar charges can be lodged against Alan Jenkins' splendid picture-book *The Twenties* (London: Heinemann, 1974). It treats both England and America but does so by turns, seldom through comparison and contrast. Malcolm Bradbury's chapter "The Modern Comic Novel in the 1920s" in *Possibilities: Essays on the State of the Novel* (London: Oxford University Press, 1973) is as chauvinistic in its way as Hoffman's book: it deals exclusively with Lewis, Huxley, and Waugh. There are no references to Americans.

HANS-JOACHIM KANN

AN UNRECORDED HEMINGWAY LETTER— IN GERMAN TRANSLATION

This Hemingway letter which appeared in German in *Heute und Morgen*[1] eluded Audre Hanneman. It is one of several items available only in German translation (like Hemingway's Schruns review;[2] excerpts from a letter to Ernst Rowohlt, his German publisher, in 1930;[3] and his "Rede an das deutsche Volk."[4]) This letter to Hans Kahle was written at the end of August or beginning of September 1940 from Cuba. The English text that follows is my translation from the printed German text.

Dear Hans![5]

I am awfully sorry to hear that you are in a prison camp.[6] Don't the Canadians know that you are one of the most valuable fighters against Fascism alive? Don't they know that you are a commanding general,

Heute und Morgen
Jahrgang 1948
Heft 8
HERAUSGEBER: WILLI BREDEL

Ernest Hemingway an Hans Kahle

Hans Kahle, dessen erster Todestag am 1. September ist, wurde 1940 in England interniert und nach einem kurzen Aufenthalt auf der Isle of Man nach Kanada gebracht, wo er neun Monate zubrachte. Während dieser Zeit erhielt er folgenden Brief von dem amerikanischen Schriftsteller Ernest Hemingway, mit dem er im spanischen Bürgerkrieg zusammen war und mit dem ihn seitdem eine große Freundschaft verband.

Lieber Hans!

Es tut mir schrecklich leid, zu hören, daß Du in einem Gefangenenlager bist. Wissen die Kanadier denn nicht, daß Du einer der wertvollsten lebenden Kämpfer gegen den Faschismus bist? Wissen sie denn nicht, daß Du ein Divisionsgeneral bist, der länger und erfolgreicher gegen den Faschismus gekämpft hat, als die ganze britische Armee während dieses Krieges? Ich jedenfalls weiß es, und ich werde alles tun, damit die höchsten Stellen es zu wissen bekommen.

Viel Wasser ist den Ebro entlang geflossen, seit wir ihn an jenem Tage kreuzten. Ich wollte, wir hätten solch einen Sport zweimal die Woche. Mit Whisky hinterher. Ich erinnere mich immer daran, wie wir hinterher glücklich wie die Kinder durch das Bombardement liefen, weil wir beide im selben Alter unsere Knabenzeit durchlebten in diesem großen Stadium der Unverwundbarkeit, der uns alten Soldaten eigen ist, statt des Stadiums der Gnade.

Hans, laß mich bitte wissen, was ich für Dich tun kann. Ich war kürzlich in New York, und da kam Duran und blieb drei Tage bei uns. Er korrigierte das Spanisch in meinem Buch, das im Oktober herauskommen wird. Die Buchgemeinschaft des Monatklubs hat es angenommen, und es wird eine erste Auflage von 200 000 Exemplaren haben. Das nennt man Glück. Ich werde Dir eine Kopie schicken. Es wird nicht so gut sein wie „Men against Metal", aber es sind Stellen darin, dir Dir gefallen werden. Es ist auch etwas über Dich darin.

Ich sende Dir einen Scheck und hoffe, daß Du ihn einlösen kannst. Solltest Du damit Schwierigkeiten haben, so schreibe mir bitte nach Sun Valley, Idaho, wo ich meine Kinder nächste Woche treffen werde. Schreibe mir, auf welche Weise ich Dir am besten Geld schicken kann. Ich weiß, daß Du nicht entmutigt bist, aber es ist doch immer ein blödes Gefühl, Gefangener zu sein. Ich wollte, Du würdest die 45. Division kommandieren, und ich hätte einen kleinen Posten in Deinem Stab.

Alles Gute, mein Lieber, schreib mir bitte nach Sun Valley und denk daran, daß ich immer Dein Freund und alter Kriegskamerad bleibe.

E. H.

who has fought against Fascism longer and more successfully than the whole British army during this war? I for my part know it, and I am going to do everything to let people in higher places know it.

Much water has flown down the Ebro since we crossed it on that day.[7] I wish we had such a sport twice a week. With whisky afterwards. I will always remember the two of us running through the bombardment afterwards, happy as children, because both of us were reliving our childhood at the same age in that great state of invulnerability that old soldiers like us are in instead of the state of grace.

Hans, please let me know what I can do for you. Recently[8] I was in New York, and Duran[9] came and stayed with us for three days. He corrected the Spanish in my book[10] that is due in October. The Book of the Month Club has accepted it, and it is going to have a first edition of 200,000 copies. That's what I call good luck. I am going to send you a copy.[11] It will not be as good as "Men against Metal,"[12] but there are some parts in there that you will like. There is also something in it about you.[13]

I am sending you a check and hope that you can cash it. If you have any difficulties with that, please write to me at Sun Valley, Idaho, where I am going to meet my children next week.[14] Tell me the best way for me to send you money. I know that you are not disheartened, but it is always a lousy feeling to be a prisoner. I wish you were commanding the 45th Division and I had a clerical job on your staff.

All the best, my dear friend, please write to me at Sun Valley and remember that I will always be your friend and old war buddy.

E. H.

---

[1] *Heute und Morgen,* 3 (August 1948), 497.

[2] See *Fitzgerald/Hemingway Annual 1971,* pp. 195-6. Hanneman S-C2.

[3] Hans-Joachim Kann, review of Hanneman, *EHACB, Die Neueren Sprachen,* 18 (February 1969), 97. Hanneman S-H526.

[4] Hanneman, C-344.

[5] Hans Kahle (d. 1 September 1947), German commander in the Eleventh International Brigade: "Hans is a book to himself. We have too much together for me ever to risk losing any of it by trying to write about it," Ernest Hemingway, "Preface," in Gustav Regler, *The Great Crusade* (New York, 1940), p. viii.

[6] Although an active anti-Nazi, Kahle was interned by the British in 1940 and sent to Canada, where he spent nine months in an internment camp, *Heute und Morgen, ibid.*

[7]5November 1938, cf. Carlos Baker, *Ernest Hemingway: A Life Story* (New Yor[k] 1969), pp. 334-5.

[8]Beginning of August; Baker, *ibid.,* p. 350.

[9]Gustavo Durán, "exiled Loyalist commander," Baker, *ibid.,* p. 350.

[10]*For Whom the Bell Tolls.*

[11]"Hemingway had heard from Hans Kahle, former commander of the XVth [*sic* Brigade and the 45th Division, that *For Whom the Bell Tolls* was a great and tru book," Baker, *ibid.,* p. 36.

[12]Unidentified.

[13]*For Whom the Bell Tolls* (New York, 1940), pp. 233-4.

[14]Early September 1940, Baker, *ibid.,* p. 351.

GERRY BRENNER

AN "IMITATION" OF DANTE'S *Divine Comedy*: HEMINGWAY'S *Across the River and into the Trees*

I imagine that many readers have scratched their heads after casually glancing at a shelf of Hemingway's works. What could motivate a writer of realistic fiction to wander into such literary by-ways as a play, a parody, and a guide-book? Browsing among the short stories, they might wonder what to make of such oddities as "A Natural History of the Dead," "One Reader Writes," or "Homage to Switzerland," all bearing little resemblance to his better-known stories. And how should they classify such items as "Old Man at the Bridge" and "The Chauffeurs of Spain," news-releases become stories? Among the curiosities in Hemingway's canon, *Across the River and into the Trees* perhaps ranks highest. Its realistic scenario, a dying ex-General's last weekend pass in Venice to duck-hunt and romance a nineteen-year-old girl, does not have much promise. Neither does its fantasy, that a dream princess can extract rancor from an aging soldier and purify him before he dies. Its non-fictional references should give any Dewey-system librarian pause. Should it be classified under fiction or, given

Venice, March 1954. Ernest Hemingway holds up the hand injured in African plane crash.

much of the criticism on it, under autobiography? Carlos Baker helpfully explains many of the elements in the novel that would make a librarian opt for the latter: Hemingway's interest in nineteen-year-old Adriana Ivancich, his recurring illnesses during 1948 and 1949, the deaths of several friends, the 1949 winter sojourn in Italy and the appearance of Sinclair Lewis at the Gritti.[1] Biographically inspired, other commentators unsympathetically dismiss this narrative oddity as a satire of middle-aged adolescence, a wish-fulfilling fictional interview, a "senile version" of "vanquished heroes," or a self-indulgent daydream.[2] But there is Hemingway's own estimate of the novel to deal with: " 'In writing I have moved through arithmetic, through plane geometry and algebra, and now I am in calculus.' "[3]

If *To Have and Have Not* and *For Whom the Bell Tolls* are saturated with the literary formulas of tragedy and the epic,[4] and if that information enables us to read those novels a bit more knowledgeably, then it seems reasonable to inquire whether there are literary, as well as autobiographical, influences behind *Across the River,* too. Taking Hemingway's mathematical metaphor in good faith, I would answer that the "calculus" of the novel—its special symbolic method of analysis—is his conscious "imitation" of Dante's *Divine Comedy.* I put the word in quotes to indicate that I do not find Hemingway imitating the design, specific scenes or even crucial strategies of the poem; he is too good an artist to copy blatantly. Using the word in its renaissance sense, I intend to suggest that Hemingway "follows classical models," that he writes the novel "in the spirit of" the *Divine Comedy.* He borrows some of its modes and devices. He incorporates several Dantean effects. He duplicates enough features to make discernible a conscious parallel.[5] Unaware of the novel's indebtedness to the poem, we may find little more than a novel of character, a quite muddled novel at that. But by overhearing the poem, we may see in Colonel Richard Cantwell—whose very name invokes the cantos—a Dantean sinner whose imminent death weighs heavily upon his failing heart. Even more, once alerted to the poem's presence we may recognize the novel's genuine experimental boldness—its Dantean marriage of mimetic fiction, historicity and dream.

Contemporaneous with the publication of *Across the River* is Lillian Ross's notorious interview with Hemingway. In that interview Hemingway reiterates the notion that for him writing is not an act of self-expression but of competition with literary predecessors: " 'I started out very quiet and I beat Mr. Turgenev. Then I trained hard and I beat

Mr. de Maupassant. I've fought two draws with Mr. Stendhal, and I think I had an edge in the last one.'"[6] No reference to Dante, of course. And some posturing and exaggeration as well. Nevertheless, this statement voices the same position Hemingway had articulated fifteen years earlier in his "Monologue to the Maestro: A High Seas Letter," declaring that "What a writer in our time has to do . . . is beat dead men at what they have done," "compete with . . . the dead that he knows are good."[7]

One sign that Hemingway is competing with Dante is the novel's most conspicuous yet most critically ignored feature, its striking mixture of fiction and non-fiction. I know of no work of literature that more effectively yokes historical and imaginary experience, actual and legendary characters than Dante's great poem. Correspondingly, along with its fictitious characters *Across the River* alludes to no fewer than sixty actual people, ranging from Ingrid Bergman and Margaret Truman to Giotto and Piero della Francesca, from Custer and General Walter Bedell Smith to Frederic the Great and T'Sun Su, from Gene Tunney and Stonewall Jackson to Gabrielle d'Annunzio and Red Smith. And while attending to its fictitious plot the novel also wanders among campaigns of World Wars I and II. Strange events for a novelist to fill an imagined thing with. Unless, of course, he has the esteemed precedent of a literary work that contains the Florentine civil strife among Guelphs and Ghibellines, the warfare between papal and temporal rulers, and numerous historical events that predate 1310. Like the poem, the novel is riddled with arcane and topical allusions, both to people—Benny Meyers, Lightning Joe, Cripps, and the "poor beat up old boy who lived [in Venice] with his great, sad, never properly loved actress";[8] and to places—the Rapido, Grosshau, Eylau, and Cooke City, Montana. In this respect the novel clearly "competes" with the poem for annotations, should it ever be properly edited for future generations.

Not only does Dante's name occur a dozen times in the novel, but a number of minor features of the novel further persuade me that the Italian's poem lurks in the novel's fabric. Although he decried Florence's degeneracy, Dante's love of the city-state has its parallel in Cantwell's love of Venice. Intimate with its history and former inhabitants, its nobility and working people, he repeats, " 'It is my city' " (p. 26). Cantwell's fulminations are reminiscent of those grand diatribes that erupt throughout the one hundred cantos too:

> [Venice] is not France, he thought.

> There you fight your way into a city that you love and are very careful about breaking anything and then, if you have good sense, you are careful not to go back because you will meet some military characters who will resent your having fought your way in. *Vive la France et les pommes de terre frites. Liberté, Venalité, et Stupidité.* The great *clarté* of the French military thinking. They haven't had a military thinker since du Picq. He was a poor bloody Colonel, too. *Mangin, Maginot* and *Gamelin.* Take your choice, Gentlemen. Three schools of thought. One; I hit them on the nose. Two; I hide behind this thing which does not cover my left flank. Three; I hide my head in the sand like an ostrich, confident in the greatness of France as a military power and then take off (pp. 26-27).

Though scaled down, Dante's encyclopedism is also mirrored in Col. Cantwell. He knows birds, wines, fish, the history of Venice, writers, artists, architecture, fuels and, above all, military history. Dante's topophiliac style may have encouraged Hemingway to give rein to his own penchant for alluding to landscape, terrain, place names and rivers, Cantwell relishing the mention of Torcello, Burano, Caorle, Maestre, Noghera and the Rivers Tagliamento, Piave, Sile, Brenda and Dese, to name a few. The novel's narrative point of view is also Dantesque. Cantwell is a character narrated about and a persona who narrates interior monologues, just as Dante is author-commentator and pilgrim-participant.[9] The novel's several boatmen and Venetian bridges recall the ferrymen and angels who assist Dante's progress, the bridges across the pits of hell, and even the metaphoric motif of the Dantean journey: "O you who in your wish to hear these things/ have followed thus far in your little skiffs/ the wake of my great ship that sails and sings,/ turn back and make your way to your own coast./ . . . / My course is set for an uncharted sea" (*Paradiso,* II, 1-4, 7).[10] The title of the novel, *Across the River and Into the Trees,* is ascribed to Stonewall Jackson. But it also evokes those rivers that Dante's pilgrim crosses: Acheron, Styx, Phlegethon, Lethe and Eunoe. Particularly apt to the memory-ridden Cantwell would be the River Lethe, whose waters of forgetfulness wash away memory and so lead to the "everlasting forest," the sacred wood of the earthly paradise. Least to be overlooked is the "sparse, direct, and idiomatic language" of both writers, a quality noted by Hemingway's middle son: "Though I have never read it anywhere in the critics, I do think that the deceptively simple style of Dante was as much a model for Papa as anything else he may have read."[11]

The poem's best-known volume, "The Inferno," deals with a place that figures prominently in the novel too: Hell. While the cornices of Purgatory and the spheres of Paradise have their share of historical personages, Dante especially delights in populating the circles of Hell. So does Cantwell. He relegates Generals Walter Bedell Smith, Bernard Law Montgomery and Jacques Leclerc to the Inferno's vestibule, telling Renata who dreads having to know such men,

> "We won't have to know them this side of hell," the Colonel assured her. "And I will have a detail guarding the gates of hell so that no such characters enter."
>
> "You sound like Dante," she said sleepily.
>
> "I am Mister Dante," he said. "For the moment."
>
> And for a while he was and he drew all the circles. They were as unjust as Dante's but he drew them (pp. 245-46).

Neither Cantwell nor Dante disparages only military figures. Of professional writers who fraudulently write of combat Cantwell remarks, " 'I do not know what category of sin that comes under' " (p. 137). It would not be difficult for anyone familiar with "The Inferno" to assign fitting stations for several of the novel's fictional characters. Cantwell's boatman on the duck-shoot solicits a place among the wrathful and sullen in the Inferno's Fifth circle. *Pescecani* (i.e., sharks), the fat, wealthy Milanese and his mistress in the bar at the Fiat garage, are marked, respectively, for bolgia five among the grafters of the Eighth Circle and for Circle Two among the carnal. Brusadelli, the Milanese profiteer "who had, in the course of a dispute over property, accused his young wife, publicly and legally through the due process of law, of having deprived him of his judgment through her extraordinary sexual demands" (p. 57), would make a fit inhabitant of Circle Nine among Cain's fellow traitors against kin. Cantwell also resembles Dante's pilgrim in that he praises people. He wishes he could "spend half my time in hell" (p. 250) with Rommel, Ernst Udet and Col. Buck Lanham, historical figures.[12] And his attitude toward Renata would likely elevate her to Paradise's Sphere of Venus among the Amorous.

A more telling parallel between the poem and the novel is the shared aim of the heroes of both works. Aware of his spiritual sloth and fearful of the afterlife awaiting him, Dante's pilgrim flees the dark wood to seek his soul's salvation. Richard Cantwell similarly fears the imminence of his own death. And his desire to reform acknowledges both spiritual sloth and the need to purge his soul for salvation:

> . . . why am I always a bastard and why can I not suspend this trade of arms, and be a kind and good man as I would have wished to be.
>
> I try always to be just, but I am brusque and I am brutal, and it is not that I have erected the defense against brown-nosing my superiors and brown-nosing the world. I should be a better man with less boar blood in the small time which remains. We will try it out tonight, he thought. With whom, he thought, and where, and God help me not to be bad (p. 65).

Cantwell's entrenchment in various of the Deadly Sins makes difficult his salvation. Gluttony is certainly one of Cantwell's more predominant vices. It is closely pursued by Pride, Cantwell telling himself, "Nobody shoots better than you here" (p. 292). Immodestly he congratulates himself, "I've been right over ninety-five percent of the time and that's a hell of a batting average even in something as simple as war" (p. 294). While thoughts of his ex-wife, the *pescecani* and the Fascist hall-porter quickly stimulate Wrath, his admission that he disparages "all who have succeeded" (p. 251) indicates Envy's presence. The other cardinal sins could be adduced. But it might be more pertinent to the impress of Dante's poem on the novel to note that though Fraud is not among those sins, Dante regards it as the worst of sins, giving it the two lowest circles in his Inferno. By having Cantwell conceal his heart condition during the medical examination, Hemingway makes him a potential inhabitant of Circle Eight. And while Cantwell's passion for Renata might be Lust, Dante's scheme would more aptly classify him as a potential occupant of the Second Circle inasmuch as Cantwell's relationship to Renata begs comparison with such other warrior-lovers as Paris, Tristram and Achilles.

Dante's pilgrim learns that his salvation requires obedience to the confessional formula of candid confession, mournful contrition and burning gratitude, a formula that Hemingway's thirty-odd years as a "Catholic" would make him no stranger to. Cantwell imitates that formula, even though he has no belief in the afterlife. He confesses that he has made three wrong decisions that have cost the lives of many men (p. 94), and he admits that he has lied to his own advantage precisely four times. His war reminiscences, Hemingway pointedly indicates, are not military swagger: ". . . he was not lecturing; he was confessing" (p. 222). Cantwell is also contrite: "I wished to be, and was, a General Officer in the Army of the United States. I have failed and I speak badly of all who have succeeded. Then his contrition did not last . . ."

(p. 251). The sincerity of his contrition takes shape in the three memories that plague his conscience. He had arrogantly assumed that the Ardennes held no danger for himself or his best friend George, who died there (pp. 292-94). He had permitted the deaths of many of his troops by obeying SHAEF military orders during the Westhall Schnee Eifel campaign (pp. 233-35). And obedient to another set of SHAEF orders for the Hurtgen Forest assault, he feels remorse for the decimation of his regiment: ". . . he was completely desperate at the remembrance of his loss of his battalions, and of individual people" (p. 242). Recalling to me the tender sensibility of Dante's pilgrim, especially during his journey through Hell, Cantwell displays remorse even over something as minor as wasted electricity: "He regretted this as he regretted all his errors" (p. 180). Though it is not "burning," he finally expresses gratitude: "I'm a lucky son of a bitch and I should never be sad about anything" (p. 254). Moments before he dies he reiterates this last step in his confession: "Three strikes is out, he thought, and they gave me four. I've always been a lucky son of a bitch" (p. 307). Much of Cantwell's speech and action may find him among the ditches of Hell, or in the novel's terms, in "the oaken staved hogshead sunk in the bottom of the lagoon" (p. 3). But there is little denying that he hopes to ascend to some ledge of Purgatory.

Like Dante's pilgrim, Cantwell's search for spiritual salvation is assisted by a "guide," a young woman whose qualities enable her to fulfill the courtly convention of Christ's secular analogue. Lying with him in his room she consoles him: " 'Don't you see you need to tell me things to purge your bitterness? . . . Don't you know I want you to die with the grace of a happy death' " (p. 240)? Handmaiden to Cantwell's need for spiritual housecleaning, Renata is the confessor-therapist who hears his unorthodox confession.[13] Repeatedly she admonishes him to be good, gentle and cheerful, not angry, rough or brutal; to ignore those things that, like the pock-marked American writer, evoke his malice. He tries to comply, beseeching "God help me to avoid brutality" (p. 85). His supine position during much of the novel, especially the long sequence on his bed during which he "educates" her about the war, also suggests her role as therapist: " 'Please talk, I'm taking care of you' " (p. 242). To further suggest her role may have been Hemingway's reason for including the five-chapter conversation Cantwell has with Renata's portrait: her image generates in him the virtuous behavior Beatrice does in Dante's pilgrim. In effect, his salvation depends upon her ability to teach him *caritas,* the charitable love of others. Reflecting this, her gifts help him to see their value as gestures of love and of willingness to serve. He reciprocates by purchasing the turbaned, ebony-faced brooch, symbol of a "confidential servant" (p. 105).

The novel clearly lacks the poem's scholastic thinking, theological and anagogical framework, allegorical method and intricate architecture. But it does share the poem's historicity. Dante-the-pilgrim, walking among the "dead," enables Dante-the-poet to reminisce, declare his historical biases and give dramatic voice to such authentic people as Ser Brunetto Latino, Farinata degli Uberti, Publius Papinius, Guido de Guinizelli or Forese Donati. Hemingway's colonel, on the brink of death, similarly enables the novelist to remember things past and to make historical footnotes on people, places and events. Both the poem and the novel, as testaments, can settle accounts with friends and enemies, dramatize personal beliefs and values, and bear witness upon time past and present.

The historical references and reminiscences, which can be ascribed to Hemingway's actual experiences, might suggest that he is venturing into the domain of the historical novel. Yet that kind of novel seeks to portray realistically the social milieu, events or crises of a historical place of period in which, to one degree or another, actual persons are represented. Or its aim may be "to portray the kind of individual destiny that can *directly* and at the same time typically express the problems of an epoch."[14] In contrast, Hemingway's novel, like Dante's poem, is not fixed to place and time. And it is similarly interested in dramatizing the private historical biases of a fictional character who, removed from a typical milieu, is preoccupied with personal problems that relate to more than one historical period. Besides, Hemingway never dramatically represents the actual people Cantwell cites. Unlike Dante in this respect, he generates the novel's historicity through allusions to, rather than dramatizations of, actual people. Admittedly the immediate effect of this gives the impression that Hemingway is merely name-dropping, for he fails to give substance to people who apparently have meaning to Cantwell. Yet the allusions fulfill their expected literary function. By drawing together and establishing a relationship between dissimilar experiences, they amplify an individual experience and make it a representative one. For example, when Cantwell thinks of "Marbot's Lysette who fought, personally, at Eylau" (p. 52) during the Napoleonic War of 1805, the allusion to the French general's fierce mare may parallel his own combat with death and a female's attempt to rescue him.[15] Allusions to past and present personages such as Robert Browning and Custer, Eisenhower and Margaret Truman, du Picq and Degas reflect Cantwell's praise or scorn of lifestyles and values that mesh or clash with his own. As a form of historical shorthand, such allusions enable Hemingway to create a main character who overlaps fictional reality without being enslaved to historical reality.

Because non-fiction theoretically defers to Truth not Beauty, and because both Dante's poem and Hemingway's novel are strongly autobiographical, it might appear that the historicity of both works would limit their esthetic effects. On the contrary, by honoring the muse of history only part of the time, both works secure esthetic effects that would be unobtainable if they adhered to the conventional expectation that a work declare its allegiance to either fiction or non-fiction. They deliberately mix the two and achieve the effects accruable to history and to fiction as well as the effects caused by the intermixture of the two and the puzzlement of when which is which. Simultaneously they can satisfy a reader's interest in fact, information, opinion and truth; they can gratify his desire to engage in wish-fulfillment, beauty and the imaginary; and they can challenge his ability to differentiate history from fiction and to interpret both. The hazard of creating a matrix of historical-imaginary experience is occasional Dantesque obscurity. And Hemingway succumbs to it, as the vagaries of some of Cantwell's mental maunderings testify. But in so doing, Hemingway is not unique. One of his earliest mentors, Pound, had likewise succumbed to it in his *Cantos.* Moreover, the hazard is worth risking inasmuch as the attempt to synthesize fictitious and historical realities does not merely prod a reader's consciousness, asking him to accept the interplay of different realities, engaging his sensibilities in more ways than do conventional works. It also acknowledges the long-standing classical debate between Plato and Aristotle, between Reality and mimesis. Hemingway's rendition of this debate seems particularly evident in Cantwell's recurring colloquies with two objects in his hotel room, Renata's portrait and his mirror. Cantwell admits that the portrait inadequately represents the living Renata: " 'There's no comparison, of course,' he said. 'I don't mean likeness. The likeness is excellent' " (p. 209). Nevertheless, as an artistic creation, the portrait is like the novel's fictitious element, a mimetic attempt to represent the essence of a person. Cantwell's mirror is like the novel's historicity: "Mirror was actuality and of this day" (p. 180).

The consorting of fiction and non-fiction is not an isolated example in which the novel mingles normally disparate entities. The January-

May relationship between a battle-ravaged American Colonel and a nubile Italian Countess also signals that the novel overlaps alien worlds. So does the novel's double action—the duck hunt "frame-tale" and the reminisced day with Renata—and the novel's juxtaposition of a single winter weekend with the rapidly shifting events that the Colonel's memory recalls. Perhaps the most interesting interpenetration, however, is Hemingway's immersion of mimetic and historical material into the novel's dream experience.

While the *Divine Comedy* has an historical dimension, even more noticeable, of course, is its dream dimension. After all, the journey of Dante's pilgrim grows out of the medieval convention of the dream vision. That the novel also possesses the quality of a dream experience is variously suggested. Renata and the Colonel daydream about a trip through the States, knowing full well it will never come to pass. Many of the Colonel's memories approximate dreams or nightmares which haunt him. Some of his recollections even have the tang of fantasy, as does his memory of beating senseless two sailors who disrespectfully whistle at Renata. Cantwell's regard for liars also hints at the possibility that his story may have elements of a tall tale: "A liar, in full flower, the Colonel had thought, is as beautiful as cherry trees, or apple trees when they are in blossom. . . . He just enjoyed, completely, hearing [liars] lie at the moment . . ." (pp. 178-79). The novel's lack of physical action further stresses a dream or daydream dimension to the novel. For almost all of the novel's events occur in Cantwell's mind as mental reminiscence while he either lies on his bed or sits—in the Buick, in Harry's bar, in a duck blind, at the Hotel Palace Gritti restaurant, in a gondola, or on the toilet. Such sedentary action is appropriate for the novel's contemplative mood and invites dreams and memories, unreal and real experiences, to blur and mingle. The novel's setting in the "Sea City," is the appropriate locale for unconscious dreams to surface, Jungians would note.

The novel's dream dimension may explain an apparent artistic lapse on Hemingway's part. At the beginning of Chapter III the novel's narrator declares that Cantwell, sitting in the duck blind on Sunday morning, has been medically examined the "day before yesterday" and that "Yesterday he had driven down from Trieste to Venice" (p. 12). According to this chronology, the exam was on Friday, the drive on Saturday, and the hunt on Sunday. Yet this chronology omits the day Cantwell spends with Renata. For if he drove to Venice "yesterday" (Saturday) and spent one night sleeping in the Hotel Palace Gritti with a portrait and another night with Barone Alvarito and the other duck hunters—"last night there had been a fair amount of good lying after the grappa had been passed around" (p. 279)—then the duckhunt would have to have occurred on Monday. Rather than regard the extra day as a flaw,[16] I would suggest that the extra day is one of Hemingway's "blinds," "any artifice you use to hide the shooter from that which he is attempting to shoot" (p. 278; this definition occurs precisely when the novel resumes the duck hunt, Chapter XL). The purpose of this "blind" would be to sustain the blurred demarcations between fictional, historical and dream materials in the novel. For this blur invites attending to the dream maiden whose presence fills that extra day, Renata.

The literal translation of her name, "reborn," has obvious significance for Cantwell in his desire for salvation. Features of her character suggest that she is someone whom Cantwell fabricates, just as Dickens' Mrs. Gamp fabricates her imaginary companion, Mrs. Harris. When Renata describes her portrait, " 'I look as though I were rising from the sea without the head wet' " (p. 97), the oft-noted allusion to Aphrodite is as unmistakable as is the pride a middle-aged man would feel in being adored by such a young goddess. Similarly, the poetic language used to define her seems fantasy-inspired. Her identity? " 'I am only the unknown country' " (p. 155). Her ambition? To " 'run for Queen of Heaven' " (p. 83), offers Cantwell. Her genealogy? " 'The moon is our mother and our father' " (p. 114). Though we might snicker at such language, it serves the purpose of rejecting Renata as a credible character, the effect the novel must achieve if Renata is to fulfill the "blessing-bearer" role of Dante's Beatrice.[17] Her solicitousness for Cantwell's maimed right hand, her gifts of the portrait and the emeralds, and her desire that he release the memories and experiences that cause his bitterness—all characterize her as *la belle dame* à *merci*. Nevertheless, her love for the battered Cantwell, who she knows will soon die, lacks sufficient motivation for a believable love story. Hemingway never even defines the origin of their relationship, allowing us to imagine that it springs full-bodied from Cantwell's forehead. But its "great miracle" (p. 288) is no less justified than Beatrice's love for Dante. Having abandoned his youthful devotion to her, Dante is unworthy of receiving Beatrice's intercession; her gift of it demands as much willing suspension of disbelief as Renata's love for Cantwell.

A feature of the novel that disturbs many readers is its use of tropes. Cantwell's heart turns over inside him when he sees Renata's profile "as though some sleeping animal had rolled over in its burrow and frightened, deliciously, the other animal sleeping close beside" (p. 83).

Because Renata is menstruating, Cantwell must search for her clitoris, "the island in the great river with the high steep banks" (p. 153).[18] And after he has manually induced her orgasm, the ecstasy is a "great bird" that "had flown far out of the closed window of the gondola" (p. 154). Pretty poetic for Hemingway. But if he hopes to approximate the metaphoric heights to which the paradisal voyage of Dante's pilgrim and Beatrice soars, he must risk lyrical language. Further, such lyricisms emphasize the novel's dream dimension, just as allusions emphasize its historicity.

The novel's dream dimension seems partly intended to mythopoeticize Cantwell as the dying hero. That role seems confirmed by Renata's devotion to him and her definition of his narrated memories, " 'Sad stories of the death of kings' " (p. 236). And his formulaic confession, the verbal exorcism of his bitterness, the ritual return to the site of his initiation into mortality at Fossalta, and the mock Order of Brusadelli all approximate ceremonies, which confer representative stature upon Cantwell. His desire to allay death, evidenced by his continual self-medication and his relationship with Renata, is a universal one, adding to his stature. Unwilling to succumb to a failing heart, Cantwell subscribes to a life-sustaining belief, declaring " 'Every day is a new and fine illusion' " (p. 232). Notwithstanding his verbal "brutalities," he values the Platonic qualities that are absorbed in Dante's trinity and that are esteemed by the race: goodness, beauty and truth. For example, acknowledging the first of these, he is ever conscious of his lapses in "kindness." When he leaves Renata he pledges continued efforts at being good: " 'I'll keep on trying' " (p. 277). Equally noticeable is his esthetic sensibility. He appreciates the beauty of art and architecture, Venice and its market, Renata and red sails on the country canals: "Why should it always move your heart to see a sail moving along through the country, the Colonel thought. Why does it move my heart to see the great, slow, pale oxen? It must be the gait as well as the look of them and the size and the color" (p. 24). Most central to his character is his desire to know and express the truth. Regarding his military experience, he tells Renata " 'I'll tell you true. . . . As true as I can tell and let it hurt who it hurts' " (p. 225). Even the occupation to which Cantwell has given his life, a metaphor of every man's combat with life's continuous conflict, suggests his universality. Like the residents of Dante's post-mortal places, he is both concretely individualized and typically representative. Thus, rather than put him into combat scenes, Hemingway has him both old and off-duty, seemingly desirous to portray him as a normal human being under relatively normal circumstances.

However, Cantwell is not an archetypal hero. Leave that to the protagonist of *Old Man and the Sea.* As Santiago's antithesis he is a more interesting character, made so partly by the novel's marriage of fiction, history and dream. Hemingway's studied refusal to create a character who allows ready identification makes Cantwell additionally interesting. Revamping the conventional types of the soldier—neither *miles gloriosus,* sadist, nor Homeric model of poetry-inspiring heroism—Hemingway literally demotes him to a prosaic career-man who drinks, defecates and cants well; he drones tediously and sententiously about his experiences and he continually slips into military jargon:

> "The weather is cloudy and the place is 986342. What's the situation? We are smoking the enemy with artillery and mortar. S-3 advises that S-6 wants Red to button up by 1700. S-6 wants you to button up and use plenty of artillery. White reports that they are in fair shape. S-6 informs that A company will swing around and tie in with B." (p. 245).

Besides, Cantwell is deprived of those traits which normally guarantee sympathetic identification: dignity, force of character, self-understanding. No apologist for the career soldier, Hemingway gives to Cantwell vanity, self-righteousness and vacillation. Like Dante's pilgrim, who immodestly regards his talents as superior to Lucan and Ovid (*Inferno,* XXV, 91-94), Cantwell is Rommel's peer and Eisenhower's superior and boasts of his military savvy. Self-righteousness enables both Cantwell and Dante to mete out judgments, just or not. And as Dante's pilgrim vacillates from sympathy to censure towards the various people he encounters, the Colonel slides from tenderness to coarseness, divided between his impulse to extend his public profession of war and violence into his private life and his self-imposed imperative to be good. Even more, so insignificant is Cantwell's current military role that his duties in Trieste go unmentioned, Hemingway thereby strips him of valor and patriotism, authority and power, attributes vital to any military hero.

Interesting as Cantwell's character is, it lacks the strength to draw together the novel's diverse elements. A character whom Hemingway would presumably hope to straddle the worlds of mimetic representation, history and dream, Cantwell certainly challenges my ability to identify with him. But he ultimately mirrors his own right hand, incurably split. His excursions into paranoia and estheticism, jargon and poetry, history and fantasy, vindictiveness and confession, obscenity and tenderness portray him at best as schizophrenic.[19] I grant that schizophrenia is consistent with the novel's experimental boldness. But the novel should also satisfy the primary requirement of all successful fiction, to be narratively engaging. Only a disingenous reader or the fond author, I believe, will grant the novel that.

The novel might have been successful had Hemingway given firmer clues of its "source" than those I have attempted to gather. For as it stands the novel's use of autobiographical flashbacks, historical allusions, lyricism, dialogue and love story seem muddled. And they invite critical disapproval largely because the novel is being measured against the conventions of realistic fiction rather than those of Dante's classical poem. For comparison, one virtue of Joyce's *Ulysses* is that the title serves notice that a meanginful reading will profit from knowledge of Homer's poem. Hemingway serves no such notice. He may be obstructing a recognition that the novel's heterogeneous elements are as much yoked by design as are those in Dante's poem.

Had he served notice, however, the novel would suffer by the comparison. Understandably it lacks the poem's scholastic thinking, theological and anagogical framework, allegorical method and intricate architecture. All but the last of these are alien to Hemingway's art. But it also lacks the subtle psychological resonances of the poem, even though Dante's method of achieving them is normally Hemingway's own. The customary method of both writers is to dramatize actions and record dialogue objectively in order to allow psychological insights to surface of their own accord, without authorial prompting. When, for example, Dante's pilgrim embraces Casella in Canto II of *The Purgatorio* and admires his song, Dante dramatizes the pilgrim's hedonistic lapse from his commitment to seek spiritual salvation and also mocks his vanity, the song being one of Dante's own *canzone* set to music. Similarly in the dialogue between Catherine Barkley and Frederic Henry during their supposedly idyllic retreat in Switzerland, Hemingway brillantly dramatizes not romance, but their boredom, the psychological burden of their relationship, and the desperate dependency each has upon the other. But in *Across the River,* by directly immersing us in the psychological process of Cantwell's mind, Hemingway loses the dimension, interest and interpretive potential of such drama. Even more, while Dante's pilgrim can filter the plethora of Dante's mind because he is spectator-student, a similar plethora splits Cantwell, the tutor-participant. Finally, while Dante, for all his artistic subtlety, maps his pilgrim's basic journey, Hemingway leaves most readers wandering the backroads of Cantwell's mind.

If we see Hemingway following the traditional formulas of tragedy and the epic in the two novels that precede *Across the River* and then fashioning this novel upon the features of a great poem, we can better assess his place in the larger tradition of literature. I hold no brief for the virtues of generic criticism; it often results in a pedantic catalogue of the resemblances between a work and the formula, tradition or model it follows. Nevertheless, a generic approach can evaluate a work according to those criteria that an author has implicitly accepted, the set of predefined characteristics established by other writers working in the same genre or mode. Hence, rather than lead only to classification that will place a work within a specific tradition and deny its claim to be *sui generis,* a generic approach can isolate and compare the shared characteristics among or between works in order to discover if one work is superior or inferior to another. Clearly Hemingway's competitive ethic, to which I referred earlier, asks for such evaluation, one which I leave to comparatists.

But to observe Hemingway using literary formulas or a classical model has an even more important consequence. It enables us to gain access to that vantage point of hazarding some reassessments of him as an artist. To give credence to the idea that his work is indebted to formal literary traditions and to specific precursors would initially add to Hemingway's artistic dimensions in that it reveals him as an artist-scholar able to conceal a classic poem or literary mode within a modern work. Such a dimension would properly show his kinship to the artist-scholar tradition of Pound, Joyce and Eliot. But that gain may be at the cost of some grave critical questions. For then, I believe, we must ask "Is his imagination original?" "Or is it bookishly derivative?" "Are his creations experimental or epigonic" "Do his works reveal structures that are organic or ones that are mechanically dependent upon pre-existing forms?" "Is his artistic genius continuously autonomous or does it eventually succumb to a life-long penchant for traditions and rituals?" "Are his fictions motivated out of an authentic compulsion to express a genuine artistic vision or an athlete's desire to compete?"

Hemingway admirers and all of us who were suckled on the myth that his writings grew out of his lived experiences may be loath to entertain the negative implications of such questions. Understandably so, for they sketch the possibility that Hemingway may be as much a crafty copyist as a craftsman, as full of devious and duplicitous motives as of esthetic ones, as inclined to subterfuge as to subtlety. Loath though we may be to consider that sketch, it looms before us quite large, particularly since the publication of Michael S. Reynold's excellent piece of scholarship, *Hemingway's First War: The Making of "A Farewell to Arms."*[20] His book proves that the early novel was the product of considerable research and that it was deeply indebted to others' writings, primarily because Hemingway had neither been present during nor ever visited the area that was the scene for the central event that he chose to write about: the retreat from Caporetto. If Hemingway repeated the process of concealing his sources and his indebtedness to other writers in subsequent novels, as I believe is the case in *Across the River,* then indeed there may be harsher questions with even more negative implications than those I have asked.

University of Montana

---

[1]*Ernest Hemingway: A Life Story* (New York: Scribners, 1969), pp. 463-73; also see Mary Welsh Hemingway, *How It Was* (New York: Knopf, 1976), which was published after this article was submitted.

[2]Respectively, Jackson J. Benson, *Hemingway . . . The Writer's Art of Self-Defense* (Minneapolis: University of Minnesota Press, 1969), pp. 52-53; Philip Young, *Ernest Hemingway, A Reconsideration* (New York: Harcourt, Brace & World, 1966), pp. 117-118; Nemi D'Agostino, "The Later Hemingway," rpt. in Robert P. Weeks, ed., *Hemingway: A Collection of Critical Essays,* Twentieth Century Views (Englewood Cliffs, N.J.: Prentice-Hall, 1962), p. 158; and Richard P. Hovey, *Hemingway: The Inward Terrain* (Seattle: University of Washington Press, 1968), pp. 177-78.

[3]Harvey Breit, "Talk with Mr. Hemingway," *New York Times Book Review,* 17 Sept. 1950, p. 14.

[4]See my articles, "Epic Machinery in Hemingway's *For Whom the Bell Tolls," Modern Fiction Studies,* 16 (Winter 1970-71), 491-504 and *"To Have and Have Not* as Classical Tragedy: Reconsidering Hemingway's Neglected Novel," in Richard Astro and Jackson J. Benson, eds., *Hemingway In Our Time,* (Corvallis: Oregon State University Press, 1974), pp. 67-86.

[5]Perhaps I would be well advised to accede to what Carlos Baker, writing of resemblances between Hemingway's works and "the European masters," defines as his "special kind" of imitation: "What he imitates is nature, the world around him, expansed before his eyes. Dante, like his renaissance audience, is dead. . . . what [Hemingway] seeks to imitate is not the texture, it is the stature of the great books he reads and the great pictures he admires," *Hemingway, The Writer as Artist*, 4th ed.

(Princeton: Princeton University Press, 1952), p. 186. Yet in the first place such a statement fails to define Hemingway's "special kind" of imitation; the statement applied with equal force to a host of writers who could similarly be said to imitate nature, Alexander Pope among them. Second, Baker negelcts to specify precisely what Hemingway does to imitate the stature of great books; as a matter of face, though one can emulate the stature of something else, one cannot imitate its stature. Most important, the very thing that makes so valuable Baker's own study is his analysis of Hemingway's artistic experimentation and literary sophistication. Indeed his critical approach might almost be called generic, for he is alert to the traditional genres, modes, literary devices and allusions that surface so recurrently in Hemingway's works that they provide the means by which Baker discerns his experimental virtus. Of *Across the River,* for example, Baker representatively remarks that its "mod is Dantesque" and that "It occupied a different genre within the broad range of possibilities which fiction may legitimately invoke" (*Artist,* p. xviii). In brief Baker's definition of Hemingway's special "doctrine of 'imitation'" goes against the very grain of his own critical approach.

Now I quibble with Baker's definition not simply to advance my notion that the *Divine Comedy* is the "original" for *Across the River.* Rather I quibble because of the consequences which assigning the label "imitation" should have upon any ultimate assessment of Hemingway as artist. I address myself to those consequences in the last paragraphs of this essay.

[6]"How Do You Like It Now, Gentlemen?" in Weeks, *Collection,* p. 23.

[7]*By-Line: Ernest Hemingway, Selected Articles and Dispatches of Four Decades,* ed. William White (New York: Scribners, 1967, pp. 218-219. To be sure the novel's allusions to *Othello* might lead us to think that if Hemingway is consciously competing with a dead man, it is Shakespeare, not Dante. But those allusions have so little to do with the novel's plot or Cantwell's preoccupations that I am inclined to see them—as the frame of duck-hunting suggests—as decoys. I recognize that Hemingway would doubtless scoff at my thesis about this novel, having rejected Young's comparable idea that "the basic symbols in 'The Snows of Kilimanjaro' were derived from Flaubert and Dante," as Baker records in *Life Story,* p. 509. But to accept in good faith Hemingway's rejections of specific interpretations would be an act of critical naivety, particularly since it would ignore his defensiveness, his acknolwedgment in his Nobel Prize Acceptance Statement that undiscerned things may lurk in his fiction, his unwillingness to discuss his writing—" 'though there is one part of writing that is solid and you do it no harm by talking about it, the other is fragile, and if you talk about it, the structure cracks and you have nothing,' " George Plimpton, "Ernest Hemingway," in *Writers at Work: The Paris Review Interviews,* 2nd ser. (New York: Viking, 1965), p. 220—and, finally, his long-standing anxiety that, as he has Jake Barnes express it, " 'You'll lose it if you talk about it,' " *The Sun Also Rises* (New York: Scribners, 1926), p. 245.

[8]*Across the River and into the Trees* (New York: Scribners, 1950), p. 51; subsequent references to this edition are in the text.

[9]This feature of the novel is well defined by Peter Lisca, "The Structure of Hemingway's *Across the River and into the Tress,*" *Modern Fiction Studies* 12 (Summer 1966): ". . . the novel is really a first person narration of events in the past . . . but disguised as third person narration through the device of using the shooter as a *persona* through whom the Colonel thinks about himself. The result is that we know

the Colonel *only as he knows himself*, but with the authority and the effects which accrue to the interior monologue by virtue of its disguise as omniscient third person narration," p. 236.

[10]All references to and quotations from the *Divine Comedy* use John Ciardi's three-volume verse translation (New York, New American Library, 1954, 1961, 1972).

[11]Patrick Hemingway, "My Papa, Papa," *Playboy,* 15 (December 1968), 264; the quoted description of language is from John Ciardi, "Translator's Note," *The Inferno,* p. ix.

[12]The Lanham reference is corroborated in "War in the Siegfried Line," *By-Line,* 392-400, and Baker, *Life Story,* p. 426.

[13]Baker, *Artist,* p. 285; for a more sustained discussion of Renata's confessional role, see Horst Oppel "Hemingway's *Across the River and into the Trees,*" trans. Joseph M. Bernstein, in Carlos Baker, ed., *Hemingway and His Critics: An International Anthology* (New York: Hill and Wang, 1961), pp. 220-23.

[14]George Lukacs, *The Historical Novel,* tran. Hannah and Stanley Mitchel (London: Merlin Press, 1962), p. 284.

[15]Hemingway includes this episode in his *Men At War* (New York: Crown, 1942), pp. 531-39.

[16]See, e.g., Lisca, p. 235.

[17]This comparison is also noted by Lisca, p. 250, and Robert W. Lewis, Jr., *Hemingway on Love* (Austin: University of Texas Press, 1965), pp. 182 et passim.

[18]There is, of course, some critical dispute over precisely what Renata's "disappointment" for Cantwell is. Lewis, *Hemingway on Love,* p. 186, argues that she is pregnant, a conclusion that Delbert E. Wylder, *Hemingway's Heroes* (Albuquerque: University of New Mexico Press, 1969), pp. 188-93, concurs with. Not only do I find more persuasive Lisca's argument, p. 236, that Renata is menstruating, but I fail to understand how her pregnancy would be a "disappointment" to a man who has no children, no way to keep alive his memory. Cantwell pities his "'poor Daughter'" (p. 110) simply because she will experience only a clitoral orgasm achieved through the manipulations of "his ruined hand" (p. 153).

[19]Baker, *Artist,* pp. 268-274, also attends to Cantwell's divided nature with different conclusions.

[20](Princeton: Princeton University Press, 1976).

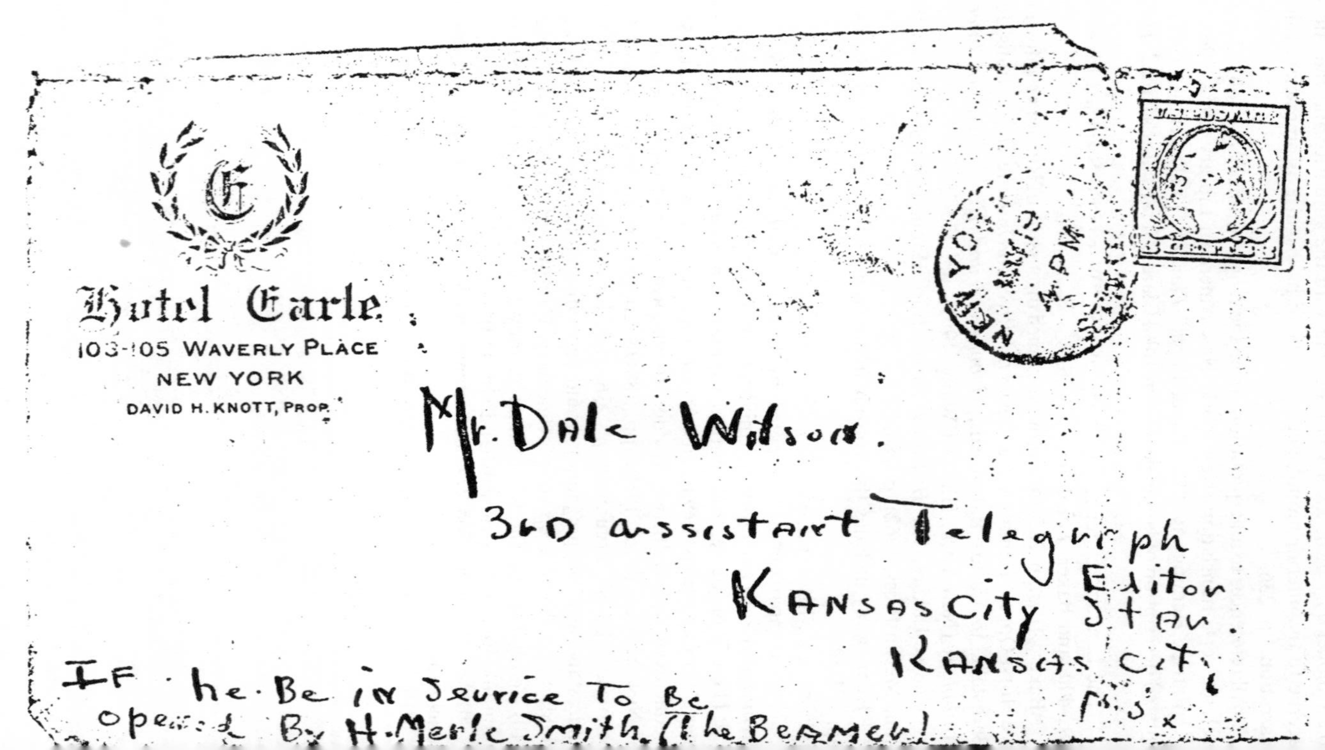
Hotel Earle
103-105 Waverly Place
New York
David H. Knott, Prop.
New York
A.M.
Mr. Dale Wilson.
3rd assistant Telegraph Editor
Kansas City Star.
Kansas City
If he Be in Service To Be
opened By H. Merle Smith

DALE WILSON

HEMINGWAY IN KANSAS CITY

The city editor, George Longan, had a squeaky voice. This squeak was more evident when he was disturbed. And right now he was disturbed. He had problems.

A new reporter was showing up nearly every Monday morning, but the wartime draft was taking men as fast as he could hire them. *The Star*—few people bothered to say "The Kansas City Star"—always a stickler for high standards, combed Missouri and Kansas dailies, and journalism schools for replacements. Longan's once careful screening had become: "Can you type? . . . What paper have you worked on? . . . You're hired. . . . Sixty-five dollars a month." Adjusting his tortoise-rimmed glasses, his polka-dot bow tie, he would turn the newcomer over to the assistant city editor, C. G. Wellington.

"Pete" Wellington was thirtyish, slight and pale. He smiled painfully. Pity the luckless reporter who misspelled a name. "Will you look it up in the city directory? . . . And don't you know that *The Star* style is 'motor car,' not 'automobile?' " He wouldn't fire the blundering cub—

nobody on *The Star* seemed to get fired—but he'd make the fumbler wish he'd never been born.

On an autumn day of 1917, Henry Haskell, chief editorial writer, stopped at Longan's desk. A friend of Haskell's had a nephew who wanted a job on a newspaper.

"For god's sake send him in," Longan said in his squeaky voice.

And that was the beginning of the career of a great American writer.

With the new reporter at his heels, solemn-faced Mr. Wellington moved from desk to desk.

"This is Mr. Hemingway," he would say. Then, to one man in the back row he added: "Mr. Hemingway will relieve you of some duties. Will you show him how we do obituaries?"

The newcomer was eighteen, cheerful and eager to get on. He had not been hired after apprenticeship on smaller dailies as had the rest of us. He got his job because Uncle Tyler Hemingway, who lived in Kansas City, knew Chief Editorial Writer Haskell. Young Hemingway's previous writing experience had been on the *Tabula* and *Trapeze* at the Oak Park, Illinois, high school. Longan figured this kid could fill in until real reporters got back from the war.

Longan didn't consider hiring girl reporters. The only females on the staff were the society editor and the woman's editor, both housed with a few girl assistants on the first floor near the elevator, out of sight of the all-male news room on the second floor. Hemingway and the rest of us found it convenient to drop in on the girls en route to assignments, beyond the watchful eyes of the Boss and Pete.

The live-wire woman's editor was Mrs. Fred Moffett who quickly became "Mother Moffett" to the young reporters. She was witty, loved to play jokes, and do impersonations. The reporters loved her. It was she who shortened Hemingway's office name to "Hemmy."

Ernest, with his hunt-and-peck typing, started on obituaries, and to his credit got the names right. Few things irritate a dead man's relatives so much as misspelling grandpa's name. Ernest was a good speller. From Obits he was shifted to "Speaking the Public Mind," the letter column. He was able to pacify contributors who insisted that "the best part was cut out." But Hemingway's big moment came when he was assigned to the "short stop" run, his duties being to phone to rewrite men the news of arrests reported at the 15th Street police station, watch the Union Station for unusual arrivals, check with undertakers, and cover news from General Hospital. He thrived on the excitement, mild as it was. Wellington complained that the desk couldn't keep in touch with him because he was eternally riding the hospital ambulances.

Fellow reporters liked the big, good-natured, enthusiastic Ernest. He quickly nicknamed most of us. H. Merle Smith was "Smith the Beamer"; Wilson Hicks, who later became executive editor of *Life,* and in 1952 paid $40,000 for magazine rights to *The Old Man and the Sea,* was "Lackpants" because Hicks' blue serge trousers were wearing very thin and his $65 pay check didn't allow for new ones; smartly dressed Leo Fitzpatrick became "Lovely Leo"; Tod Arneson, whose adroitness with girls the talk of the office, was "The White Slaver"; unlucky poker-playing William Moorhead was "Broken Bill"; Fleisler was "the pensive Hebrew"; I myself was "Woodrow Junior" or "Wilse"; Hemingway called himself "Hemingstein" or "the Great Hemingstein," but to others he was "Hemmy." When an Australian was hired as a reporter, the playful Hemingway showed us a supposed telegram warning *The Star* against "the Tasmanian woodchopper and boomerang thrower."

EH was just out of high school but looked about the age of the college graduates around him. He was six feet tall and muscular. He had dimples in his cheeks, and a slight speech impediment that made his "l's" sound like "w." His hairline at the middle of his forehead formed a widow's peak. His arms were too long for his sleeves, and his trousers too short for his legs. He walked in a rolling gait, leaning a bit forward like a woodsman carrying a pack.

His first task was to familiarize himself with the Style Book. *The Star*'s Style Book was a stickler for simple, declarative sentences. Wellington rode herd on the young reporters in enforcing the rules. Most regulations were solid, even stolid: Use short sentences; short first paragraphs; be positive, not negative; use vigorous English. Use "widely known," not "well known"; in estimating numbers write "more than," not "over." Some rules were out of date. For example, the ban on "automobile" as a French bastardization of "motor car" complicated reporting of the Kansas City Automobile Show, and was finally dropped.

But the advice to use words of action was sound. In later years EH himself said: "Those were the best rules I ever learned for the business of writing." Words of Latin derivation were suspect. A Missouri farmer, in *The Star,* was never an agriculturalist.

One rule, not in the Style Book, but rigidly enforced, was: Never write stories of snakes. City Editor Longan had a horror of snakes, even of reading about them.

Looking back a half century one sees Hemingway traits in formation. He bristled at injustice. A bully at a lunch counter one Saturday night belittled "Lovely Leo." Hemmy swung at him, missed and smashed a showcase. His bandaged hand was his hero's badge. He would modestly explain that it was nothing.

His eagerness to ride ambulances was also an omen of things to come. That ambulance riding led to his first news stories of importance, stories that he didn't telephone to a rewrite man, but wrote himself in the office. He saw hospital inefficiencies and ambulance laxity, and wrote with vigor about them. Perhaps he overdid it. The copy desk edited out parts, much to Hemingway's irritation. He blamed Wilson Hicks, his close friend, who was then a local copyreader. Hicks brushed off the criticism, saying Hemmy meant well but got too enthusiastic in his writing.

Ernest remembered the grievance four months later when he left *The Star*. He wrote me from New York on the eve of sailing for Italy (For some unknown reason I put the letter, envelope and all, in a trunk, and ran across it thirty-four years later, about the time Charles Fenton was researching Hemingway's apprenticeship.)*

"And how is the Great Hicks? He of the tortoise shelled disposition and lack of anal covering!" Hemmy asked whether Hicks still classified the Great Chicagoan, noblest scion of the Windy City, as a well-meaning fellow? He said to tell him he'd buried the hatchet, but as a favor when the story of Hemmy's sad end comes over the wires let not "Lackpants" read copy on it, for it was feared that Hicks would cut out even the name of ye deceased.

But, wrote Hemingway, to get down to the bare, naked, unclothed facts, does "Smith the Beamer" slip the great Gus Seesteed the warm palm and tell him, Gus, how he, Smith, likes to work for the paper he, Gus, manages? Miles Vaughan, the United Press manager, was undersized, a fact which handicapped him in his pursuit of girls. Hemingway asked whether "Peg" Vaughan still fared forth in search of booty, and was "Lovely Leo" still haunted by booty in search of him?

Some present-day critics and researchers, tracing the origin of the mature Hemingway technique, think *The Star*'s Style Book and Wellington's rigid discipline may have been the starting point. One delver even suggested that EH's Anglo-Saxon words came from the 15th Street Police blotters. More likely, though he first heard about adjective-free writing on *The Star,* he developed his style by self-

---

*The letter is now at the Princeton University Library.

discipline long after he had left Kansas City. At least he showed no signs of such restrained writing in the letter referred to above. There were six pages, in longhand, postmarked May 19, 1918. The letter was flamboyant, free-wheeling with spoofs and double-talk.

When he left *The Star* he asked me to forward to him the Liberty Bond he was buying. His letter was a note of thanks. He started much as a show-off high school boy might:

"Dear Wilse—. Ha Ha! Ha Ha! Ha Ha! 'Tis none other than the greatest of the Hemingsteins that indites this epistle. Woodrow me lad, how are you?"

There was a certain timidity in the Hemingway I knew. To cover it he put on the take-charge talk. At one point in the letter he sounded a bit homesick, as if whistling for courage. He had just been given his honorary first lieutenant's uniform and would sail next week. The Gt. Hemingstein said he stalked down Broadway and returned 367 salutes, then decided to ride the bus. It was easier on the right arm.

On May 18, his contingent of 70 was among the 75,000 men and women who marched down Fifth Avenue from 82nd St. to 8th in the Red Cross fund-raising parade. They were reviewed by "Woodrow Senior and the Mrs." and also a bunch of "large insects." Woodrow resembled nothing so much as his pictures. By virtue of his manly form and perfect complexion, the one and only Hemingsteith was made Ye Top Cutter. "And you all should hear his rasping voice." In the parade, he said, as ye right guide he stalked all alone down the old avenue and "felt lonesome as hell." But at eyes right, he had a fine look at Woodrow.

Hemingway changed the tone of his letter after saying "we'll be plowing the briny" next week and told of his New York romance with a famous movie queen. Warning that this is not for publication he wrote that he had been out to see Mae Marsh several times and was going out again to her house tomorrow night for dinner. He had spent every damn cent he had too.... "Miss Marsh, no kidding, says she loves me." He suggested the Little Church Around the Corner but she opined as how ye war widow appealed not to her. So he sank the 150 plunks his Pop had given him in a ring and was engaged anyhow. Also broke. He did have another 100 but bought a 30-buck pair of cordovan leather boots, a few sundries and a couple of drinks and now all was gone. "Anyway my girl loves me and says she believes I am going to be a great newspaper man and says she will wait for me, so what the hell, Bill." He hoped he could win an honest-to-god commission and be worthy of her. "Gee, she's a wonderful girl, Wilse. Too damn good for me."

Hemmy wrote that I could tell Punk Wallace, a *Star* friend, about his being engaged, but "don't let it get out among the gang and in the sheet." That was a very, very important warning.

It took me forty-eight years to finally get in action and check the accuracy of that engagement. I phoned to California in 1966 to Mae Marsh, the movie queen of *The Birth of a Nation.* "Yes," she said she had been in New York in 1918, in fact had married Lee Armes, still her husband, there in September, that year.

"Did you ever meet Ernest Hemingway?"

"No," she said, "but I would have liked to."

It would seem that Reporter Hemingway in that 1918 letter was trying out his fiction writing on us back in Kansas City.

GREGORY S. SOJKA

Who Is Sam Cardinella, and Why Is He Hanging Between Two Sunny Days at Seney?

The vignette, Chapter XV, is located between Part I and Part II of "Big Two-Hearted River" in Ernest Hemingway's *In Our Time.* At first glance, the reason for this vignette's appearance and position is not apparent. Nick Adams is not included in this sketch, which features the execution of a man named Sam Cardinella. This shocking miniature describes the frightened Cardinella losing control of his sphincter muscles when being bound to a chair on the scaffold for execution, and it seems to be an out-of-place intrusion between the two extended descriptive sections of Nick's pastoral excursion.

Charles Fenton tells us that young Ernest Hemingway, the Kansas City *Star* police-beat reporter, mentioned a criminal with this same name to his fellow staffers in 1918.[1] The man's hanging remained in the young writer's memory for five years. So much for Sam Cardinella the man. The more important aspect of his fictional reincarnation remains to be explained.

The general function of all the *In Our Times* vignettes provides a useful clue to Chapter XV's purpose. In a letter to Edmund Wilson, Hemingway reports: "Finished the book of 14 stories with a chapter of *I O T* [sic] between each story—that is the way they were meant to go—to give the picture of the whole between examining it in detail."[2] This unique arrangement of the Cardinella vignette placed between the two parts of one complete story allows Hemingway the privilege of supplementing "Big Two-Hearted River" by a strategically placed inter-chapter which illuminates the detailed fictional exploration by means of a short, striking contrast in action and reinforcement of theme.

Basically the common theme of all the vignettes and short stories of *In Our Time* is the necessity for a man to confront the circumstances of life using whatever means necessary to maintain self-respect. "Grace under pressure," as Philip Young points out, becomes the key objective of men who must hold to their values and principles in the face of threatening circumstances.[3] Within this theoretical framework, the realistic brutality of Sam Cardinella's vignette intentionally interrupts the tranquility of Nick Adams' fishing trip. This brief glimpse of a man who wilts under pressure, literally losing control of himself, serves as a graphic contrast to the protagonist of the short story, who is striving valiantly to remain in full control of all his faculties despite his own panic and suffering.[4]

The Nick Adams revealed in Part I of "Big Two-Hearted River" shows the results of his earlier traumatic adventures. The sleepless and mentally disturbed Nick of "Now I Lay Me" and "A Way You'll Never Be" is, however, on the road to recovery in this story. The meaningless physical therapy and mechanical exercises of "In Another Country" are replaced by camping and fishing activities whose ritual provides a comforting order and security to both body and soul. As Malcolm Cowley perceptively observes, the whole fishing expedition can be regarded as "an incantation" and "a spell to banish evil spirits."[5] Nick discovers the peaceful stream that he could only dream about as the wounded, unstable *tenente* in "Now I Lay Me." Nick's fishing and camping activities create an entire physical reality. They shut out threats of chaotic mental disturbances and provide a comforting shelter against the ever-encroaching *nada*. Nick escapes from suffocating civilization and its bad memories by re-establishing a healthy organic union with nature.

In the opening pages of the story Nick is greeted by the burned-out countryside and charred remains of Seney, a ghost town. There is no trace of life: "even the surface had been burned off the ground."[6] The setting reflects the moral and mental state of the harried protagonist. Like the sleepless veteran of "Now I Lay Me" Nick seeks assurance and security in the stability of nature. He is not disappointed for "the river was there" (p. 179), "permanent and of value" like the Gulf Stream in *Green Hills of Africa.*[7] He stares down into the clear water watching the trout use their fins to keep steady in the strong current.

> As he watched them they changed their positions by quick angles, only to hold steady in the fast water again. Nick watched them a long time.
>
> He watched them holding themselves with their noses into the current, many trout in deep, fast moving water. . . . At the bottom of the pool were the big trout. Nick did not see them at first. Then he saw them at the bottom of the pool, big trout looking to hold themselves on the gravel bottom in a varying mist of gravel and sand, raised in spurts by the current. . . .
>
> It was a long time since Nick had looked into a stream and seen trout. They were very satisfying (p. 179-180).

This description of Nick's reaction has more purpose than a mere subjective background for the objective description of the fish. For the trouts' struggle to hold themselves steady in the current is the externalization of the inner conflicts in Nick's mind. Like many of Hemingway's stories, "Big Two-Hearted River" is ostensibly about physical activity in the outdoor world. But the real battleground of this story is inward. Nick's observations are a self-reflection of his struggle to maintain control of himself against the rippling waves of fear. The trout's successful self-control is reassuring and satisfying to Nick, while their momentary waverings cause the man's heart to "tighten" and experience the "old feeling" of doubt. This brief, but graphic exposition sets the stage for the rest of the story, which consists of Nick's struggle to hold his own on a camping and fishing excursion despite his recurring waves of panic and doubt.

Nick's physical exercise is his spiritual exorcism. Thus his hike to the river becomes a ritualistic test of his physical endurance and mental fortitude. "It was hard work walking up-hill," for "his muscles ached and the day was hot, but Nick felt happy" (p. 181). He takes no short-cuts to the river, but keeps "on toward the north to hit the river as far upstream as he could go in one day's walking" (p. 185). Nick's primary motivation is to escape from the imposing chaos of war memories and return to the primitive stable basics of survival. "He felt he had left everything behind, the need for thinking, the need to write, other needs. It was all back of him" (p. 179). His constant physical activity and attention to present sense phenomena keep his mind occupied and away from threatening memories.

When Nick finally reaches a fertile meadow of sweet fern next to the river, he decides to make camp. He methodically smoothes out a sleeping place, pitches his tent, and adjusts the mosquito bar, almost as if he were following his creator's article, "When You Camp Out Do It Right," written five years earlier for the Toronto *Star Weekly*.[8] A good camp is "where a man feels at home, outside of where he's born, is where he's meant to go."[9] This camp is Nick's clean well-lighted place.

> Already there was something mysterious and homelike. Nick was happy as he crawled inside the tent. He had not been unhappy all day. This was different though. Now things were done. There had been this to do. Now it was done. It had been a hard trip. He was very tired. That was done. He had made his camp. He was settled. Nothing could touch him. It was a good place to camp. He was there, in the good place. He was in his home where he had made it. Now he was hungry (pp. 188-9).

Hemingway's constant repetition stresses the finality and reassurance Nick achieves.

Nick's bubbling bean and spaghetti dinner is tempting, but he carefully guards against an indiscreet act. "He looked at the fire, then at the tent," Hemingway comments; "he was not going to spoil it all by burning his tongue" (p. 190). Even Nick's post-meal coffee is prepared with the religious attention to details that a mother utilizes while preparing a baby's formula. After coffee, his mind "was starting to work," and the danger of a relapse like that in "A Way You'll Never Be," is imminent. Nick "knew he could choke it," however, because his regimented physical activities have left him "tired enough" to relax and sleep peacefully. The demands of his aching body dominate his restless mind, and as Part I concludes, he settles down for a good night's sleep.

Which brings us to Sam Cardinella whose sudden appearance in the vignette jolts us from the relaxed context of Nick's slumber. The stark jail corridor contrasts strikingly with the homey campsite we have just left.

> *The corridor was high and narrow with tiers of cells on either side. All the cells were occupied. The prisoners had been brought in for the hanging. Five men sentenced to be hanged were in the five top cells. Three of the men to be hanged were negroes. They were very frightened.*

One of the white men sat on his cot with his head in his hands. The other lay flat on his cot with a blanket wrapped around his head (p. 195).

The jail evokes a stiflingly oppressive atmosphere which pressures the condemned inmates into various postures of psychic despondency and physical paralysis. Unlike Nick's meticulously ordered campsite the prison walls and individual cells seal in the threat of death and deny any means of escape. The claustrophobic prison contrasts sharply with the expansive outdoors. Nick walks freely in advance of his lingering fears. The prisoners' bondage, however, increases their terror. The two condemned men block their vision in a futile attempt to deny this enactment of their own fates, while Nick gathers courage from his observations of the trout's successful response to the pressures upon them. Nick willingly performs certain rituals to provide structured activity in defiance of chaos. His camping and fishing preparations, called "a series of little ceremonies" by Malcolm Cowley, are part of his self-rehabilitation program.[10] On the other hand, the ceremony of Sam Cardinella's execution procession is preamble only to his hanging and to the subsequent deaths of his fellow prisoners. As long as Nick can regulate his actions, he can control his emotions.

Conversely, Sam Cardinella has no recourse to any meaningful activities to "choke off" the panic of impending death. Unlike Nick who can escape from the source of his fears with a retreat into nature, Sam Cardinella is without physical outlet for his tensions and must be pathetically carried to his fate, paralyzed for two hours with fear of the inevitable. He must be strapped tightly and placed in a chair in order to be properly executed. With the release of his sphincter muscles he loses the last vestiges of human dignity. All self-control is lost. Cardinella can't "be a man" as the priest encourages, but regresses into an infantile stage of helplessness. Orthodox prayer, a ceremony comparable to Nick's meal preparation, tent pitching, and bait gathering, is void of meaning. Religious faith affords no reassurance or sustenance to Cardinella, and it "skips away" from the man, like the priest who offers only token comfort and ceremonial propriety.

With the death cape extinguishing the light of the world, Sam Cardinella sinks into the darkness of *nada.* Unlike the veteran bullfighter of "The Undefeated" who loses his fight but retains his dignity and self-respect by performing bravely according to the codes of his sport, Sam Cardinella's pathetic and messy death is a truly graphic example of loss of grace under pressure. Nick holds a tight rein on his emotions while Sam Cardinella loses even his fundamental control. True to

Hemingway's theory of "iceberg" composition, Sam Cardinella's emotional panic is a reminder of what lies beneath the surface of Nick's calm.

Sunrise beginning Part II finds Nick still disciplined by meal preparation, grasshopper gathering, and tackle adjustments. All of these preparatory activities are scrupulously performed with professional expertise. The jarring sensation of the shocking cold water does not trigger mental disruption in this fortified angler. Earlier, the mere memory of a river in "A Way You'll Never Be" provoked an incoherent outbreak in the shell-shocked veteran. Nick judiciously wets his hand so not to disturb the delicate mucus coating on an undersized fish. He knows the true importance of a protective covering whether it is the mucus on a trout or a tent over his own head.

Throughout his afternoon of fishing, Nick's punctilious movements derive from a similar knowledge of self. These ordered routines and procedures are specifically chosen tasks that free his mind from unpleasant memories. A swamp located at a narrowing of the river does, however, reactivate Nick's dormant apprehensions. The location fills Nick with foreboding despite its mysterious promise of large trout.

> He felt a reaction against deep wading with the water deepening up under his armpits, to hook big trout in places impossible to land them. In the swamp the banks were bare, the big cedars came together overhead, the sun did not come through, except in patches; in the fast deep water, in the half light, the fishing would be tragic. In the swamp fishing was a tragic adventure. Nick did not want it. He did not want to go down the stream any further today (p. 213).

Nick's instinct and judgment warn him against abandoning his clean well-lighted camp and open river to venture into the murky, cramped confines of the swamp. The swamp, like the burned-out ground of Seney, is a sinister atmospheric symbol of the many fears that still lurk in Nick's subconscious. As the Italian major of "In Another Country" phrases it, Nick does not want to put himself in the "position to lose" all the confidence that he has worked so meticulously to gain. "There were plenty of days coming when he could fish the swamp" (p. 214), so Nick returns to the security of his camp for a good night's sleep. He knows what is good for himself, and is "his own nutritionist" on the "strictest sort of emotional diet."[11] He must limit his daily activities to the certainty of his senses in the physical world and keep emotional excesses at bay. "He did not want to rush his sensations any," says Hemingway, and Nick literally rations his intake of physical sensations on his fishing trip (p. 206).

Sam Cardinella is not so lucky. All of his physical sensations, from the guards' strapping his legs together to the touch of the rope around his neck, are imposed upon him in a cascade of horror. Nick is free to nibble emotional tidbits in small pieces; Sam Cardinella is force-fed his fate in one deadly frightening chunk. Nick valiantly seeks an equilibrious life, while Sam Cardinella falls vertiginously and remains suspended as a graphic example of a messy death, without dignity, without control.

Bowling Green State University

---

[1]Charles Fenton, *The Apprenticeship of Ernest Hemingway* (New York: Farrar, Straus & Young, 1954), p. 239.

[2]Carlos Baker, ed., *Hemingway and His Critics* (New York: Hill and Wang, 1961), p. 60.

[3]Philip Young, *Ernest Hemingway* (New York: Rinehart, 1952), p. 35.

[4]David J. Leigh, S. J. "*In Our Time:* The Interchapters as Structural Guides to a Psychological Pattern," *Studies in Short Fiction,* 12 (Winter 1975), 1-8, sees Sam Cardinella's death as a foreshadowing of Nick's own fate, not as a contrast in action.

[5]Malcolm Cowley, "Introduction," *The Portable Hemingway* (New York: Viking, 1944), rptd. as "Nightmare and Ritual in Hemingway," Robert P. Weeks, ed., *Hemingway: A Collection of Critical Essays* (Englewood Cliffs: Prentice-Hall, 1964), p. 48.

[6]Ernest Hemingway, *In Our Time* (New York: Boni & Liveright, 1925), p. 179. Subsequent references from Chapter XV and "Big Two-Hearted River" will be from this first edition with pagination provided within the text.

[7]Ernest Hemingway, *Green Hills of Africa* (New York: Scribners, 1935), p. 149.

[8]Ernest Hemingway, "When You Camp Out Do It Right," Toronto *Star Weekly,* 26 June, 1920, p. 17.

[9]Ernest Hemingway, *Green Hills of Africa,* p. 284.

[10]"Nightmare and Ritual in Hemingway," p. 48.

[11]Philip Young, *Ernest Hemingway,* p. 19.

GEORGE MONTEIRO

The Wages of Love: "Hills Like White Elephants"

In *Death in the Afternoon* (1932) Ernest Hemingway defined a theory that had guided his practice as a writer: "If a writer of prose knows enough about what he is writing about he may omit things that he knows and the reader, if the writer is writing truly enough, will have a feeling of those things as strongly as though the writer had stated them."[1] This had been his theory as early as the mid-1920s, he would later recall in *A Moveable Feast* (1964).[2]

Throughout his career Hemingway would apply his theory of omission in various ways, depending on the specific nature of the tale involved. He might omit an element of plot, as he did in the early story, "Out of Season," leaving out the information that the drunkard—guide would hang himself shortly after the events depicted in the story.[3] Following the same theory, Hemingway could leave out of "Big Two-Hearted River" the thematic information that even though there was no mention of it the story was "about coming back from the war."[4] In "The Short Happy Life of Francis Macomber," to take a third example, he would omit a key reference point in the psychological motivation of one of its principals. Did Margot Macomber intend to murder her husband or was she merely one party to a shooting accident? Indeed, in this story, which once carried the working title of "The Manner of the Accident,"[5] one doubts that the author himself could answer this question.

Functional omissions in a Hemingway story took still other forms. In "Hills Like White Elephants," first published in *transition* in August 1927, shortly after Hemingway's first divorce and his second marriage, the first omission takes the form of a single key word. Notably, however, that omission serves not to create a puzzle calling for concentration and solution—for the word itself occurs immediately to even the most casual reader—but as a way to enhance the reader's *felt* experience of the dramatized episode.

Surely some of the power of "Hills Like White Elephants" derives from Hemingway's decision not to employ the common term for the operation that the young man wants the young woman to undergo. To this young couple, drinking beer and *Anis del Toro* in a station by the Ebro river as they await the express from Barcelona to Madrid, the operation is socially, and personally, it turns out, a taboo. The operation can be described, as the man describes it, " 'It's really not anything. It's just to let the air in,' "[6] but it must not be named—not by either party to the decision to have the woman submit to this illegal procedure.

Hemingway's point, of course, is to make the reader state the term for himself. This device serves another principal exchange in the story. The man, having just described the operation, insists that "it's all perfectly natural." Its naturalness, of course, makes it all "awfully simple" and "perfectly simple," which the man echoes three times and the woman, sardonically, once.

The phrases "perfectly natural," "awfully simple," and "perfectly simple" do their appointed work. How "simple," really, and how "natural" is this clandestine operation? The author's point is that there is of course nothing "simple" or "natural" about what the woman is about to submit to, just as in no way will the operation make it possible, we suspect, for the couple to become as they were before the woman's pregnancy. The man asserts that " 'We'll be fine afterward. Just like we were before.' " But the woman thinks differently. " 'And once they take it away," she insists, "you never get it back.' "

Provoked abortion, under the circumstances, is in no way "natural." Apart from its physical consequences, complicated as they are, the personal consequences, Hemingway's story tells us, are totally determinant. It is the woman, however, who affirms Hemingway's own characteristic values in all matters: simplicity and naturalness. And, despite the denotations of the words he uses, it is the man who stands for what is artificial and unnatural, and therefore, to the author, repugnant. In its sympathetic treatment of the woman in a deteriorating relationship with a man, "Hills Like White Elephants" suggests that we modify our customary view that in his treatment of the sexes under marital and extramarital stress Hemingway always favors the man.

Underlying the entire incident, however, is still another unstated truth: that above all the young woman fears death. Fear emerges in the dialogue only as her concern for what she sees as the inevitable consequences that an abortion will have for their relationship, but the forceful reality of that fear cannot be denied. It is our perception that she is, throughout all, terrified which makes the story, as H. E. Bates calls it, "one of the most terrible Hemingway or anyone else ever wrote."[7] It is, moreover, the theme of death that "Hills Like White Elephants" shares with most of Hemingway's finest stories. As Hemingway remarked in *Death in the Afternoon,* "all stories, if continued far enough, end in death, and he is no true-story teller who would keep that from you."[8]

"Hills Like White Elephants," as we know it in its final form, tells us nothing regarding the woman's ultimate fate. Was that fate the part of his materials that the author knew well enough to omit it from his story? One possible answer might emerge from a consideration of the source of the story. The difficulty in taking that route, however, lies in the fact that there is no single agreed-upon source for it. In 1958, for example, Hemingway described the "incident" behind his story:

> I met a girl in Prunier where I'd gone to eat oysters before lunch. I knew she'd had an abortion. I went over and we talked, not about that, but on the way home I thought of the story, skipped lunch, and spent that afternoon writing it.[9]

Without denying that Hemingway had his oysters and a conversation with an unidentified woman who had had an abortion, however, it should be noted that Robert McAlmon, Hemingway's friend of the 1920s, saw himself as the source of the story:

> One night in Rapallo [in February, 1923] the lot of us were talking of

> birth control, and spoke of the cruelty of the law which did not allow young unmarried women to avoid having an unwanted child. Recalling an incident of college days I told a story of a girl who had managed to have herself taken care of. Her attitude was very casual. "Oh, it was nothing. The doctor just let the air in and a few hours later it was over." . . . Later Hemingway informed me that my remark suggested the story.[10]

Before choosing between McAlmon's account and Hemingway's, however, we should consider some other factors. Why, for instance, did Hemingway note at the bottom of the final page of the extant manuscript of "Hills Like White Elephants. A Story" the cryptic information: "Mss. for Pauline—well, well, well"?[11] It should be noted, moreover, that the story, started as early as March 1927—shortly after Hemingway's divorce from Hadley Richardson, as we have already noted, and two months before his marriage to Pauline—began originally with this sentence not in the *third* person as we now have it but in the *first* person: "*We* sat at a table in the shade of the station."[12] It may be, of course, that after this start in the first person Hemingway changed his mind for purely aesthetic reasons. Given his customary mode of composition, however, that is, to employ in the first drafts of his stories and novels the names of actual people and places (*The Sun Also Rises* provides the best known example of this), it is rather likely that the "we" of the original draft for "Hills Like White Elephants" referred to Hemingway himself and an unidentified "other." That the "other" might have been Hadley is suggested by an incident during the summer of 1924. The report is Robert McAlmon's.

> Walking one night in Roncesvalles, the scene of medieval romance and legend, Chanson de Roland Hemingway was most unhappy because he feared he was again to become a father. He told Hadley it would be no fun at all any more if they had too many children at his age. She wouldn't be a good playmate any more either. He was tragic about it, and Hadley, too, became upset. Finally Sally Bird, who was walking ahead with Bill [Bird] and me, turned back and said to Hemingway, "Stop acting like a damn fool and a crybaby. You're responsible too. Either you do something about not having it, or you have it."[13]

In no way do I wish to imply that Hadley actually underwent an abortion or even that she considered doing so. Nor do I wish to imply anything along those lines about Pauline Pfeiffer, who by 1925 was already displacing Hadley in Hemingway's sphere, and who at the time of the writing of "Hills Like White Elephants" was engaged to Hemingway. What is apparent is that, as McAlmon has informed us, Hemingway had behaved childishly when confronted with the *possibility* that Hadley was again pregnant. Such an occurrence, diminishing Hadley's value to him as a "playmate," would border on the tragic for the "young" Hemingway. If it cannot be said that abortion was on the young husband's mind, there can be no doubt that the personal consequences of an unwanted pregnancy were very much so. Be that as it may, it would be no more than a matter of months before his marriage to Hadley would begin to collapse. In the midst of such marital difficulties Hemingway set down "Hills Like White Elephants."

The possibility remains that Hemingway drew upon personal experience but extended those details imaginatively to a conclusion that had no basis in the actualities of autobiography beyond Hemingway's fear at what *could* have happened. Indeed, what might have been a considered solution—a possible decision—was made literal in the "action" of the story. Such a procedure, common enough in writers of all stripe and in all times, was particularly characteristic of Hemingway. To see it as a mark of the way Hemingway's imagination normally worked we need only consider how the autobiographical hints of marital conflict in the later work *Green Hills of Africa* (1935)—this time involving his hunter's apprehension and real fear at P. O. M.'s (Pauline's) following him on the hunt armed with a loaded gun—were imagined into the nightmarish drama we know as "The Short Happy Life of Francis Macomber."

Conclusion. Given the autobiographical matrix of "Hills Like White Elephants" and the thrust of the tale itself—authorial tenderness toward the despondent young woman—the student of Hemingway's work and life might well be justified in entertaining the possibility that this story, from one significant point of view at least, was Hemingway's attempt to "explain" away his own apparent callousness to that unidentified "other."

Brown University

---

[1]*Death in the Afternoon* (New York: Scribners, 1932), p. 192.
[2]*A Moveable Feast* (New York: Scribners, 1964), p. 75.
[3]*Feast,* p. 75.

[4]*Feast,* p. 76.

[5]Philip Young and Charles W. Mann, *The Hemingway Manuscripts: An Inventory* (University Park and London: Pennsylvania State University Press, 1969), p. 118.

[6]"Hills Like White Elephants," *Men Without Women* (New York: Scribners, 1927), p. 72.

[7]H. E. Bates, *The Modern Short Story: A Critical Survey* (Boston: The Writer, 1972), p. 173.

[8]*Death in the Afternoon,* p. 122.

[9]Quoted by George Plimpton, "An Interview with Ernest Hemingway," *Hemingway and His Critics: An International Anthology,* ed. Carlos Baker (New York: Hill & Wang, 1961), p. 34.

[10]Robert McAlmon, *Being Geniuses Together* (London: Secker & Warburg, 1938), p. 159; quoted by Carlos Baker, *Ernest Hemingway: A Life Story* (New York: Scribners, 1969), p. 595.

[11]*Manuscripts,* p. 43.

[12]Quoted by Baker, *Life Story,* p. 595; emphasis added.

[13]Robert McAlmon, *Being Geniuses Together 1920-1930,* revised and with supplementary chapters by Kay Boyle (Garden City: Doubleday, 1968), p. 277.

SAM S. BASKETT

The Great Santiago: Opium, Vocation, and Dream in *The Old Man and the Sea*

Eight times in *The Old Man and the Sea* Santiago invokes the formulaic name: "the great DiMaggio."[1] He credits the baseball star with doing "all things perfectly even with the pain of the bone spur in his heel,"[2] and he encourages himself to "be worthy" (p. 75) of this ideal of performance in his own travail. On nearly twenty pages, some phase of "the baseball" is mentioned, evidence of Santiago's, and Hemingway's, strong interest in the sport.

This interest, however, has received ambiguous critical recognition. As George Monteiro has summarized, critical opinion is about equally divided between those who find the fiction "enhanced" and those who find it "diminished" by the admiring references to DiMaggio.[3] A similar split is evident regarding the baseball talk generally. Ray B. West, Jr. has offered the most radical objection, contending in an early commentary that "the baseball talk between the old man and the boy and the baseball images in the old man's mind during this trial of strength and cunning are unsuccessful—because not integrated into the story. . . . for American sports are not capable . . . of carrying the mythological burden Hemingway puts on them."[4] A few years later, he added his doubt that baseball could "convey that larger and more universal world that it is designed to image. As symbolic hero (and despite Hemingway's use of Dimaggio [sic] in *The Old Man and the Sea*), the baseball player is at least once removed from the bullfighter, who is not merely playing a game but is facing death each time he steps into the ring."[5] Other assessments are more positive, but even those approving Hemingway's use of the baseball motif have usually been implicitly somewhat negative in their consideration, finding the baseball references sufficiently obvious or insignificant to warrant only passing attention.

Two recent studies set a somewhat different course in recognizing that the baseball motif is an aspect of the novel requiring more careful explication than it has received. Monteiro cites at length the "historical events behind Santiago's admiration [of DiMaggio]," interpreting those events as providing an image of "the unalloyed victory" denied the old fisherman.[6] James Barbour and Robert Sattelmeyer discuss in considerable detail the functions of baseball in the novel, the most significant being the establishing "a course of heroic action": "baseball hero and humble fisherman demonstrate the possibility of human achievement."[7] These two studies are both important in two major ways. By concentrating on an area of the novel that is ultramontane to many literary critics, they are expressing what should have been obvious much earlier, the necessity of dealing fully with the entire novel, not as it might have been written but as Hemingway wrote it. Moreover, by bringing relevant baseball knowledge to bear, these studies illuminate parts of the work that have often heretofore been misunderstood or passed over. Agreeing with this corrective emphasis, I would stress that the important thing in this connection is not merely an understanding of the glamorous world of big league baseball forming part of the background of *The Old Man and the Sea,* but, rather, the discernment of Hemingway's careful and discriminating employment of that glamorous world. In parts of the novel, Hemingway has made what has been called a "non-Christian use of Christian symbolism"; likewise, the baseball references are in a sense a "non-baseball use of baseball symbolism." As Santiago is not finally Christ, neither is he ultimately a DiMaggio disciple, nor, certain evidence suggests, was he meant to be.

There are two early hints that the baseball passages require more than a sports page reading. Only a few lines after the first mention of "the great DiMaggio," Manolin reminds Santiago that he must keep warm because "we are in September." Santiago answers, "The month when the great fish come. . . . Anyone can be a fisherman in May" (p. 19). DiMaggio's name, of course, translates "Of May," a reading that could scarcely escape the author of *A Farewell to Arms* and *Across the River and Into the Trees*. During his stay in Venice the year prior to writing Santiago's story, any calendar could have reminded him "Maggio" equals "May." Hemingway asserted that he named his characters "the best I can." Why, we must consider, did he insert the belittling comment about fishermen "in May" at the same point that DiMaggio's name is introduced into the story? A second clue that the baseball talk has concealed implications occurs a few pages later in another reference to greatness, a discussion about the "greatest managers." Neither "the great John J. McGraw"—the adjective comes from Manolin's father—nor the currently successful but somewhat notorious "Durocher" qualifies, in Santiago's judgment. Instead, "Luque" and "Mike Gonzales" "are equal" (pp. 24-25). Yet Adolpho Luque never managed in the big leagues and Gonzales was acting manager for a total of twenty-three games, winning only nine of those,[8] facts which both Santiago and Hemingway, baseball aficionados, surely know. Why, then, this blunder that must be intentional?[9]

These questions should be entertained, not as mere curiosities, either of baseball or of the novel, but because the answers point, in contrast to the prevailing interpretation, to the integral ironic function of baseball in this strongly crafted fiction as a symbol of that which is finally unessential to Santiago. For Santiago's stature is defined in large part by the emphatic distinctions he makes between baseball and his two more important concerns: his vocation as fisherman and "the main thing that is left" (p. 73), his dream of the lions.

The ambiguous discussion of the greatest managers provides a perspective on the baseball ambience *of the fiction*—the setting of DiMaggio's "greatness." Manolin's father, who "hasn't much faith" and therefore, as is "normal" (p. 11), will not permit the boy to continue with the old fisherman, believes that McGraw is "greatest." Baseball experts generally concur with this "normal" judgment, but Santiago summarily rejects it: The father picks McGraw "Because he came here the most times. . . . If Durocher had continued to come here each year your father would think him the greatest manager." Santiago describes McGraw as "rough and harsh-spoken and difficult when he was drinking. His mind was on horses as well as baseball. At least he carried lists of horses at all times in his pocket and frequently spoke the names of horses on the telephone" (pp. 24-25).[10] Nothing further is said about Durocher, noted throughout his early career for the aphorism—recently to serve as a title for his ghost-written autobiography—"Nice guys finish last."[11] Both McGraw and Durocher, then, renowned for their winning records, are too easily applauded for being unaccustomed, at whatever moral cost it is implied, to "fishless" days. Santiago is apparently teaching Manolin that the skill to win is not enough to make McGraw and Durocher the "greatest."

If these two are not "worthy" of Santiago's highest praise for excellence in baseball, why Luque and Gonzales? Although Santiago offers no explanation, his reasons may be inferred from the careers of the two men, who were among the first Cubans to play in the big leagues, Luque as a pitcher, Gonzales, as a catcher. As a "poor" Cuban fisherman who "understands" in a way that the "rich" cannot (pp. 23-24), Santiago must have had a profound sense of the difficulties encountered in the 1910's by Cubans breaking into the national American game. It is likely that, in Santiago's view at least, Luque and Gonzales exercised more than mere baseball skill in achieving their successes a far geographical and metaphorical distance from their homeland. Moreover, since they were not even managers in the "Gran Ligas," their designation as the "greatest managers" can have no relation to *baseball* skill. Santiago's "mistake" in choosing them emphasizes that their qualities must have to do with them as *men* who have performed well, perhaps with "bone spurs" of a sort, not as managers. All this, of course, is implicit rather than explicit in the text. But whatever Santiago's unstated reasons for his "mistake," the effect of it is to raise doubts about the ultimate status of baseball in his world. If the greatest managers are those who are not really managers, the importance of the "Gran Ligas"[12] is diminished, not only in the eyes of the sophisticated reader, but also in the view of the two naive baseball fans making the judgment.

This is not to say that Santiago and Manolin—and Hemingway[13]—do not love the sport. The two characters talk about it repeatedly and "happily" (p. 23)—just as Hemingway used it as a major motif in his novel. Each day at sea Santiago wonders "how the baseball came out" (pp. 52, 75). He wishes he had a radio to keep him informed of the results, and on his return he asks for the newspapers he had missed. Even so, he never permits the interest in baseball to interfere with his commitment as a fisherman. The explicit separation between the two begins with the first reference to baseball, when Manolin offers to "serve" in the preparation for the next day's fishing. Santiago responds, "No. Go and play baseball. I can row and Rogelio will throw the net" (p. 12). The boy passes this test of his manhood[10] and remains to assist the old man. That baseball is playtime activity is emphasized a little later when Santiago reads the sports pages while he is resting sleepily in the sun. At sea, wondering about the scores, he rebukes himself: "Now is no time to think of baseball. . . . Now is the time to think of only one thing. That which I was born for" (pp. 43-44). After the fish settles on his course, the old man's mind drifts again to baseball, but he pulls himself up short. "Think of what you are doing" (p. 52). Subsequently, when "very tired . . . he tried to think of other things. He thought of the Big Leagues" (pp. 74-75).

Baseball, Santiago's principal diversion, is thus often in his mind, but it never substitutes for nor impedes the practice of his vocation. It functions as an interlude, as a relief, but he is alert to the danger that his interest could become, in the expression of "The Gambler, the Nun, and the Radio," an *opium* of sorts. The vocabulary of "Mr. Frazer" is beyond the old fisherman, but the contrasting relation between the story in which the "hero" speculates that not only gambling, religion and the radio, but all life is an opium—"Bread is the opium of the people"—and Santiago's story is suggested by two passages coupling radio and baseball. Santiago laments, "the rich have radios to talk to them in their boats and to bring them the baseball" (p. 43); and the next day, "It would be wonderful to do this with a radio" (p. 52), but both times, as noted above, he immediately puts the thought aside. Santiago, like Mr. Frazer, is sufficiently human to yearn for an anesthetic, but, unlike Mr. Frazer, if he is to be "more man than I am and I will be so" (p. 71), he must reject the pleasant distraction of the radio bringing the baseball.

In sum, then, baseball in *The Old Man and the Sea* symbolizes the allurements which might deter the old man from his true calling—like hand wrestling which, although Santiago is *El Campéon,* he abandons as bad for his fishing. Of course, Santiago is only an observer of the "Gran Ligas," through the papers. He also considers, however, that "the baseball" can be an "opium" for those who take it as their vocation, however skillful their practice of it—hence the somewhat derogatory remarks about McGraw and Durocher. Santiago suggests that two other well known baseball players have also lost a measure of their openness to life, of their "understanding," despite, and even because of, their successes in the game. Manolin mentions Dick Sisler who used to come to their village. Santiago wanted "to take him fishing but I was too timid to ask him." He continues,

> "I would like to take the great DiMaggio fishing," the old man said. "They say his father was a fisherman. Maybe he was as poor as we are and would understand."
>
> "The great Sisler's father was never poor and he, the father, was playing in the big leagues when he was my age" (pp. 23-24).[15]

Great as the Sislers are as baseball players—"the great Sisler" hits "great drives"—their success has insulated them from "understanding," from true greatness: Santiago knows he would have to take them fishing, but he also questions if they "understand" enough to want to go, and therefore he is too timid to approach them.

But DiMaggio is possibly different, in Santiago's view. Although he too would have to be "taken" fishing, "Maybe he . . . would understand." That he might understand—or that he is only one generation, or even the achievement of success and riches on the baseball diamond, away from understanding—is vastly different, however, from the role DiMaggio has usually been understood to play in the novel, as enhancing the significance of the simple Cuban fisherman. On the contrary, it is apparent that Hemingway intends Santiago's naive praise of the greatest baseball star, who "makes the difference" (p. 23) to the Yankees, to emphasize the much greater achievement in far starker circumstances of the old fisherman himself. The two kinds of greatness become more distinct if the several references to DiMaggio are read as a unit:

1. "The Yankees cannot lose. . . . Think of the great DiMaggio" (p. 18).

2. "In the American League it is the Yankees. . . . The great DiMaggio is himself again. . . . he makes the difference" (p. 23).

3. "I would like to take the great DiMaggio fishing. . . . They say his father was a fisherman. Maybe he was poor as we are and would understand" (pp. 23-24).

4. I must be worthy of the great DiMaggio who does all things perfectly even with the pain of the bone spur in his heel. What is a bone spur. . . ? We do not have them (p. 75).

5. Do you believe the great DiMaggio would stay with a fish as long as I will stay with this one. . . ? I am sure he would and more since he is young and strong. Also his father was a fisherman. But would the bone spur hurt him too much?

"I do not know," he said aloud, "I never had a bone spur" (pp. 75-76).

6. "I think the great DiMaggio would be proud of me today. I had no bone spurs. But the hands and back hurt truly." I wonder what a bone spur is, he thought. Maybe we all have them without knowing of it (p. 107).

7. I wonder how the great DiMaggio would have liked the way I hit him. . . . It was not great thing. . . . Any man could do it. But do you think my hands were as great a handicap as the bone spurs (p. 114)?

8. You were born to be a fisherman as the fish was born to be a fish. San Pedro was a fisherman as was the father of the great DiMaggio (p. 116).

The first two comments focus entirely on DiMaggio's world of baseball. In the third, Santiago introduces the idea of DiMaggio into his own world, as well as the possibility that DiMaggio's father was a fisherman. Thereafter, the emphasis is on Santiago as he moves "Beyond all people in the world" (p. 55) to the "dark water of the true gulf" (p. 109), a shift signalled by the change of setting from the playing field to the sea, from the game to fishing and from the third person to the pronouns "I" and "you" (referring to himself) which introduce the last six passages. In the fourth through the seventh references, Santiago is not concerned about DiMaggio's action nor the Yankees' success but his own performance. To the end, the old fisherman is more "worthy" than he knows, and this innocence as well as his appreciation of great skill in a sport he enjoys serve to keep bright for him the image of his hero. The reader, however, even one fully appreciative of DiMaggio's eminence in the baseball world,[16] cannot fail to find him diminished as he is imaginatively transported from the clean, well-lighted ball park to the open boat of the "true gulf." And despite his naive adulation, Santiago finally realizes that DiMaggio's bone spur is not unique, that his own wounds are as painful; and the reader of course is aware that his suffering is, in fact, profoundly greater.[17] By the last reference, DiMaggio is no longer important to Santiago as a baseball player, nor even the center of the reference made to him. He has become, rather, the son of a fisherman, a son who is still "of May" in terms of a truly big fish. Santiago's concern in the DiMaggio allusions has shifted completely from "great" baseball in the direction of "great" fishing—that is to say, to his vocation which he has come to believe he shares with DiMaggio's father and San Pedro.

The reference to San Pedro, in the last sentence which mentions

DiMaggio, and in effect dismisses the baseball player, points to a vision of greatness beyond either games or vocations, however. Carlos Baker has observed:

> For many years prior to the composition of *The Old Man and the Sea* Hemingway had interested himself in the proposition that there must be a resemblance, in the nature of things, between Jesus Christ in his human aspect as the Son of Man and those countless and often nameless thousands in the history of Christendom who belong to the category of "good men," and may therefore be seen as disciples of Our Lord, whatever the professed degree of their Christian commitment.[18]

Despite the reference to "San Pedro," and Hemingway's "non-Christian use of Christian symbolism,"[19] Santiago's "Christian commitment" is largely unprofessed. He does not reject the Christian framework, but he says his prayers "mechanically"[20] (p. 71) in a bargaining attitude, and even postpones them until after he will have caught the fish: "Consider them said. . . . I'll say them later" (p. 96). The Christian context in which Hemingway places his character is obviously not something profoundly felt and explicitly expressed; rather it is a relic of his heritage, just as the religious pictures on the wall of his shack are "relics of his wife" (p. 16). What Santiago does feel deeply and personally, what he has professed from his boyhood to the last sentence of the book is "the main thing that is left," the dream of the lions.

That the lions embody for Santiago a sufficiency beyond both baseball and fishing—and yet somehow is related to them—is implied in the passage continuing the discussion of the Sislers quoted previously. To Manolin's comment that Sisler's father was playing in the big leagues when he was the boy's age, Santiago responds,

> "When I was your age I was before the mast on a square rigged ship that ran to Africa and I have seen lions on the beaches in the evening."
>
> "I know. You told me."
>
> "Should we talk about Africa or about baseball?"
>
> "Baseball I think. . . . Tell me about the great John J. McGraw" (p. 24).

Manolin, who has yet to learn the "everything" (p. 139) that Santiago can teach him, boyishly chooses baseball, and Santiago "happily" indulges him, teaching about "the greatest managers" instead, as I have noted, although he himself had already chosen the lions, the passage makes explicit, when he was Sisler's and Manolin's age. But Manolin soon leaves, and the old man is shortly asleep dreaming of the lions.

The lions, like the Christian symbolism, have received extensive explication. There seems to be general agreement that they stand for a dream of harmony. As has been variously observed, this is a harmony of the old man and nature,[21] of youth and age, of bracing and relaxing;[22] but beyond these reconciliations, the lions suffice for Santiago as a dream of his faith in an ultimate harmony of life and death.[23] The profound dimensions of this dream are at once individual and traditional. The dream is unique to Santiago arising from his voyage to Africa at an age when other boys are playing or talking about baseball. The climactic treatment of the dream is also individual—the sequence of the dream of life symbolized by the sea of mating porpoises, then of his coldness during the norther signalling his coming death, and the "happy" third dream of the lions coming down to the yellow beach (pp. 89-99) all are instances of Santiago's life transmuted into a higher form. It should be noticed, however, that Hemingway has very possibly connected these apparently artless and even quaint reconstructions of the experience of the old man with the traditional Biblical vision of harmony through the prophecy of Isaiah of a time when "it shall come to pass. . . . that the Lord shall set his hand. . . . to recover the remnant of his people," and the lion shall dwell in a peaceable kingdom with the other animals (Isaiah 11: 1-11). I have examined these possible connections at greater length elsewhere,[24] but here I wish to emphasize rather than any particular interpretation of Santiago's dream, the fact that he has a recurrent vision that is more significant to him than anything else.

> He no longer dreamed of storms, nor of women, nor of great occurrences, nor of great fish, nor fights, nor contests of strength, nor of his wife. He only dreamed of places now and of the lions on the beach. They played like young cats in the dusk and he loved them as he loved the boy. He never dreamed about the boy (pp. 27-28).

In other words, Santiago does not dream of what is or has been on the naturalistic surface of his life, including "contests" and "great fish." His dream searches beyond that surface to a past that is somehow present, to places that remain largely unparticularized: "he dreamed of Africa when he was a boy and the long golden beaches and the white beaches, so white they hurt your eyes, and the high capes and the great brown mountains. *He lived along that coast now every night. . . .*" (pp. 26-27;

italics added). The intensity of his vision where he truly "lived . . . now" is such that he is partially blinded, but the glimpse of the visible that is "a little hard to see," in Wallace Stevens' phrase, is sufficient to enable him, despite his human suffering, to be what he was "born to be."

In one of its aspects, then, *The Old Man and the Sea* can be read as a comparison of different orders of greatness. Both explicit and implicit, the comparison is even more repeatedly explicit than I have noted thus far; for some form of the word *great* appears nearly thirty times in the novel. There is the superb if temporary skill at playing a game, strikingly exhibited by the "young and strong" (p. 75) DiMaggio and ambiguously represented by the "greatest managers": about half the references to greatness apply to performance connected with the entertainment that so preoccupies Santiago in his spare time, the kind of preoccupation required by some earlier Hemingway heroes as an "opium." "Why should the people be operated on without an anesthetic?" Mr. Frazer had asked. Another kind of greatness is necessary for success in the lifetime earning of one's daily bread, if one is "definitely and finally *salao,* which is the worst form of unlucky" (p. 9): and about half the references to greatness apply to Santiago's vocation. The term, however, is never applied to Santiago.[25] He is unique in the novel and among Hemingway heroes: the greatness of this "strange old man" is somehow beyond that "normally" encountered in championship baseball and successful fishing. "There are many good fishermen and some great ones," Manolin says, "But there is only you" (p. 25). Santiago avidly, but never mindlessly, follows "the baseball"; the old man considers he was born to be a fisherman and he is utterly committed to the practice of his vocation even unto his death; but it is his dream that sustains him from his boyhood to the last line of the book and that, by enabling him to withstand the "Plenty" (p. 139) of suffering that is his human lot, establishes the different dimension of this greatness.

In his short review Faulkner praised *The Old Man and the Sea* as Hemingway's "best," and even "perhaps the best of any of us" because "This time he discovered God, a Creator."[26] It is doubtful that Hemingway would have described his achievement in this manner,[27] but he had created a fiction of a character who plays and works and suffers in the world without denying that world nor deadening himself to it, a character whose "main thing that is left" is the dream-like act of envisaging a supreme aim beyond entertainment and occupation—at long last a Hemingway hero who follows the example of the Christ figure in "Today is Friday" and thus makes it in a truly "Gran Liga."

"You must get well fast for there is much that I can learn and you can teach me everything," Manolin implores the dying[28] Santiago. "Everything" about baseball and fishing to be sure, but, much more, about how to live "now" in a dimension of the imagination transcending pastime and craft.

Michigan State University

---

[1]Mr. Joseph Mallia, a student in my Twentieth Century American Fiction class at Michigan State University, first called my attention to the translation of DiMaggio's name and to the possibility that he functions as a foil to Santiago as well as an example. His fresh and sensitive reading was instrumental in my taking another look at the baseball symbolism in the novel.

[2]Ernest Hemingway, *The Old Man and the Sea* (New York: Scribners, 1952), p. 75. Subsequent references will appear in the text.

[3]George Monteiro, "Santiago, DiMaggio, and Hemingway: The Ageing Professionals of *The Old Man and the Sea," Fitzgerald/Hemingway Annual 1975,* pp. 273-280.

[4]"The Sham Battle Over Ernest Hemingway," *Western Review,* XVII (Spring 1953), 240.

[5]"Six Authors in Search of a Hero," *Sewanee Review,* LXV (Summer 1957), 503.

[6]Monteiro, p. 278.

[7]"Baseball and Baseball Talk in *The Old Man and the Sea," Fitzgerald/Hemingway Annual 1975,* pp. 281-287.

[8]*The Baseball Encyclopedia* (New York: Macmillan, 1969), p. 1145, p. 2216.

[9]Monteiro has called attention to another instance of this technique in the book when Hemingway puts the Cincinnati Reds, a National League club, in the American League. Actually, Monteiro observes, Santiago is thus allaying Manolin's fears with the absurdity that a team from the *other* major leagues might beat out the Yankees. *Notes on Contemporary Literature,* IV (May 1974), 8.

[10]Similarly, in *A Farewell to Arms,* (New York: Scribners, 1929), Mr. Meyers, who is "supposed to have been in a penitentiary at home" and let out to die, is characterized by the way in which he plays the horses. "Meyers won on nearly every race but disliked to give tips because it brought down the prices. The racing was very crooked" (pp. 130, 133).

[11]In the early 1950's Durocher's unprecedented suspension for the 1947 season as manager of the Brooklyn Dodgers for conduct "detrimental to baseball," and his acquittal in 1945 for calling a vociferous fan under the stands and attacking him with a blunt instrument—the acquittal possibly related to the payment of damages to the victim—were relatively fresh and unsavory memories. Allison Danzig and Joe Reichler, *The History of Baseball* (Englewood Cliffs, N.J.: Prentice-Hall, 1959), p. 364.

[12]Barbour and Sattelmeyer stress the successful playing careers of the two Cubans and note that they did manage in the winter leagues in Latin America. But the fact remains that Santiago's praise of them as "the greatest managers" has no basis in fact, at least in the "Gran Ligas," the subject of his conversation with Manolin. Pp. 284-285.

[13]Hemingway's interest in baseball is too well known to require extensive documentation. See, for example, his dozen or so references to the sport in his conversations with Lilian Ross in 1950. *Portrait of Hemingway* (New York: Simon and Schuster, 1961). But he also had reservations about games such as baseball surprisingly close to the criticism made by Ray B. West, Jr. (Notes 5 and 6, above.) Much earlier he had written that bull fighting "would never have much success among the amateur sportsmen of America and England who play games. We, in games, are not fascinated by death, its nearness and its avoidance. We are fascinated by victory and we replace the avoidance of death by the avoidance of defeat. It is a very nice symbolism but it takes more cojones to be a sportsman when death is a closer party to the game." *Death in the Afternoon* (New York: Scribner's, 1932), p. 22.

[14]In the immediately following comment Santiago praises, "You are already a man."

[15]This conversation provides another example of Hemingway's manipulation of baseball "facts" for his own purposes, possibly to make the parallel between the baseball players and the fishermen seem closer. The senior Sisler first played in the big leagues when he was twenty-two, much older than Manolin. *The Baseball Encyclopedia,* p. 1485.

[16]The measure of that eminence is suggested by the fact that it is sufficiently remembered a generation later to bring the historical figure alluded to in the novel, now no longer in May, additional rewards for extolling the merits of Mr. Coffee on TV commercials.

[17]In point of historical fact, after missing nearly half of the 1949 season because of the bone spurs, "When DiMaggio returned to the Yankee lineup the pain in his right heel had disappeared," as DiMaggio had told reporters after the first week of play and as he repeated in a ghost-written article in *Life* a month later. Santiago is obviously and necessarily unaware of this fact, necessarily "for it is not DiMaggio's skill which most appeals to Santiago; rather it is his conviction that DiMaggio has succeeded in reestablishing his prowess in spite of his age, infirmity, and, above all, pain," Monteiro, p. 277. Actually, as Monteiro has established, DiMaggio was not playing under the handicap of infirmity and pain; and the fifth reference listed above makes clear that Santiago considers him to be "young and strong," "in May" as it were. Although it cannot be established that Hemingway knew DiMaggio had not been performing under pain, that knowledge was easily available to any baseball follower. If Hemingway was in possession, over a year later, of this common baseball knowledge, the ironic thrust of Santiago's self-abnegating praise is all the more unmistakeable. Monteiro's conclusion also suggests that however brilliant DiMaggio's baseball exploits, Santiago is playing in a league of different dimensions: "The level of success reached by the ballplayer is possible, we infer, only within the posited limits of a sport in which men compete against—not the immutable forces of nature, as does the fisherman—but

merely other men," p. 279.

[18]Carlos Baker, *Hemingway* (Princeton: Princeton University Press, 1972), p. 299.

[19]Arvin R. Wells, "A Ritual of Transfiguration: *The Old Man and the Sea,*" *The University Review,* 30 (Winter 1963), 100.

[20]When his prayers are said he is "feeling much better, but suffering exactly as much and perhaps a little more. . . ." (p. 72).

[21]Wells, 101.

[22]Baker, pp. 308-11.

[23]That the lions are indeed a dream of harmony is indicated more expressly in the novel than has previously been noted. As Santiago sits with Manolin on the Terrace, "His hope and confidence had never gone. But now they were freshening as when a breeze rises" (p. 14). The image of the breeze explicitly connects this resurgence of hope and confidence to the two most detailed dreams of the lions. See pp. 27, 89.

[24]Sam S. Baskett, "Toward a 'Fifth Dimension' in *The Old Man and the Sea,*" *The Centennial Review,* XIX (Fall 1975), 274-77.

[25]In addition to the references to baseball and fishing, the term is used three times: "the great negro from Ciefuegos" (p. 76); "the great strangeness" (p. 109) Santiago experiences with the fish; and "The dark water of the true gulf is the greatest healer that there is" (p. 109).

[29]William Faulkner, "Review of *The Old Man and the Sea,*" *Shenandoah,* III (Autumn 1952), 55.

[27]Hemingway wrote to the Editors of *Life,* XXXIII (25 August 1952), 124, "Whatever I learned is in the story but I hope it reads simply and straight and all the things that are in it do not show but only are with you when you have read it. . . . It's as though I had gotten finally what I had been working for all my life."

[28]See Bickford Sylvester, "They Went Through This Fiction Every Day: Informed Illusion in *The Old Man and the Sea,*" *Modern Fiction Studies,* XII (Winter 1966-67), 473-77; and Baskett, 269n.

RICHARD LAYMAN

"C. and M." in "The Light of the World"

There has been some question about Hemingway's use of the term "C. and M." in "The Light of the World." In Joe Gores' novel *Hammett* (New York: Putnam, 1975), there are two references to C-and-M. On p. 19 Egan Tokzek "snorted a generous pinch of the white C-and-M crystal. His face contorted as the potent mixture of cocaine and morphine bit into the tortured flesh of his inner nose." And on p. 159 Tokzek is said to have been high on "C-and-M" crystals at the time of his death. When questioned about the term, Gores responded with a detailed explanation, citing two authorities: Eugene Landy, *The Underground Dictionary* (New York: Simon and Schuster, 1971); and Goldin, O'Leary, and Lipsius, *Dictionary of American Underground Lingo* (New York: Twayne, 1950).

Both sources support Gores' definition of C-and-M as a "mixture of cocaine and morphine," and the latter adds an example of the usage: "Them juneys (drug addicts) hooked on (habituated to) c-and-m would rat (inform) on their mothers for the whizz-bang (potent drug mixture)."

Gores also added his own comments on the story: "I fully believe that the Hemingway reference . . . does indeed refer to the whore's 'chipping' with C and M. It fits the way the reference appears in the dialogue. It is also obvious the girl is not an addict. The reference by the other whore could [be] (and probably was) derogatory and not referring to what she knew as fact (i.e., that the girl actually *had* experimented with C and M.)."

University of South Carolina

DAVID McCLELLAN

The Battle of the Little Big Horn in Hemingway's Later Fiction

Hemingway once said that his idea of heaven was a front seat at a bullfight with a private trout stream out back. Later on he might have offered as his image of paradise a role in a high plains Sioux sundance on the eve of an Indian engagement with the United States cavalry.

From *To Have and Have Not* on, an increasing concern with the Battle of the Little Big Horn, usually from the Indian side, is near the surface of the combat episodes in Hemingway's longer fiction. In *To Have And Have Not,* as Harry Morgan goes out to his death in the fight with Cuban revolutionaries, he looks at a painting of Custer's "Last Stand" on the wall of a saloon as if he is seeing it for the first time.

The painting referred to is an Anheuser-Busch sponsored creation which hung for decades after the battle in taverns across the nation. Hemingway refers to the painting twice more in his fiction. In *For Whom The Bell Tolls* Robert Jordan recalls that he admired the idealized Custer of the painting and at first resented the image of Custer as an inferior cavalry leader, destroyed at the Big Horn by his own stupidity, conveyed to him by his grandfather who had known Custer. In the "At Sea" section of *Islands In The Stream,* as Thomas Hudson's crew finally closes with the escaping German submariners, a crewman says, "They're fighting Custer's Last Stand in the mangroves. Christ, I wish I had some Anheuser Busch."

In *Across The River And Into The Trees,* while the painting does not appear, Custer himself emerges in Richard Cantwell's reveries as a contemptible figure who justly was defeated at the Big Horn. But there is more evidence that Hemingway was increasingly obsessed with the battle and identified with the Indian victors.

In an article in the 1974 *Fitzgerald/Hemingway Annual,* I have argued that the battle between El Sordo's guerrillas and the Fascist captain in *For Whom The Bell Tolls* is substructured on Custer's phase of the Battle of the Little Big Horn. To recapitulate, the Fascist captain with his blond hair, blue eyes, and British cavalry mustache, looks like Custer. He also acts like him, disregarding his subordinate's warning that he is walking into a trap, then dying on a hillside. And, with his broad face and thin mouth, El Sordo looks like Sitting Bull, who masterminded the Sioux victory over Custer. El Sordo is even described as having a "thin-bridged, hooked nose like an Indian's."

In the same article there is exterior evidence. Hemingway in a letter quoted in a newspaper claimed authoritative knowledge of the battle. He also reprinted as an example of great writing about combat in his anthology *Men at War* a chapter on the Battle of the Little Big Horn from a life of Custer.

Since writing the article, I have discovered, through the cooperation of Matthew Bruccoli who permitted me to examine an unpublished list of the books in Hemingway's Cuba library, that Hemingway owned three books on Custer and the Battle of the Little Big Horn.[1]

The Little Big Horn as battle substructure also is at work in *Across the River* and *Islands.* The role of Major Marcus Reno in the battle is reenacted in *Across the River.* Acting on Custer's orders, Reno attacked a Sioux village inhabited by hordes of warriors vastly outnumbering the Seventh Cavalry. Reno and his men narrowly escaped total extinction before Reno pulled them out of the woods and led them across a river to a rocky hillside. Although Reno attacked the village under Custer's orders and performed as ably as was possible under the circumstances, he concluded his military career under a cloud because he was considered to have failed in his duties at the Big Horn. Like Reno, Richard Cantwell in *Across The River And Into The Trees* led his command into a disastrous military action and experienced the ruin of his career because he followed orders of incompetent superiors. Obeying the instructions of the Allied high command, Cantwell attacked a heavily fortified wooded German town and then had to fight across a rocky hillside, losing a majority of his men in the process and ultimately as a consequence suffering reduction in rank from general to colonel.

In *Islands In The Stream* the Big Horn reappears, but with a curious yet explainable twist. In *For Whom The Bell Tolls* and *Across The River And Into The Trees,* the protagonist in the context of the Big Horn substructure is a pro-Indian or at least an anti-Custer figure. But in *Islands In The Stream,* Hudson follows to his doom the outlines of the pattern Custer fatally pursued. This may be explained by the fact that while at the Big Horn the Indians defeated Custer, the battle really was their "Last Stand" in that never again were they able to mobilize such power and perform with such strategic skill in their encounters with the white soldiers.

The battle pattern definitely appears as Hudson pursues and finally finds the fleeing German submarine crew. Like Custer, Hudson meets his end in an ambush along a river after patiently tracking his human prey, who left signs of their passing presence, for several days. Not long before nearing the big Indian camp, Custer and his men encountered a dead Indian in a lean-to, a sure sign that a war camp was ahead. As he approached the submariners' island-river hideout, Hudson on another island found in a lean-to a dying German who had been left behind by the submariners. The presence at this point in the novel of the dying German does not contribute to furthering the action or heightening the suspense of the narrative—other signs, such as a burned village and discarded cartridges from a German pistol, having already been discovered to indicate that Hudson was on the track of a German submarine crew. That the incident reflects a detail in the Custer fight thus would appear to be the best explanation of this inclusion.

When Hemingway received the Nobel prize, he spoke of the artist's activity as alchemy.[2] It appears that one of the elements which went into the transformation of actual combat observation, reading, and imaginings into Hemingway's later art were some of the events and people of the Little Big Horn battle.

Eastern Tennessee University

---

[1]Books on Custer with which Hemingway was definitely familiar included F. Van

De Water's biography of Custer *Glory Hunter* (Indianapolis: Bobbs Merrill, 1934), Jay Monaghan's *Custer: The Life of George Armstrong Custer* (Boston: Little Brown, 1959), David Humphreys Miller's *Custer's Fall,* (New York: Duell, Sloan and Pearce, 1957) and Charles Windolph's *I Fought With Custer* (New York: Scribners, 1959). Hemingway's knowledge of Van De Water's book is shown by the fact that he included the chapter on the Battle of the Little Big Horn in the book in his anthology of outstanding writing about combat, *Men at War* (New York: Crown, 1942). The three other books about Custer were in his Cuba library.

[2]Since it is generally known that Hemingway was directly involved in various ways in the Spanish Civil War and World War II, against the claims of this article it may be argued that all of the elements of the combat episodes examined came from actual experience, with Hemingway's study of the Custer fight making no contribution. However, according to Carlos Baker's biography, *Ernest Hemingway: A Life Story* (New York: Scribners, 1969), Hemingway invented the guerrilla action of *For Whom The Bell Tolls,* pursued but did not actually close with German submarines in the Caribbean early in World War II, and later in the same war served as a war correspondent covering an American infantry regiment in France and Germany under Colonel Charles T. (Buck) Lanham. Lanham, whose outfit did not suffer casualties quite as severe as Colonel Cantwell's, instead of being reduced in rank later became a general.

Bibliographical Material

Bruccoli Addenda

Section A

A8. The *B & D* dust jacket with the title in solid black lettering is later than the jacket with outlined lettering. Perkins to FSF, 10 February 1922: "In the second twenty thousand, we are printing the lettering of the title in black and the disk is in quite a deep orange. . . ."

A11. *GG* has been reset in Scribner Library. See Editorial in this volume of the *Annual*.

A15. *TITN* was a Literary Guild alternative in June 1934.

A17. *TAR* was a Literary Guild alternative in June 1935.

A26. Book-of-the-Month Club copies of *Letters* can be identified by a blindstamped square on the back cover.

Bits of Paradise. New York: Pocket Books, [1976]. #80250. Adds "Dice, Brass Knuckles, and Guitar."

The Cruise of the Rolling Junk. Bloomfield Hills & Columbia: Bruccoli Clark, [1976].

F. Scott Fitzgerald's Preface to This Side of Paradise. Iowa City: Windhover Press & Bruccoli Clark, 1975. Ed. John Hopkins. 150 copies.

SECTION AA

Janus-sarja 5/F. Scott Fitzgerald/Babylon Revisited/and/Two Other Short Stories/[Device]/HELSINGISSA/KUSTANNUSOSAKEYHTIO OTAVA. 1962. Includes "'The Sensible Thing'" and "The Baby Party."

SECTION B

B48. *Beloved Infidel* was included in *Books Abridged,* XXX-XIV (n.d.).

Graham, Sheilah. *The Real F. Scott Fitzgerald.* New York: Grosset & Dunlap, 1976. Includes "Dame Rumor" and facsimile of Fitzgerald's revisions for "Not in the Script," by Graham.

SECTION C

C183 (Note). Additional Woodbury Soap Beauty Contest ads in *Ladies' Home Journal:* February-May, July, September, December 1929; January 1930.

SECTION D

CATALOGUE THIRTY-THREE . . . BLACK SUN BOOKS [1975] #53: *VEG,* inscribed for Ernest Truex: "The best postman in the world Atlantic City Nov. 19 1923 F. Scott Fitzgerald." This is the third known copy so inscribed.

ARGUS CATALOG NUMBER 3. . . . [1946] #338: TS of "The Peroxide Blonde" by Scottie Fitzgerald; each sheet signed by FSF.

Antiquarian Bookman (7 July 1975), 99. Ad by Old New York Book Shop in Atlanta, Georgia offers inscribed *TSOP*: "For John Myers O'Hara who first introduced me to Sapho in his translations, with a thousand thanks. 'Much have I travelled in the Realms of gold'? his most cordially, F. Scott Fitzgerald, Washington, D.C."

CATALOGUE 46 1974 . . . John Howell-Books . . . #609: *B & D,* autographed.

SECTION E

Wilson, B. F. "F. Scott Fitzgerald on Minnie McGluke," *Picture-Play,* XIX (October 1923), 83-84, 102.

MARGARET M. DUGGAN

FITZGERALD CHECKLIST

Adams, Val. "Radio Roundup," (N.J.) *Sunday News* (17 August 1975), TV8. On proposed 52 half-hour radio dramas based on Fitzgerald's short stories.

Anon. "People," *Time* (17 November 1975), 63. On movie version of LT.

____. Stationery featuring Fitzgerald's home in St. Paul. St. Paul: Artprints, 1973.

Atkins, Irene Kahn. "In Search of the Greatest Gatsby," *Literature/Film Quarterly*, 2 (Summer 1974), 216-228.

Bakker, J. "F. Scott Fitzgerald and the American Dream," *Levende Talen*, No. 283 (1971), 784-793.

Brogunier, Joseph. "An Incident in *The Great Gatsby* and *Huckleberry Finn,*" *Mark Twain Journal,* 16 (1972), 1-3.

Brown, Dennis. "Uncut Fitzgerald," *St. Louis Post-Dispatch* (7 September 1975), 4F. Review of *Gatsby* manuscript facsimile.

Burton, Mary E. "The Counter-Transference of Dr. Diver," *Journal of English Literary History,* 38 (September 1971), 459-471.

Canby, Henry S. *American Memoir.* Boston: Houghton Mifflin, 1947.

Casty, Alan. " 'I and It' in the Stories of F. Scott Fitzgerald," *Studies in Short Fiction,* 9 (1972), 47-58.

Chadwick, Bruce. "Fitzgerald's Works Nourished in Jersey," *New York Sunday News*—Jersey Edition (31 August 1975), J34.

Coleman, Tom C. "Nicole Warren and Scott Fitzgerald: The Girl and the Egotist," *Studies in the Novel,* 3 (Spring 1971), 34-43.

Corrigan, R. A. "Somewhere West of Laramie, on the Road to West Egg: Automobiles, Fillies, and the West in *The Great Gatsby,*" *Journal of Popular Culture,* 7 (Summer 1973), 152-158.

Donnelly, Tom. " 'Infidelity': A Screenplay by Fitzgerald," *Washington Post* (2 December 1973), K8.

Drabble, Margaret. "The Beautiful Couple," (BBC Radio Brighton) *Radio Times* (26 April-2 May 1975), 60, 63. Cover story on Robert Muller's play about Fitzgeralds and part of BBC *Private Affairs* series.

Engle, William. "The Tragic Fitzgerald Story," *The American Weekly* (13 June 1948), 16-17.

Fitzgerald, F. Scott. *The Cruise of the Rolling Junk.* Bloomfield Hills & Columbia: Bruccoli Clark, 1976.

——. *El gran Gatsby,* trans. E. Piñas. Guadalupe & Barcelona: Plaza & Janes, 1975. Spanish edition featuring color cover photo from movie.

——. *Preface to This Side of Paradise,* ed. John Hopkins. Iowa City:

Windhover Press and Bloomfield Hills & Columbia: Bruccoli Clark, 1975.

Fitzgerald, F. Scott and Zelda. *Bits of Paradise,* ed. Matthew J. Bruccoli and Scottie Fitzgerald Smith. New York: Pocket Books, 1976. Adds "Dice, Brass Knuckles, and Guitar."

Forrey, Robert. "Negroes in the Fiction of F. Scott Fitzgerald," *Phylon,* 28 (Fall 1967), 293-298.

Gollin, Rita K. "The Automobiles of *The Great Gatsby," Studies in the Twentieth Century,* No. 6 (Fall 1970), 63-83.

——. "Modes of Travel in *Tender Is the Night," Studies in the Twentieth Century,* No. 8 (Fall 1971), 103-114.

Graham, Sheilah. "Letters to the Editor/College of One," *The New York Times Book Review,* (April 1967), 42.

——. *The Real F. Scott Fitzgerald.* New York: Grosset & Dunlap, 1976.

——. "Sheilah Graham's Own Story of Her Stormy Romance with F. Scott Fitzgerald," *Midnight* (7 April 1975), 16-17.

Hartford, G. F. "Reflections and Affinities: Aspects of the American Past, the American Dream, and *The Great Gatsby," English Studies in Africa,* 16 (1973), 23-36.

Higgins, Brian and Hershel Parker. "Sober Second Thoughts: Fitzgerald's 'Final Version' of *Tender Is the Night,*" *Proof 4,* (1975), pp. 129-152.

Hobsbaum, Philip. "Scott Fitzgerald and His Critics: The Appreciation of Minor Art," *British Association of American Studies Bulletin,* 6 (June 1963), 31-41.

Houston, Penelope. "Gatsby," *Sight and Sound,* 43 (Spring 1974), 78-79.

Isaacs, Stan. "Fitzgerald to Truex Gets Quite a Play," *Long Island Newsday* (4 November 1975), 7A.

——. "Schulberg, Fitzgerald and 'The Disenchanted,' " *Long Island Newsday* (2 September 1975), 7A.

Jones, Edward T. "Green Thoughts in a Technicolor Shade: A Revaluation of *The Great Gatsby," Literature/Film Quarterly,* 2 (Summer 1974), 229-236.

Korenman, Joan S. " 'Only Her Hairdresser . . .': Another Look at Daisy Buchanan," *American Literature* (January 1975), 574-578.

Kuehl, John, ed. *The Apprentice Fiction of F. Scott Fitzgerald.* New Brunswick, N.J.: Rutgers University Press, [1975]. Paperback reprint of original edition.

Lowry, Malcolm and Margerie Bonner. *Notes on a Screenplay for F. Scott Fitzgerald's Tender Is the Night,* Introduction by Paul Tiessen. Bloomfield Hills & Columbia: Bruccoli Clark, 1976.

Margolies, Alan. "F. Scott Fitzgerald's Prison Play," *Papers of the Bibliographical Society of America,* 65 (1972), 61-64.

Margolis, Jon. "The America of the Future is Before Your Eyes," *Chicago Tribune Perspective* (29 June 1975), Section 2, 8. Quotes from *GG.*

Martin, Robert. "Gatsby and the Dutch Sailors," *American Notes and Queries,* 12 (December 1973), 61-63.

——. "The Hot Madness of Four O'Clock in Fitzgerald's 'Absolution' and *Gatsby," Studies in American Fiction,* 2 (Autumn 1974), 230-237.

Mass, Roslyn. "A Linking of Legends: *The Great Gatsby* and *Citizen Kane," Literature/Film Quarterly,* 2 (Summer 1974), 207-215.

McNally, John J. "Boats and Automobiles in *The Great Gatsby:* Symbols of Drift and Death," *Husson Review,* 5 (1971), 11-17.

——. "Prefiguration of Incidents in *The Great Gatsby," University of Dayton Review,* 7 (1971), 39-49.

Niven, David. *Bring On the Empty Horses.* New York: G. P. Putnam's Sons, 1975. Relates acquaintance with FSF.

Oakes, Philip. "The Way They Were," *London Sunday Times* (12 October 1975). Bijou O'Connor on the Fitzgeralds in Paris. Recording of her reminiscences available on Audio Arts cassette (92-104 Carnswath Road, London SW6 3HW). Side two is 1946 CBS radio version of Bogart-Bacall *To Have and Have Not.*

Rodda, Pater. *"The Last Tycoon," English Studies in Africa,* 14 (1971), 49-71.

Robinson, Jeffrey. "Fitzgerald's Riviera—'disappeared with time,' " *Christian Science Monitor* (8 April 1975), 19.

Robson, Vincent. "The Psychosocial Conflict and the Distortion of Time: A Study of Diver's Disintegration in *Tender Is the Night," Language and Literature,* 1 (1972), 55-64.

Schulberg, Budd. "The Best Gatsby," *The New York Times Book Review* (18 May 1975), 3. On *GG* facsimile.

Smith, G. Roysce. "Known & Unknown Best Sellers," *New York Times Book Review* (22 June 1975), 10. Ad which includes report of FSF's book sales.

Stouck, David. "White Sheep on Fifth Avenue: *The Great Gatsby* as Pastoral," *Genre,* 4 (December 1971), 335-347.

Strode, Hudson. *The Eleventh House: Memoirs.* New York & London: Harcourt Brace Jovanovich, 1975. Includes conversation with FSF.

Tasaka, Takashi. "The Ethic and Aesthetic Aspects of *Tender Is the Night," Studies in American Literature,* 8 (1972), 15-23.

Trower, Katherine B. "Visions of Paradise in *The Great Gatsby," Renascence,* 25 (Autumn 1972), 14-23.

West, James L. W., III. "Notes on the Text of F. Scott Fitzgerald's 'Early Success,' " *Resources for American Literary Study,* 3 (Spring 1973), 73-99.

Whitman, Alden. "Sara Murphy, Patron of Artists and Writers in France Dies," *New York Times* (11 October 1975), 30m.

Will, George F. "A California Gatsby," *Washington Post* (22 March 1975), A15. Article on Hugh Hefner quotes from *GG.*

Notices of Fitzgeralds' Reburial: Anon. "Acceptable for Burial," *The Nation* (25 October 1975), 390; ___. "Fitzgerald's Grave Site to Change," *The* (Columbia, S.C.) *State* (12 October 1975), 8-A; ___. "F. Scott Fitzgerald to Get His Wish," *Washington Star* (12 October 1975); ___. "New Burial Site Chosen for Fitzgerald," *Washington Post* (12 October 1975); ___. "Author F. Scott Fitzgerald Is Reburied," *Detroit Free Press* (10 November 1975), 14-D; ___. "Fitzgerald Buried With Ancestors," *The* (Raleigh, N.C.) *News and Observer* (12 November 1975); ___. "F. Scott Fitzgerald Gets Wish: Catholic Reburial," *Des Moines Tribune* (8 November 1975); ___. "F. Scott Fitzgerald Reburied," *San Francisco Chronicle* (8 November 1975), 15; Ben A. Franklin. " 'Happy Thought': Fitzgerald Reburied," *New York Times* (8 November 1975), M 29; Cynthia Gorney. "Fitzgerald Reburied in Simple Ceremony," *Washington Post* (8 November 1975), A 15, A 28; Paul Hendrickson. " 'He had come a long way to this blue lawn. . .,' " *National Observer* (22 November 1975), 20; John Sherwood. "Very Tender Was the Day," *Washington Star* (8 November 1975), A 1, A 8.

University of South Carolina

WILLIAM WHITE

HEMINGWAY CHECKLIST

Amon, Rhoda. ". . . And His Granddaughters Keep Up Traditions," *Miami Herald* (9 November 1975), G 2.

Anon. "Hemingway's Last Novel," *TLS: Essays and Reviews from The Times Literary Supplement*. Oxford: Oxford University Press, 1971, 9: 26-32. Review of *Islands in the Stream.*

——. "Notes to Myself by Ernest Hemingway." *National Lampoon,* I (September 1975). Parody.

——. "Widow's Gift to JFK Library: Hemingway Papers Released," *The Detroit News* [and other Associated Press papers], 13 July 1975, 17-D.

——. Review of Jackson J. Benson, ed., *The Short Stories of Ernest Hemingway: Critical Essays, Choice,* 12 (October 1975), 996.

——. Review of Madelaine Hemingway Miller, *Ernie: Hemingway's Sister "Sunny" Remembers, Choice,* 12 (October 1975), 1001.

Agroskina, S. N. "Semantiko-strukturnaya kharakteristika absatsa tipa povestvuyushchii monolog v proze E. Khemingguey a," *Leningradskii Pedagogicheskii Institute Imeni A. I. Gertsena* (Leningrad), 474 (1972): 67-78. The semantico-structural characteristic of the paragraph of the type narrating monologue in the prose of E. Hemingway.

Alinei, Tamara. "The 'Corrida' and *For Whom the Bell Tolls,*" *Neophilologus,* 56 (1972), 487-492.

Asselineau, Roger. "Ernest Hemingway: A Rebel Rediscovers Tradition or the Destruction and Rehabilitation of Traditional Values in E. Hemingway's Fiction," *Studien zur englischen und amerikanischen Sprache und Literature: Festschrift fur Helmut Papajewski,* eds. Paul G. Buchloh, Inge Leimberg, and Herbert Rauter. Neumünster: Karl Wachholtz Verlag, 1974, pp. 387-404.

Baker, C. H. "Hemingway's Empirical Imagination." Kenneth H. Baldwin and David K. Kirby, eds. *Individual and Community: Variations on a Theme in American Fiction.* Durham: Duke University Press, 1975, pp. 94-111.

Baker, Lera Helen. "The Flapper Figure in American Fiction 1919-1933," *Masters Abstracts,* 13 (March 1975), 26. MA thesis, University of Louisville, 1974. 72 pp. *The Sun Also Rises* and *A Farewell to Arms* are two of the novels treated.

Bakker, Jan. "In Search of Reality: Two American Heroes Compared," *DQR: Dutch Quarterly Review,* 2 (1972), 145-161.

Beebe, Maurice, ed. "Ernest Hemingway," "1973 Annual Review," *Journal of Modern Literature,* 4 (November 1974), 345-349.

Bodonescu, ion. "Amintirea lui Hemingway," *Ramuri,* 9 (No. 6, 1972), 23-24. Hemingway's memory.

Boyce, Robert L. Review of Audre Hanneman, *Supplement to Ernest Hemingway: A Comprehensive Bibliography, Library Journal,* 100 (1 November 1975), 2036.

Bruccoli, Matthew J. Review of *Ernie, Panorama—Chicago Daily News,* 3-4 May 1975, 8.

Buchesky, Charles Stanley. "The Background of American Literary Naturalism," *Dissertation Abstracts International,* 32 (1972), 6368-A-6369-A. Ph.D. dissertation, Wayne State University, 1971.

Burhans, Clinton S., Jr. "Hemingway and Vonnegut: Diminishing Vision in a Dying Age," *Modern Fiction Studies,* 21 (Summer 1975), 173-191.

Cantalejo Ruiz, Zacarias. "Estudio bibliográfico sobre Ernest Hemingway," MA thesis, Salamanca, 1972.

Capellan Gonzalo, Angel. "Hacia una interpretación orgánica de 'El Viejo y el Mar,'" *Filología Moderna* (Madrid), 1972.

Castillo-Puche, José Luis. Ernest Hemingway: Presencia y señorio de la muerte," *Estafeta Literaria,* No. 545 (1 August 1974), 9-12.

Chamberlain, J. E. Review of Emily Stipes Watts, *Ernest Hemingway and the Arts, Hudson Review,* 25 (1972), 698-700.

Chatterton, Wayne. "Textbook Uses of Hemingway and Faulkner," *CCC: College Composition and Communication,* 23 (1972), 292-296.

Chu, Rudolph Yen. "Women in Hemingway's Fiction," *American Studies* (Institute of American Culture, Academia Sinica, Nankang, Taipei, Republic of China), 5 (March 1975), 43-53. In Chinese.

Connolly, Cyril. "Ernest Hemingway," *The Evening Colonnade.* New York: Harcourt Brace Jovanovich, 1975, pp. 255-257.

Conroy, Jack. "Monograph on Hemingway," *American Book Collector,* 25 (March-April 1975), 20. Review of Ina Mae Schleden and Marion Rawls Hurzog, *Ernest Hemingway as Recalled by His High*

School Contemporaries.

Cooperman, Stanley. "American War Novels: Yesterday, Today, and Tomorrow," *Yale Review,* 61 (1972), 517-529.

Coren, Alan. "The Short Happy Life of Margaux Hemingway," *Harper's,* 251 (October 1975), 72, 75. To be reprinted in his *Golfing for Cats* (New York: St. Martin's Press, 1975).

Crozier, Robert D., S.J. "Home James: Hemingway's Jacob," *Papers on Language and Literature,* 11 (Summer 1975), 293-301.

Faherty, Robert. "French TV Plans Hemingway Series," *Atlanta Constitution,* 11 July 1975, 4-B.

Gertzman, Jay A. Review of *The Fifth Column and Four Stories of the Spanish Civil War* and *The Nick Adams Stories, Studies in Short Fiction,* 10 (Spring and Summer 1975), 224-226, 297-298.

Greenfeld, Howard. *They Came to Paris.* New York: Crown, 1975. For juvenile readers.

Gribanov, B. Introduction to Russian translation of *A Farewell to Arms, The Fifth Column,* and *The Old Man and the Sea.* Moscow: Khudozhestvennaya Literature, 1972.

Gruenberg, Robert. "Viva Papa: He's Still a Hero in Cuba," *Panorama—Chicago Daily News.* 31 May-1 June 1975.

Gunn, Giles B. "Hemingway's Testament of Human Solidarity: A Literary Critique of *For Whom the Bell Tolls, Christian Scholar's Review,* 2 (1972), 99-111.

Hanneman, Audre. *Supplement to Ernest Hemingway: A Comprehensive Bibliography.* Princeton: Princeton University Press, 1975.

Hemingway, Ernest. *Der alte Mann und das Meer.* Suhrkamp Verlag, [1970]. Band 214 der Bibliothek Suhrkamp. German translation by Annemarie Horschitz-Horst of *The Old Man and the Sea.*

—— *The Butterfly and the Tank.* Shanghai: Mei-Hsüeh, 1943; Chen-

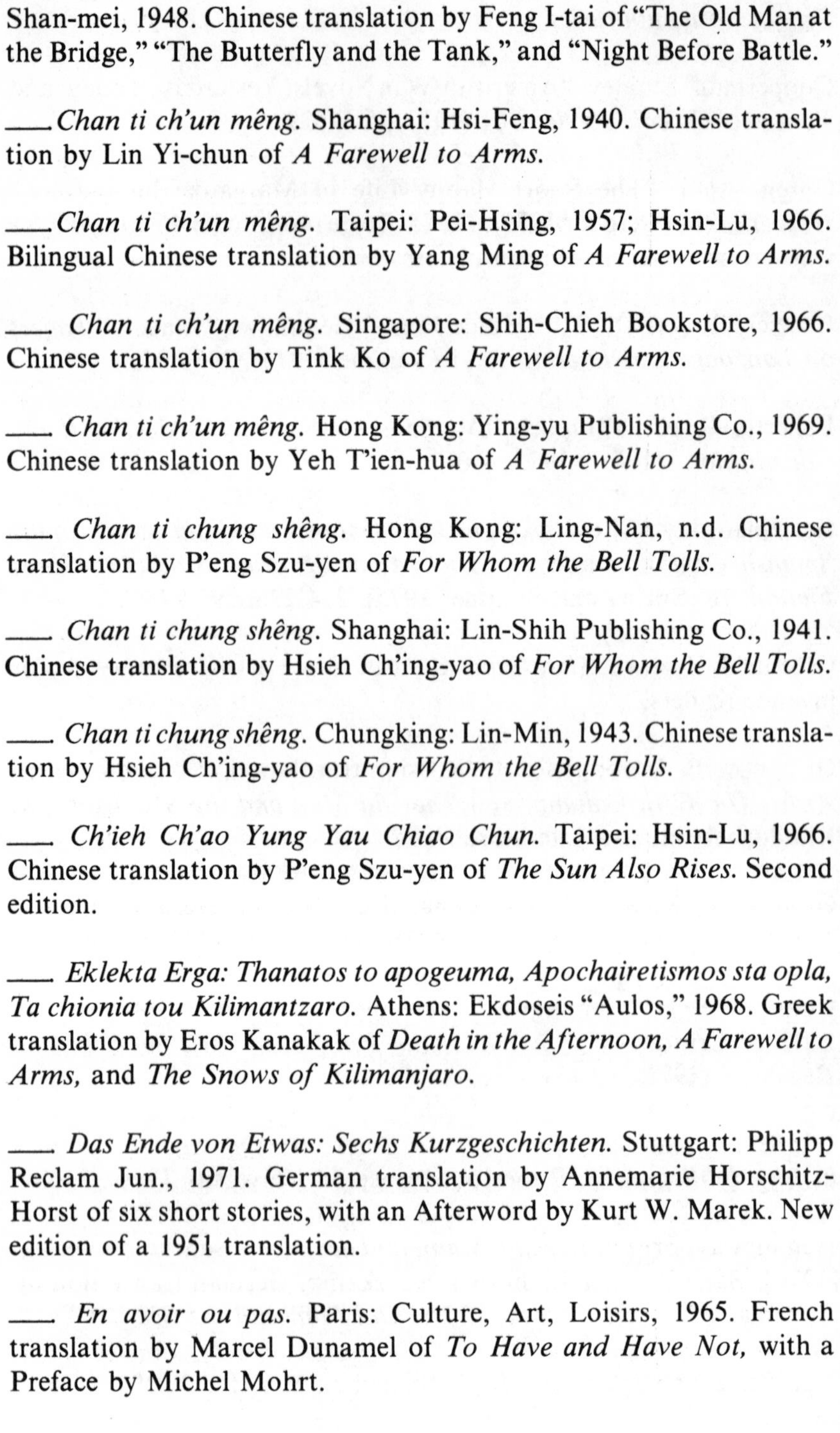

Shan-mei, 1948. Chinese translation by Feng I-tai of "The Old Man at the Bridge," "The Butterfly and the Tank," and "Night Before Battle."

——— *Chan ti ch'un mêng.* Shanghai: Hsi-Feng, 1940. Chinese translation by Lin Yi-chun of *A Farewell to Arms.*

——— *Chan ti ch'un mêng.* Taipei: Pei-Hsing, 1957; Hsin-Lu, 1966. Bilingual Chinese translation by Yang Ming of *A Farewell to Arms.*

——— *Chan ti ch'un mêng.* Singapore: Shih-Chieh Bookstore, 1966. Chinese translation by Tink Ko of *A Farewell to Arms.*

——— *Chan ti ch'un mêng.* Hong Kong: Ying-yu Publishing Co., 1969. Chinese translation by Yeh T'ien-hua of *A Farewell to Arms.*

——— *Chan ti chung shêng.* Hong Kong: Ling-Nan, n.d. Chinese translation by P'eng Szu-yen of *For Whom the Bell Tolls.*

——— *Chan ti chung shêng.* Shanghai: Lin-Shih Publishing Co., 1941. Chinese translation by Hsieh Ch'ing-yao of *For Whom the Bell Tolls.*

——— *Chan ti chung shêng.* Chungking: Lin-Min, 1943. Chinese translation by Hsieh Ch'ing-yao of *For Whom the Bell Tolls.*

——— *Ch'ieh Ch'ao Yung Yau Chiao Chun.* Taipei: Hsin-Lu, 1966. Chinese translation by P'eng Szu-yen of *The Sun Also Rises.* Second edition.

——— *Eklekta Erga: Thanatos to apogeuma, Apochairetismos sta opla, Ta chionia tou Kilimantzaro.* Athens: Ekdoseis "Aulos," 1968. Greek translation by Eros Kanakak of *Death in the Afternoon, A Farewell to Arms,* and *The Snows of Kilimanjaro.*

——— *Das Ende von Etwas: Sechs Kurzgeschichten.* Stuttgart: Philipp Reclam Jun., 1971. German translation by Annemarie Horschitz-Horst of six short stories, with an Afterword by Kurt W. Marek. New edition of a 1951 translation.

——— *En avoir ou pas.* Paris: Culture, Art, Loisirs, 1965. French translation by Marcel Dunamel of *To Have and Have Not,* with a Preface by Michel Mohrt.

——. Facsimile of manuscript, *The David A. Randall Retrospective Memorial Exhibition: Twenty Years' Acquisitions* (Bloomington, Indiana: The Lilly Library, 1975).

——. *A Farewell to Arms. (Proschai oruzhiye.)* Leningrad: Prosveshchenie, 1971. English text, with a Russian title-page, and notes and glossary (in Russian) by I. M. Vlader and K. A. Guzejeva.

——. *Gia poion chtypa ē kampana.* Athens: Diethnēs Leschē Bibliou, 1971. Greek translation by Alex Karer of *For Whom the Bell Tolls.*

——. *Green Hills of Africa* inscribed to Sterling Gaet. *Swann Galleries Sale Number 992* (5 June 1975).

——. *Hai-Ming-Wei Ch'uang-Tso-Lun. (The Writing Theories of Hemingway.)* Taipei: Chung-Kuang Wen-I Publishing Co., 1957. Chinese translation by Ho Hsin.

——. *Ḥai shang yü wêng.* Taipei: Chung-Kuang-Wen-I publishing Co., 1957. Chinese translation by Yu Kuang-chung of *The Old Man and the Sea.*

——. *In Our Time.* Shanghai: Ch'en Kuang Publishing Co., 1949. Chinese translation by Ma Yen-hsiang of "Indian Camp," "The Doctor and the Doctor's Wife," "The End of Something," "The Three Day Blow," "The Battler," "A Very Short Story," "Soldier's Home," "The Revolutionist," "Mr. and Mrs. Elliot," "Cat in the Rain," "Out of Season," "Cross Country Snow," "My Old Man," "Big Two-Hearted River," and "L'Envoi."

——. *In Our Time.* Taipei: I-Kuang Publishing Co., 1962. Chinese translation by Tung I-hsin.

——. *Islands in the Stream.* New York, Toronto, London: Bantam Books, 1971. Paperback edition with cover in green, lettered in yellow and white; line on front cover, reading upwards: 'Q4905 *1.25* A BANTAM EXPORT EDITION'.

——. *Islas en el golfo.* Madrid: El Libro de Bolsillo/Alianza Editorial; Buenos Aires: Emecé Editores, 1972. Spanish translation by Marta

Isabel Gustavino and Héctor Quesada Zapiola of *Islands in the Stream.*

—— *Men Without Women.* Taipei: Wen-Hsing, 1965. Chinese translation.

—— *Meesterwerken van Hemingway: En de zon gaat op . . ., Afscheid van de wapenen, Hebben en niet hebben.* Amsterdam: Uitgeverij Contact, 1970. Dutch translation by W. A. Fick-Lugten (1949), Katja Vranken (1958), and H. W. J: Schaap (1966) of *The Sun Also Rises, A Farewell to Arms,* and *To Have and Have Not.*

—— *Na eches kai na mēn echēs.* Athens: Korali, Ekdotikes Epharmoges, 1968. Greek translation by Dimitris P. Kostelenos of *To Have and Have Not.*

—— *Nick Adams.* Buenos Aires: Emecé Editores, 1974. Spanish translation by Rolando Costa Picazo of *The Nick Adams Stories.*

—— *Las nieves del Kilimanjaro: Novela.* Barcelona: Luis de Caralt-/Plaza & Janés, S. A. Editores, 1971. Spanish translation (translator unidentified) of 15 short stories; bound in dark blue leather.

—— *The Old Man and the Sea.* Hong Kong: Chung-I, 1952. Chinese translation by Fan Ssu-p'ing.

—— *The Old Man and the Sea.* Kaohsiung: Shih-Sui, 1953. Chinese translation by Hsin Yüan.

—— *The Old Man and the Sea.* Hong Kong: Chung-I, 1955. Chinese translation by Chang Ai-ling.

—— *The Old Man and the Sea.* Taipei County, Chung-Ho Township: Hsüan-Feng Publishing Co., 1956. Chinese translation by Ling Yün.

—— *The Old Man and the Sea.* Kaohsiung: Ta-Hsiang Book Co., 1964. Chinese translation by Lü Chin-hui.

—— *The Old Man and the Sea.* Singapore: Shih-Chieh Bookstore, 1969; Hong Kong: Ying-yü Publishing Co., 1969. Chinese bilingual translation by Liu Yen-chiao.

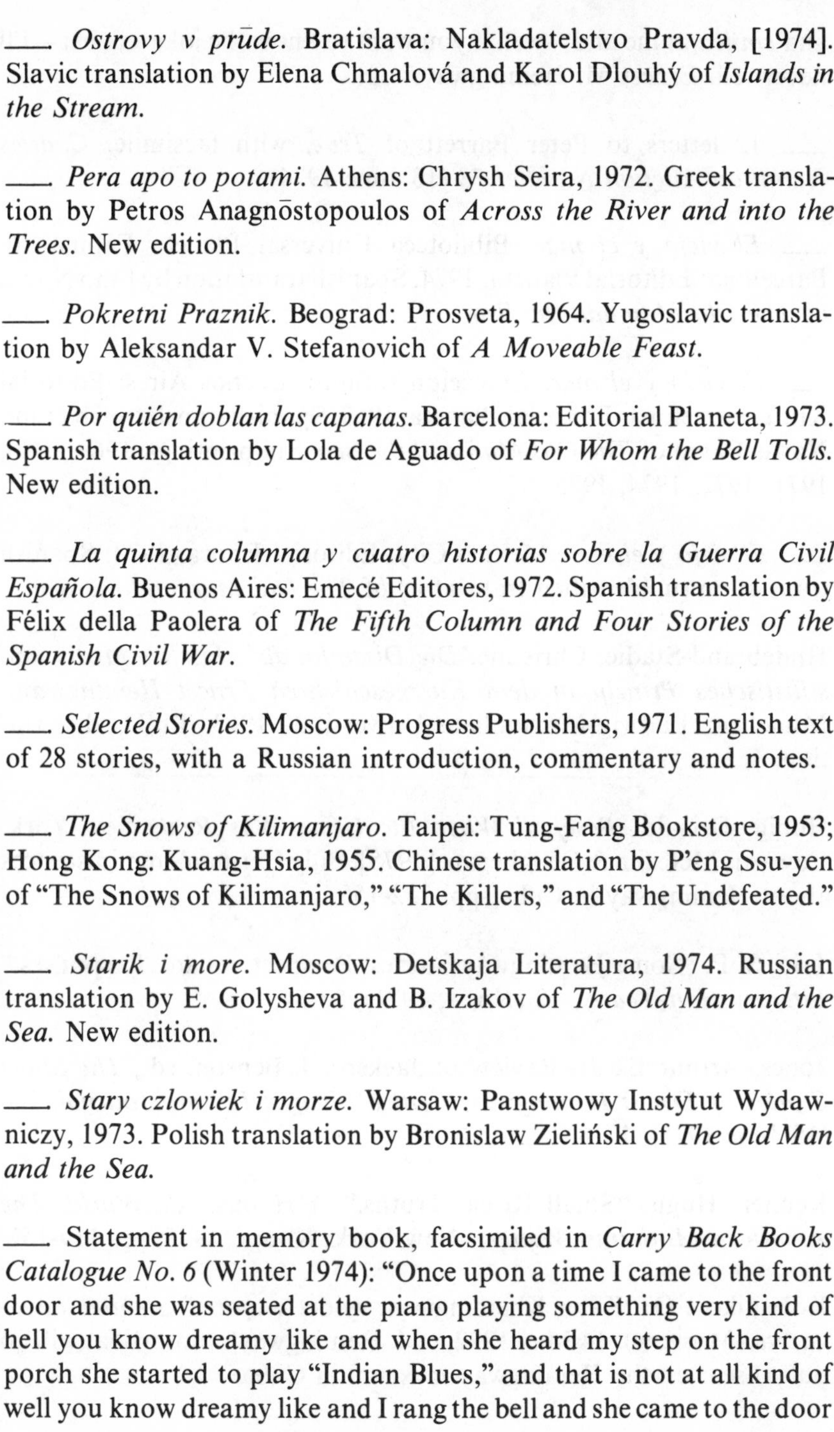

——— *Ostrovy v prūde.* Bratislava: Nakladatelstvo Pravda, [1974]. Slavic translation by Elena Chmalová and Karol Dlouhý of *Islands in the Stream.*

——— *Pera apo to potami.* Athens: Chrysh Seira, 1972. Greek translation by Petros Anagnōstopoulos of *Across the River and into the Trees.* New edition.

——— *Pokretni Praznik.* Beograd: Prosveta, 1964. Yugoslavic translation by Aleksandar V. Stefanovich of *A Moveable Feast.*

——— *Por quién doblan las capanas.* Barcelona: Editorial Planeta, 1973. Spanish translation by Lola de Aguado of *For Whom the Bell Tolls.* New edition.

——— *La quinta columna y cuatro historias sobre la Guerra Civil Española.* Buenos Aires: Emecé Editores, 1972. Spanish translation by Félix della Paolera of *The Fifth Column and Four Stories of the Spanish Civil War.*

——— *Selected Stories.* Moscow: Progress Publishers, 1971. English text of 28 stories, with a Russian introduction, commentary and notes.

——— *The Snows of Kilimanjaro.* Taipei: Tung-Fang Bookstore, 1953; Hong Kong: Kuang-Hsia, 1955. Chinese translation by P'eng Ssu-yen of "The Snows of Kilimanjaro," "The Killers," and "The Undefeated."

——— *Starik i more.* Moscow: Detskaja Literatura, 1974. Russian translation by E. Golysheva and B. Izakov of *The Old Man and the Sea.* New edition.

——— *Stary czlowiek i morze.* Warsaw: Panstwowy Instytut Wydawniczy, 1973. Polish translation by Bronislaw Zieliński of *The Old Man and the Sea.*

——— Statement in memory book, facsimiled in *Carry Back Books Catalogue No. 6* (Winter 1974): "Once upon a time I came to the front door and she was seated at the piano playing something very kind of hell you know dreamy like and when she heard my step on the front porch she started to play "Indian Blues," and that is not at all kind of well you know dreamy like and I rang the bell and she came to the door and *smiled* at me and—well if you want to know the joke ask her—I'll never tell. Ernest M. Hemingway."

____ 12 letters to Peter Barrett of *True,* with facsimile. *Charles Hamilton Auction Number 78* (13 June 1974).

____ *El viejo y el mar.* Biblioteca Universal Planeta Fábula 36. Barcelona: Editorial Planeta, 1974. Spanish translation by Lino Novas of *The Old Man and the Sea.*

____ *El viejo y el mar.* Coleccion Infinito. Buenos Aires: Editorial Kraft; Barcelona: Editorial Planeta, 1969. Spanish translation by Lino Novas Calvo of *The Old Man and the Sea.* Six printings: 1969, 1970, 1971, 1972, 1974, 1975.

____ *El viejo y el mar.* Mexico City: Editorial Epoca, 1973. Spanish translation (unidentified translator) of *The Old Man and the Sea.*

Hildebrand-Stadie, Christine. *Die Disziplin als ethisches Motiv und stilistisches Prinzip in dem Kurzgeschichten Ernest Hemingways.* München: Ludwig-Maximilians-Universität, 1963. Ph.D. dissertation.

Honig, Donald. *Baseball When the Grass Was Real.* New York: Coward, McCann & Geoghegan, [1975]. Billy Herman's reminiscences about Hemingway in Cuba, pp. 152-155.

Jain, S. P. "Some Hemingway Stories: Perspectives and Responses," *Literary Half-Yearly,* 12 (No. 1, 1971), 53-64.

Jones, Arthur E., Jr. Review of Jackson J. Benson, ed., *The Short Stories of Ernest Hemingway: Critical Essays, Library Journal,* 100 (15 June 1975), 1218.

Kenner, Hugh. "Small Ritual Truths," *A Homemade World: The American Modernist Writers.* New York: Knopf, 1975, pp. 119-157.

Kolesnikov, O. "Kater Khemingueya vyidet v more," *Stroitel 'naya-gazeta* (Moscow), 14 May 1972, p. 4. Hemingway's motorboat will go out to sea: on the Hemingway museum in Cuba.

Korn, Gary Alan. "Hemingway's Women—Broken and Unbreakable," *Masters Abstracts,* 12 (December 1974), 431. MA thesis, Adelphi University, 1974.

Kromi, Edythe Darlene. "Hemingway and the Aristotelian Tragedy," *Masters Abstracts,* 12 (December 1974), 431. MA thesis, North Texas State University, 1974.

Leigh, David J., S. J. *"In Our Time:* The inter-chapters as Structural Guides to a Psychological Pattern," *Studies in Short Fiction,* 12 (Winter 1975), 1-8.

Lewis, Margaret Calien. "Ernest Hemingway's *The Spanish War:* Dispatches from Spain 1937-1938," *Masters Abstracts,* 8 (September 1970), 127. MA thesis, University of Louisville, 1969.

Lonie, Charles Anthony. "Accumulations of Silence: Survivor Psychology in Vonnegut, Twain, and Hemingway," *Dissertation Abstracts International,* 35 (June 1975), 7871-A. Ph.D. dissertation, University of Minnesota, 1974. 288 pp.

Losada Duran, José. Critical Views About the Symbolism in *The Old Man and the Sea.* MA thesis, Salamanca, 1972.

Mansell, Darrel. "The Computer Goes Fishing," *Dartmouth Alumni Magazine,* 68 (September 1975), 19-21. On *The Old Man and the Sea.*

Mendel'son, M. Afterword to Vol. 2 of Lettish 5-Volume Translation of Hemingway's Collected Works. Riga: Liesma, 1972.

Monteiro, George. "The Education of Ernest Hemingway," *American Studies,* 8 (April 1974), 91-99.

Morris, Lewis Randolph. "Philosophical Concepts in American Short Stories," *Dissertation Abstracts International,* 33 (1972), 1692-A. Ph.D. dissertation, Howard University, 1971.

Murray, D. M., Chan Wai-heung, and Samuel Huang. "A Checklist of Chinese Translations of American Literature," *American Book Collector,* 22 (March-April 1972), 15-37.

Myers, Marshall. "A Tagememic Analysis of Hemingway's 'A Very Short Story.' " Daniel G. Hays and Donald M. Lance, eds. *From Soundstream to Discourse: Papers of the 1971 Mid-America Linguistic Conference.* Columbia: University of Missouri, 1972, pp. 158-166.

Parker, Ken. "Michigan Scenes Set 'Papa' on Literary Path," *The Detroit News,* 12 October 1975, 5-H.

Ratliff, Rick. "In Key West, A Friend Recalls Hemingway," *Miami Herald* (9 November 1975), G 1-2. Interview with Charles Thompson.

Richards, Robert F. "Hemingway and Stevens' 'Poetry of Extraordinary Actuality,' " *Descant,* 17 (Summer 1973), 46-48.

Rouse, Blair. Review of Robert O. Stephens, *Hemingway's Non-Fiction: The Public Voice, Style,* 6 (No. 2, 1972), 207-211.

Rovit, Earl. *Ernest Hemingway.* Buenos Aires: Compañia General Fabril Editora, 1971. 245 pp. Spanish translation by Alicia McGaw.

Ryan, Frank, Frank Leo. "Ernest Hemingway's Literary Reputation in America 1924-1966," *Dissertation Abstracts International*, 36 (August 1975), 893-A-894-A. Ph.D. dissertation, The Catholic University of America, 1975.

Sachs, Lisbeth J., and Bernard H. Stern. "The Little Preoedipal Boy in Papa Hemingway and How He Created His Artistry," *Costerus,* 1 (1972), 221-240.

Sequeira, Isaac. Review of *Islands in the Stream, IJAS Reviews,* #2 (June 1972), 4-5.

Shepherd, Allen. "Hemingway's 'An Alpine Idyll' and Faulkner's 'Mistral,' " *University of Portland Review,* 25 (Fall 1973), 63-68.

Simonov, K. Afterword to Lithuanian translation of *For Whom the Bell Tolls.* Vil'nyus; Vaga, 1972.

Singer, Kurt. *Ernest Hemingway: Su vida y sus amores.* Mexico City: Editorial Diana, 1961. 248 pp. Spanish translation by Carlos Barrera.

Slavutych, Yar. "Ernest Hemingway in Ukrainian Literature," Wolodymyr T. Zyla and Wendell M. Aycock, eds. *Proceedings of the*

Comparative Literature, Vol. 5, *Modern American Fiction: Insights and Foreign Lights.* Texas Technical University, 27-28 January 1972, pp. 67-76.

Smith, Leverett T., Jr. *The American Dream and the National Game.* Bowling Green: Bowling Green University Popular Press, 1975. Hemingway and sport.

Startsev, A. *Ot Uitmena do Khemingueya.* Moscow: Sovetskii Pisatel', 1972. From Whitman to Hemingway.

Stead, Alistair. Review of Robert O. Stephens, *Hemingway's Non-Fiction: The Public Voice, Notes and Queries,* n.s. 19 (1972), 77-78.

Stephens, Robert O. Review of Matthew J. Bruccoli, *Ernest Hemingway's Apprenticeship: Oak Park 1916-1917, Resources for American Literary Study,* 2 (Spring 1972), 115-116.

——. Review of Matthew J. Bruccoli and C. E. Frazer Clark, Jr., *Hemingway at Auction 1930-1973, Resources for American Literary Study,* 5 (Spring 1975), 113-115.

Stewart, Donald Ogden. *By a Stroke of Luck!* New York: Paddington Press, [1975]. Autobiography by Bill Gorton.

Strode, Hudson. *The Eleventh House: Memoirs.* New York and London: Harcourt Brace Jovanovich, 1975, pp. 91, 93, 167-171, 175. Includes conversation with and letter from Hemingway to Strode, Havana, 8 October 1934, p. 170.

Sturua, Mèlor. "Rasprodazha pisem Kheminguèya," *Literturnaya Gazeta* (Moscow), 22 March 1972, p. 15.

Sutherland, Fraser. "Hemingway and Callaghan," *Canadian Literature,* 53 (1972), 8-17.

Thomas, Phil. "Brother Ernie," *The Detroit News* [and other Associated Press papers], 13 July 1975, p. 2-C. Review of Madelaine Hemingway Miller, *Ernie: Hemingway's Sister "Sunny" Remembers.*

Wagner, Linda W. Review of J. Bakker, *Ernest Hemingway: The Artist as Man of Action;* Sheldon Norman Grebstein, *Hemingway's*

Craft; and Wayne E. Kvam, *Hemingway in Germany, Journal of Modern Literature,* 4 (November 1974), 345-347.

___ Review of *Fitzgerald/Hemingway Annual 1973* and José Luis Castillo-Puche, *Hemingway in Spain, Modern Fiction Studies,* 21 (Summer 1975), 287-289.

___ "The Marinating of *For Whom the Bell Tolls,*" *Journal of Modern Literature,* 2 (November 1972), 533-546.

Wallack, John P. "The 'Old Man' Remembers Hemingway," *Genesis,* 1 (August 1973), 22-24, 45, 118.

Warner, S. D. "Hemingway's *The Old Man and the Sea,*" *The Explicator,* 33 (October 1974), 9.

Weeks, Lewis E., Jr. "Two Types of Tension: Art vs. Campcraft in Hemingway's 'Big Two-Hearted River,' " *Studies in Short Fiction,* 11 (Fall 1974), 433-434.

Weeks, Robert P. Review of Bertram D. Sarason, *Hemingway and the Sun Set,* and Emily Stipes Watts, *Ernest Hemingway and the Arts, Modern Fiction Studies,* 18 (1972), 595-598.

White, William. "Hemingway's Sister Reveals New Facets," *The Oakland Press* (Pontiac, Michigan), 3 November 1975, p. D-10. Review of Madelaine Hemingway Miller, *Ernie: Hemingway's Sister "Sunny" Remembers.*

Williams, G. "Programming Papa," *Science Digest,* 77 (June 1975), 56-57.

Winkler, Reinhold. *Lyrische Elemente in den Kurzgeschichten Ernest Hemingways: Eine Untersuchung der Textstruktur.* Nürnberg: Friedrich-Alexander-Universität zu Erlangen-Nürnberg [Erlangen: Josef Hogl], 1967.

Young, Philip. Review of *Ernie, New York Times Book Review,* 27 April 1975, 16, 18.

Oakland University

MARGARET M. DUGGAN

General Checklist

Bruccoli, Matthew J. *The O'Hara Concern A Biography of John O'Hara.* New York: Random House, 1975. Significant mention of FSF and EH.

Cheney, Anne. *Millay in Greenwich Village.* University, Ala.: University of Alabama Press, 1975.

Greenfeld, Howard. *They Came to Paris.* New York: Crown, 1975. Account of expatriate life and works for juveniles.

Guiles, Fred Lawrence. *Hanging on in Paradise.* New York: McGraw-Hill, 1975. Hollywood chronicle includes chapter on FSF and considerable mention of EH.

Hobhouse, Janet. *Everybody Who Was Anybody A Biography of Gertrude Stein.* New York: Putnam, 1975.

Marx, Samuel. *Mayer and Thalberg.* New York: Random House, 1975. Some mention of FSF.

Salloch, Roger. "Ernest & Scott in Paris," *New York Times* (5 October 1975), Section 10-1, 14.

Stewart, Donald Ogden. *By a Stroke of Luck! An Autobiography.* London & New York: Paddington Press Ltd., 1975. Significant mention of FSF and EH.

Woodress, James. *American Fiction, 1900-1950 A Guide to Information Sources,* Vol. 1. Detroit: Gale Research Company, 1974. Includes chapters on FSF and EH.

University of South Carolina

Reviews

C. E. FRAZER CLARK, JR.

Supplement to Ernest Hemingway: A Comprehensive Bibliography.

Audre Hanneman.

Princeton, N.J.: Princeton University Press, 1975. $20.00.

In her *Supplement,* Miss Hanneman deals with work by and about Ernest Hemingway published between 1966 and 1975, incorporates material omitted from the first volume, and provides new information about material previously described. The format and the section classifications established in the first volume have been maintained with the prefix S- used in numbering entries in the *Supplement* to distinguish them from entries in the first volume of the bibliography. However, care will have to be taken in making reference to Hanneman entries since the entry numbers for a given title in Section A of the first volume and the *Supplement* do not correspond. For example, "the various editions of *The Old Man and the Sea* are numbered and lettered A24A to A24E [in the first volume, while in the *Supplement*] they are S-A9F to S-A9H." Also, Sections B through H in the *Supplement* begin again with the number 1, so that there is a B1 and an S-B1, etc., making the use of the supplement prefix S- imperative to avoid confusion.

The most significant fact revealed by the *Supplement* is the extent of continued and growing interest in Hemingway studies. As Miss Hanneman points out, "It is interesting to note that the number of principal books on Hemingway has more than doubled in the last eight years." Twenty-one principal works on Hemingway were published between 1931 and 1966; the *Supplement* lists twenty-five published between 1966 and 1974. A noticeable increase in doctoral dissertations, critical essays, and textual studies is evident. Contributing to this interest is the amount of important new or recovered Hemingway writings published during the last eight years: *By-Line: Ernest Hemingway, The Fifth Column and Four Stories of the Spanish Civil War, Islands in the Stream, The Nick Adams Stories, Ernest Hemingway, Cub Reporter: Kansas City Star Stories, Ernest Hemingway's Apprenticeship: Oak Park, 1916-1917,* and the material located in *Ernest Hemingway: A Life Story, Hemingway at Auction: 1930-1973,* and *The Fitzgerald/Hemingway Annual.* As a record of the last eight years, Hanneman's *Supplement* is not only invaluable, but, as prophesied by Charles Scribner, Jr. in his 1967 Foreword to the first volume, an inevitable act of Hemingway bibliography.

While scholars of bibliography can argue that Miss Hanneman may not use technical terms or describe a book with satisfactory precision, there is no question about the magnificent job she has done in searching out and compiling the overwhelming bibliographic record of Ernest Hemingway. In this respect, her work is a major accomplishment.

The chief limitation of the Hanneman bibliography, both in the first volume and in the *Supplement,* continues to be an inadequate index. The principal function of a comprehensive bibliography is to make easily accessible to a user information about which he is presumed to know considerably less than does the compiler; and the user should be able to get at whatever information he seeks with the only clues available to him. Full accessibility is particularly important in the case of an author like Hemingway whose publication history is so vast, spans so many international boundaries, and involves such a wide variety of media. Hanneman will unnecessarily frustrate or defeat users seeking publication information that should be easily accessible because the index was prepared with presumptions about the user's level of knowledge. For example, in her preface, Miss Hanneman refers to *Fact,* a monograph published in London (July 1938), as the "most notable omission" in the first volume of the bibliography. *Fact* is included in the *Supplement,* but there is no entry in the index under

Fact; to find *Fact* in the index the user has to know that it contains the NANA Spanish Civil War Dispatches (which appears in the index under "NANA . . .") or that the title given the material in *Fact* is "The Spanish War" (a title that also appears in the index). In other words, the user has to know what Hemingway's contribution to *Fact* is before he can locate *Fact.* The problem represented by the *Fact* example can be expanded if you consider the Part Three Appendix included in the first volume and the *Supplement* which is a "List of Newspapers and Periodicals Cited in Sections C and H." The titles listed are importatnt, but if you want to discover what Hemingway material appears in *Bifur,* the *Exile, This Quarter, Co-operative Commonwealth,* the *Golden Book Magazine* and a hundred more equally significant newspapers and periodicals, the index won't help you. There is no way you can find out what appears, for example, in *Bifur* (or the other titles) unless: A) you happen to know that it was published in 1929, in which case you can laboriously go through the Section C entries on a fishing expedition; or, B) you already know that *Bifur* prints a French translation of "Hills Like White Elephants," in which case you wouldn't need Hanneman in the first place. Consider the impossible task faced by the user who wants to track down in the first volume the entry for the classic Hemingway rarity, the *Co-operative Commonwealth;* although listed in the appendix, there is no reference given in the index to either the title or the first appearance of Hemingway's "Will You Let These Kiddies Miss Santa Claus?" Dealers, collectors, and scholars who want to quickly locate such simple but essential Hemingway bibliographical information as what Hemingway's contributions to *Esquire, Ken, Scribner's,* etc., were will not be able to do so with the present Hanneman index.

What makes the inaccessibility of Hanneman information so utterly frustrating to users familiar with both the first volume and the *Supplement* is the knowledge that what you are seeking is buried somewhere in the work. This inability to get at needed information must inevitably drive users to other sources of Hemingway bibliographical information in order to see Hanneman. Like unpublished scholarship, comprehensive bibliographies that conceal information do not serve scholars. Hanneman has accumulated an enormous and important amount of Hemingway publication information. It is unfortunate and unnecessary that this otherwise monumental work is in certain respects crippled by an inadequate index. We can hope that a proper index—or a supplementary index—will be forthcoming.

ROBERT F. LUCID

The Cruise of the Rolling Junk.
F. Scott Fitzgerald.
Bloomfield Hills, Mich. & Columbia, S.C.:
Bruccoli Clark, 1976. $25.00.

Because its publication actually does make available the last significant piece of Fitzgerald's uncollected work, *The Cruise of the Rolling Junk* will probably trigger a certain amount of reference to the bottom of the barrel. This is unfortunate, for it could delay some readers from experiencing the best piece of nonfictional narrative that Fitzgerald ever wrote.

Generically, the narrative fits in with "How to Live on $36,000 a Year," and "How to Live on Practically Nothing a Year." At least as good as the former and certainly much better than the latter, it is as close to a full-length autobiographical effort as Fitzgerald made outside of his fiction, and it throws itself into the scales as a kind of balance to the "Crack-Up" essays. Balance is not achieved, however, through the mere depiction of a gay and irresponsible pair, blind to the reversals which history had in store. On the contrary, *The Cruise* shows that as early as 1922 Fitzgerald was already able to effect a detachment from the first public identity he had been so eager to create.

The Scott and Zelda who tour from Connecticut to Alabama in an untourworthy car are zany enough, and the central design is firmly comic. But the comedy is achieved through narrative distancing, and the point of the story, all humor aside, is that the young couple once was impulsive and irresponsible and it nearly ruined them. Nearly, but not actually, and with this narrative Fitzgerald assumes the identity of the thoughtfully mature observer whose wild oats had been irrevocably sown. This came close to being the best profile he created during his public life: those other identities of the eager young fool, the glittering sophisticate, and the ruined profligate—all masks he fashioned for an audience itself voracious for as many identities as he could supply—were worn less successfully.

Especially compelling in the present narrative is the dimension of his picaresque illumination of the American landscape, dotted with gas station and garages which prove, if proof were needed, that the trap of Myrtle Wilson and her husband was not confined to Long Island. Compelling in an answerable way is the mode of travel, and Fitzgerald's use of the automobile, funny though it may be, is more than funny. Resonant with metaphor, it stands before us as a crucial way of coming to know that which demands knowing about America.

But the key to this short book's success is Fitzgerald's narrative identity. Not unlike Nick Carraway, he is a man on the other side of the narrative divide, intimately including the reader in residence there, where together they nourish themselves on spectacles of the disintegratingly unreliable vehicles of our technology, the folly of the young, and the wildness of the unexplored American night.

A richness of the book is the set of absurd photographs which accompanied the text in its original appearance in *Motor* magazine, depicting the young couple in various attitudes of distress. We view them now, of course, over a burnt and wasted distance unrequired of readers at the time, and as one holds the pictures up to the light of 1976 one is moved by the faces and the knowledge of what happened to them.

The best, the most moving face that Fitzgerald finally showed us in his career was that of the artist engaged in retrospective, generous understanding of the whole mess. That face appeared rarely: we saw it in "Afternoon of an Author" and in "Author's House," and seldom elsewhere outside the fiction. But one glimpses it in these pictures of two finally gallant people, as one sees in the narrative itself a poignantly American panorama, and it all recalls with great vividness the view from the turret at the end of "Author's House": "As far as your eye can see there is a river winding between green lawns and trees and purple buildings and red slums blended in by a merciful dusk. Even as they stand there the wind increases until it is a gale whistling . . . and blowing birds past them."

University of Pennsylvania

BENJAMIN B. DUNLAP

Notes on a Screenplay for F. Scott Fitzgerald's Tender Is the Night

Malcolm and Margerie Lowry.
Introduction by Paul Tiessen.

Bloomfield Hills, Mich. & Columbia, S.C.:
Bruccoli Clark, 1976. $25.00

In July 1949, two years after getting *Under the Volcano* into print, Malcolm and Margerie Lowry collaborated on a movie treatment of *Tender Is the Night*. By the following April their cinematic whim had grown into a 455-page screenplay of which Lowry wrote to his publisher, "we put our all, our everything in it." Christopher Isherwood, another novelist turned scriptwriter, declared the Lowrys' work a masterpiece: "I wait to see it filmed, of course—but equally I want to see your full script published with all your notes and comments." A quarter-century later the script has still appeared neither on screen nor in print, but the eighty pages of notes Lowry produced as epistolary arguments for the screenplay have now been published. The notes, together with a useful introduction by Paul Tiessen and a letter from Lowry to MGM producer Frank Taylor, comprise a tantalizing package—a jumble of garrulous, sometimes obsessive, often scintillating monologues designed to justify an unpublished script for an unproduced film: One hopes the horse can eventually be coaxed from its stable to join the cart.

But the notes may well be the best part of the venture, for what they reveal of the ill-fated script somewhat restores one's faith in the commercial wisdom of Hollywood. Which is not the same thing as endorsing Selznick's tawdry version of the book, a movie bad enough to confirm Fitzgerald's morose suspicion that film "was capable of reflecting only the tritest thought, the most obvious emotion." The script must speak for itself when it can, but the notes show Lowry at his most self-indulgently assured, exuberantly impelled by the recent completion of his script, optimistically emphatic about his extensions and interpretations of Fitzgerald. Though often convoluted in expression, the notes are less like the prefaces of Henry James than like random pages from Sir Thomas Browne or Robert Burton, to whom Lowry twice alludes. Energetic and idiosyncratic, full of alternative developments of what Lowry considers inchoate or non-cinematic in Fitzgerald's novel, the notes provide a sort of holographic criticism of the book. There are provocative flashes of perception—Dick Diver is compared to Lindbergh as an American adventurer, Fitzgerald to Conrad and Keats as novelist and poet, and *Tender Is the Night* to the tragi-comedies of Shakespeare. There is a brilliantly digressive defense of Fitzgerald's choice of title; and on the heels of Lowry's contention that this is "at bottom an incredibly religious book" is the related kicker that "preeminently it is tragic," a conviction underpinning the entire script: "the task would be in a film . . . to make Dick heroic in terms of fate—not to diminish him in terms of a social or psychological problem." In short, Lowry would like to subscribe to the classical dictum that a man's character is his fate, but not if his character is defined by facile Freudianism—much less if he becomes himself "a shyster alienist," as Fitzgerald suggested. The paradoxical result of Lowry's insistence on tragedy is that destiny rules the screen less by tragic flaw than by melodramatic circumstance.

Several of Lowry's alterations of detail can be explained if not applauded—the substitution of an auto crash for incest was necessitated by the Production Code, though the auto is unlikely to convey the recondite symbolism Lowry ascribes to it. Similarly, his corrected impressions of the English at play were prompted by a sense of fairness, though he contradicts Fitzgerald's own pronounced bias. But his most presumptuous revision, Dick's quasi-suicidal death by shipwreck, is not only arrant misrepresentation of the author's intention but, in a Hollywood infamous for imposing happy endings, an heroically upbeat resolution that ignores what Lowry elsewhere recognizes as "something like the beginning of an ironic philosophical system" in Fitzgerald's work. Lowry unpersuasively argues that "a spectacular error such as Dick's deserves a more spectacular ending" than the book allows. In *Under the Volcano* Firmin is dispatched with an ignominious *nunc dimittis,* but Lowry summons Nietzsche, Ortega y Gasset, and Fitzgerald himself to plump for Dick's more grandiloquent exit. Or rather, he quotes Diver's "I want it to die violently, not just fade out sentimentally" to counter Fitzgerald's "I wanted to make Dr. Diver fade out in the end as a shyster alienist." Perhaps Lowry wanted to play with alternatives to Quauhnahuac and Dollarton, but the point of Fitzgerald's conclusion is that Dick's self-desertion precludes shipping out with Shelley on the *Ariel* or Hart Crane on the *Orizaba.* It is one thing for Helen Wales to commit suicide at sea in "Cosmopolitan" [Fitzgerald's screenplay for "Babylon Revisited"], but for Diver (the name assumes new irony in this context) his obscurely drawn-out purgatory in the American hinterlands is a far more terrible and appropriate "karmic involvement" (the phrase is Lowry's) than the "Dionysian tragedy" the script proposes.

Midway through his "three years' heartbreak" of seeking a producer, Lowry conceded there may have been "an overreaching at the end" of his screenplay; and two years later he admitted "part of the ending is probably tripe." But the error is typical of an irrepressible tendency in Lowry's work, here as elsewhere: he ransacked Fitzgerald's novel with the same cabalistic intensity with which he interpreted his own experience, and in the end he appropriated and transformed what he described so that it became his experience, no longer Fitzgerald's. That is, after all, the law of Hollywood; and Lowry, with the best of intentions, was claim-jumping with the rest. Significantly, he later squeezed much of his script's conclusion into an autobiographical story, "Through the Panama"—movies, the ship's-engine syncopation of "Frères Jacques," the neoplatonic symbolism, even a reference to Fitzgerald as "the last Laocoön."

Despite his conviction that film was a major influence on his work, Lowry's notes frequently betray trite or uninformed notions of film technique. Certainly there is little evidence of the "purely cinematic" conception praised by Frank Taylor; rather, Lowry's best ideas derive from an instinctive theoretical understanding of what *ought* to work on the screen. The ironic use of "Japanese Sandman" as a theme song requires the sort of verbal attention more easily secured on the page, but its repetition with different modes of orchestration at crucial points in the movie is a sophisticated idea. The New York City montage—

another major addition to the novel, occurring as Dick returns from his father's funeral—is, as literal exposition, a hackneyed device. But Lowry's intention is also expressionistic:

> the film needs relating to the *world,* as does Nicole's illness to some of its outward manifestations in her indigenous world. . . . as we once went into Nicole's mind, so now we go into the divided mind of the world of which America is the symbol and coefficient. . . . the obvious danger would be to draw a too direct contrast between the insanity within and that without: writers love to do this, but let's make it perpendicular here rather than lateral. . . .

Lowry's articulation of his idea in terms of perpendicular and lateral imagery anticipates by three years Maya Deren's similar remarks in her celebrated encounter with Dylan Thomas and Arthur Miller at the Cinema 16 symposium; and he evidently knew as well as she what the terms implied:

> This, then, is the pay-off of the thing psychologically, and any psychiatrist of poetic understanding will see what we have done. Instead of going in Nicole's mind again, this time when she cracked up we have plunged into the psyche—into the unconscious—of America itself. . . .

As he had in *Under the Volcano,* Lowry emphasizes the parallel deterioration of the central character and the culture he represents. Doubtless he also detected parallels between his own career and Fitzgerald's, and in their respective relationships to their work. Since Lowry rarely brought any project to completion, it is intriguing that he considered *Tender Is the Night* an inchoate masterpiece: "it looks very much as though Fitzgerald jettisoned half the deck cargo," he wrote, with Fitzgerald's own indecision about the novel's structure in mind, "and woke up too late to the fact that he'd jettisoned the most valuable part: heroically, though with a pronounced list, he makes port with his residue of lumber intact, and the machinery more or less undamaged below: but from the main deck Cleopatra's Needle has mysteriously gone overboard." That sentence is characteristic of what Lowry is attempting in these notes and, presumably, in his script. Even if we permit him to shanghai Fitzgerald's book, there has to be some limit to the cabalistic indignities he can heap upon it—and Cleopatra's Needle is simply beyond the limit. Fitzgerald was full of profundities, but they weren't to be found in the rubbish heaps of hermetic philosophy where Lowry went poking after his.

Nevertheless, these notes offer valuable insights into Lowry's own stylistic development. As he finished the screenplay, Lowry noted in a letter to Taylor that "many of our writers [of movie scripts] cannot think visually and aurally, if they could the sacrifice of words would not seem so great. These writers cannot make you see and hear in their novels either." As Fitzgerald had used his film work to evolve stylistic devices for *The Last Tycoon,* Lowry seems to have used his script and its notes to explore the implications of techniques already employed in *Under the Volcano.* Like Joyce, who recognized affinities between his own work and that of Eisenstein, Lowry's essentially symbolist aesthetic required an ambiguous manipulation of visual and audial detail, evoked as vividly as language would permit. "The medium of the movies is physical reality as such," Erwin Panofsky had written in the year *Tender Is the Night* was published; but Lowry, a movie-goer who was also a student of Joyce and the Cabala, further perceived that film tends to adumbrate the conceptual as literature adumbrates the concrete:

> the value of objects and of people in relation to them, one assumes, is a hundredfold greater on the screen than in a book: what would be impossibly crude in a novel, Barban's pipe, his uniform, because they are fully realised—ten pages of condensed naturalistic technique at a blow each time they appear—can be even profound in a film.

Hence Lowry's efforts to adapt the effects, and where possible the techniques, of film to literature without crudities of prolonged description. And thus, by studying Lowry's transformation of novel into film, one can better comprehend how film contributed to his novels.

It would seem from these notes upon his screenplay, however, that Lowry was not the man to translate *Tender Is the Night* for the screen. Perhaps, as Edward Murray has suggested, Antonioni should do it—Fitzgerald is the Italian director's favorite author, and many an admirer of the novel was grateful to find it in Monica Vitti's luggage in *L'Avventura.* As for Lowry's career as a screenwriter, he continued to hope something might come of his abortive efforts. In a postscript to his notes, he offered Taylor a high-spirited confession: "it seems to us we've been awfully bloody sanctimonious in places"—which is true. And two years later, with somewhat more humility, he trusted Joseph Mankiewicz would "overlook any possible tangential pretentiousness in the film." And still later, as he watched his "good and noble" project spiral down the Hollywood drain, he begged Harold Matson to ask Selznick for another crack at the book. But Ivan Moffat got it, and Henry King, who also directed pedestrian adaptations of *The Sun Also Rises* and "The Snows of Kilimanjaro." Malcolm Lowry's dust continues to settle, but for the present these notes are all we have to honor his "deep instinct that what we did was too good to be written off, Hollywood or no Hollywood." For that we must be grateful.

University of South Carolina

MARGARET M. DUGGAN

The Real F. Scott Fitzgerald Thirty-Five Years Later.
Sheilah Graham.
New York: Grosset & Dunlap, 1976. $8.95.

Promises of sensational revelations and other such book-hawking hype have long been the staple of dust-jacket copy, especially for the genre of the personal memoir. The jacket of *The Real F. Scott Fitzgerald* is, in view of Miss Graham's avowed concern for respectability, ironically no exception. The reader's interest is titillated with portents of suicide attempts, "even threats of murder," and "the intimate details" of Fitzgerald's past that "have never been revealed to any other biographer." In her third, latest, and, with luck, last retelling of her three-and-a-half-year sojourn with Fitzgerald, Miss Graham's book eventually overreaches itself less through lack of morals than through lack of taste.

If *Beloved Infidel* was conceived expressly to refute the Schulberg and Mizener portraits of Fitzgerald as a drunken and dying man, then, *The Real F. Scott Fitzgerald* seems to have been born of Miss Graham's desire to reinstate her own reputation. Threaded throughout her discussion are the testimonies of Scottie Fitzgerald Smith, Edmund Wilson, the Murphys, and others as to her devotion and saving influence on Fitzgerald during those last critical and precious days in Hollywood Captivity. But, without diminishing the truth of these commendations, the cumulative effect of such pointedly self-serving comments is to undercut the very emotions they were originally to inspire. She is at once and everywhere eager to dispel both the notion of herself as either Fitzgerald's "nurse" (as Aaron Latham would have it) or his "mistress" (as Webster would have it). The emphasis of the book is clearly less on adding materially to an expanded insight into the real Fitzgerald than it is on a marked, and rather defensive, reply to *all* other versions of their relationship—including, curiously, her own previous books. This book does little save to provide, as promised, more and more explicitly expressed "intimate details." The major events of their life together as well as the tenor of his character have been amply treated before by Miss Graham. This effort is not so much new as graphic in content.

While it is very apparent that her discussion of the different phases of Fitzgerald's life has incorporated the work of other biographers and critics, it is often impossible to isolate what Miss Graham knew then from what she has only since learned. Reference sources are rare or vague if not altogether non-existent. Indeed, the key to her treatment of the real Fitzgerald is contained in the telling subtitle: THIRTY-FIVE YEARS LATER. This point is not a quibble for the main justification for this "new" version is reputedly Miss Graham's mature perspective, an ability now to render "the man as he really was—the bad as well as the good, the cruel . . . the kind, the modest, the vulgar, the ruthless, the tender." Yet the fact remains that in these succeeding thirty-five years Miss Graham's recollections, served up to the reader as they are with all the deceptive immediacy of last week's gossip column, have been profoundly colored, if not adulterated, not only by the evaluation of others but also by her own sense of personal accomplishment: her emergence from a dependent apprentice to a highly independent woman. In place of the often unguarded, but by no means uncritical, presentation of Fitzgerald in the earlier books, one finds rhetorical speculations on Fitzgerald's true motivations and latter-day qualifications of her first impressions/perceptions. As a consequence any sense of the real Sheilah Graham circa 1937-40 is lost as well along with the probable dynamics of their relationship. To state the case quite bluntly, Miss Graham's assessment of Fitzgerald the man *today* is less intrinsically signficant than the less tutored and tempered observations of *Beloved Infidel* and *College of One.*

Her comments on *The Last Tycoon,* its composition, origins, and real-life counterparts are valuable and do include largely fresh rather than reworked material. The book is, with all its flaws, notable—and collectable—because of the previously unpublished Fitzgerald letters as well as the facsimile of Miss Graham's short story, "Not in the Script," that bears Fitzgerald's holograph revisions. An investigation of the facsimile clearly shows Fitzgerald's talent as an editor—with very few changes the tone and focus of the story is brought into higher relief. Aside from simple choices of diction and paring down of lengthy phrases, Fitzgerald deletes most of the bald editorial comment by the narrator so that the final resolution of the narrator's point of view is only crystallized in the closing sentences. Also included in an appendix is the fragment of a play titled "Dame Rumor" on which Miss Graham and Fitzgerald planned to collaborate; however, we do not have a facsimile to make clear their respective contributions. Miss Graham explains that she was to write the first draft which Fitzgerald would revise, but there is no detailed description of the nature of his revisions given nor any indication of his appraisal save that the play was never finished because he felt that "the material wasn't really good enough."

In trying to account for Fitzgerald's enduring attraction to her, Miss Graham notes with some pleasure the aspirations and affinities she shares with Jay Gatsby. But Gatsby—in his simplicity—thought that money alone would gain his admission into the socially acceptable world of the Buchanans; Miss Graham—in her sophistication—ought to know only too well that such things as security and respectability, for which she has "always longed," have no price.

University of South Carolina

BERTRAM D. SARASON

Published in Paris
American and British Writers, Printers, and Publishers in Paris, 1920-1939.
Hugh Ford.

New York: Macmillan, 1975. $14.95.

To those who dream of writing the definitive work on the 20s Hugh Ford's new book, *Published in Paris,* may appear to dash their visions; for the subtitle, *American and British Writers, Printers, and Publishers in Paris, 1920-1939,* betokens the comprehensive. The reader is left with little doubt that a vast amount of work has gone into this book. But Ford's focus is primarily on the publishers, those who put out limited editions of reprints and of new writers that were not likely to be published elsewhere. Ford's work then, centers around pivotal people: Sylvia Beach, Robert McAlmon, Bill Bird, Edward Titus, the Crosbys, Jack Kahane, Nancy Cunard, and Barbara Harrison—to name the foremost. We are given some biography of each publisher, a little about the printer, something about the authors published, sometimes summaries of their books, and, when available, the contemporary reviews. Physical descriptions of books are consistently presented: the amount of the edition, the paper used, the type selected by the printer, and details of the art work. In all, we are given a vast range of information, and for those of us knowledgeable about the era of the young Fitzgerald and Hemingway and the decade beyond that, for those who were already familiar with the Contact Publishing Company and The Three Mountains Press, our knowledge of the extraordinary publishers of those times is vastly augmented.

Ordinarily this type of book would be published by a university press, and, I suppose, Macmillan is to be congratulated on this undertaking. If the book is aimed at the general public, as presumably it is, then certain sacrifices evidently have had to be made. The book is filled with quotations which are left unannotated. Certain topics, like homosexuality, are toned down. When, for example, we are told that the marriage of Bryher and Bob McAlmon was on the rocks, this news is offered as if we were reading about Liz and Richard Burton or Sonny and Cher. Topics of interest to the student of the 20s, perhaps too heavy for the average reader, are excluded. The pivotal publishers, just about every one of them, are depicted as motivated by a single-minded virtue: to get the best writers published in defiance of the censors. Nor is that solitary virtue evoked with much passion. The book is bland, almost all bland exposition. Except in the section on Jack Kahane, the human voices are so few that when we hear Helena Rubinstein (Mrs. Edward Titus) explode against her husband's star writers, "To me, they were meshugga . . . and I always had to pay for their meals!" that voice startles with the surprise of a filibuster from a Trappist with good references.

This book which is frequently about censorship has more earmarks of censorship probably exercised by Macmillan's sales manager or the firm's junior editors. We miss, for example, the usual author's introduction in which he tells us what novelty we are to expect. Accordingly, one has to guess whether or not Mr. Ford has reported anything new. My guess is that he has, but properly to make such a judgment would require being deeply versed in every publisher from 1920 to 1939 and the thirty major authors listed on the book jacket which also tells us that there are "dozens more." Some of the material has a familiar ring. The introductory chapter about Sylvia Beach is unquestionably much in debt to her *Shakespeare & Company.* Information about Bird and McAlmon recall passages in Carlos Baker's *Ernest Hemingway A Life Story* and Bryher's *The Heart of Artemis: A Writer's Memoirs.* Sections on Jack Kahane, particularly those relative to his publishing Henry Miller, echo George Wickes' *Americans in Paris.* Eight pages of acknowledgements and bibliography toward the end of the book suggest that Mr. Ford has drawn on materials from a wide variety of sources. But if there were nothing original in this volume, Mr. Ford has to be praised for the enormous job of organization of such materials. He presents them—perhaps he had to present them—with detachment. The anonymous dreamer mentioned in my opening sentence might have more to say about the 20s.

He might want to have pointed out that our conventional view of the 20s needs revision. By the conventional view I refer, of course, to the story of the exodus of painters, poets, critics, intellectuals, and malcontents who set out for Paris in the early 1920s to seek a more creative mileu. Harold Stearns was the prototype. He had edited one book on what was wrong with America and published another. Fictionalized by Hemingway, he was transmuted into one of the Lost Generation for whose blight somehow World War II was responsible. Of course, Hemingway's version of expatriate existence was not the only one. For John Dos Passos those days in Paris could be included under the banner of "The Best Times." There were writers seeking franker realism, there were others attempting experiments in language. "Don't be conventional" was the maxim of the day, but as Mr. Ford's work makes evident, unconventionality began before World War II and before the arrival of the bibulous or traumatized expatriates. Gertrude Stein's *Three Lives* had been published in 1909 and the 1913 Armory Show (remembered today chiefly for Duchamp's *Nude Descending A Staircase*) started Bob Brown in the direction of experimenting with language.

Was the flight of the expatriates merely one of escaping from the censors? The prosecution of the *Little Review* for its publication of portions of *Ulysses* certainly defined the perils of creative expression but there were other areas of unofficial censorship for which there is considerable documentation. At the turn of the century *Beverley of Graustark* headed the best-seller list, and the middle-European romance (so successfully satirized in *Prater Violet*) established the escapist taste of the American reading public. Subsequent sentimentalism and poetic justice guaranteed many a publisher a pretty profit, and Harold Bell Wright was often singled out by Sherwood Anderson and Mencken for literary dishonesty. So it was against public taste and not merely official censorship that serious writers of the 20s sought new publishers. Those publishers selected by Mr. Ford served not one, therefore, but a duality of purpose.

It might be argued that a change of purpose took place at the close of the 20s when the Depression drove many of the expatriates homeward and when changed economic conditions created a new era in literature.

For Elliot Paul and Eugene Jolas the revolution of the word remained as heretofore their brand of radicalism. Samuel Putnam (and others) were thinking of revolution in economic and political terms. We all remember Michael Gold's attack on Wilder and Fitzgerald's falling into desuetude. The heroic publishers of that day provided the opportunity for the non-Marxian to be printed. By 1933 when Judge Woolsey sanctioned *Ulysses* (*In Our Time* had found an American publisher eight years earlier) official censorship began to relax even if *Lady Chatterley's Lover* had still a long wait and *The Memoirs of Hecate County* demonstrated that the friends of Comstock and the descendents of Mrs. Grundy were still abundant.

The brave publishers served different purposes in the 20s than they did in the 30s, but they invite our attention for still other reasons. One is struck by the fact that so many of these publishers were women: Nancy Cunard, Sylvia Beach, Gertrude Stein, Caresse Crosby and Barbara Harrison. It was actually the financing by Anais Nin that made possible Kahane's publication of *The Tropic of Cancer*. It was Helena Rubinstein's money that provided the funds for Edward Titus' Black Manikin Press. It is a theme for Women's Lib, and it is a facet that a historian of the 20s cannot overlook. To that list of women we must add Bryher Ellerman, for it was her money—actually, her family's money—that made possible Bob McAlmon's enterprise, just as it was Cunard's money that enabled Nancy's venture. To the economist here is an interesting picture. The funds to publish D. H. Lawrence, Henry Miller, James Joyce, and Ernest Hemingway (to name but a few) came from two shipping magnates, the manufacturer of lipsticks and skin cleansers, and, if we assume that the Crosbys enjoyed a trickle of Morgan money, from the intangibles of Wall Street. That is one side of the story: the respectable side. On the other side, one is impressed by the significant number of inverts gravitating about these publishers. Hemingway in the *bal musette* scene in *The Sun Also Rises* was trying to communicate the annoying presence of the numerous homosexuals in Paris at the time. His dislike of them is frowned on in our own more tolerant age, but he had a right to his prejudices just as, to those of us who believe that hunting and fishing are worthy of the Indians, Hemingway's role as the Last of the Mohicans seems a bit anachronistic.

The Paris of the 1920s was the site of hospitality for the irate, the invert, the creative, and the talented woman. The age had its jokers and its mavericks too, but Josephson and Cowley have lately presented it as a serious age—the writer was proud of his talent, Cowley reminds us.

And I suppose the Parisian publishers were proud too. Without intending to disparage those publishers who risked their time and capital on writers not likely to yield bumper-profits, one must point out that not all of the output was motivated by idealism. McAlmon published himself, the Crosbys published themselves, Gertrude Stein published only Gertrude Stein, Bob Brown was chiefly concerned with Bob Brown, and Barbara Harrison saw to it that her future brother-in-law Glenway Wescott had two publications. Nor were all publications vanguard items. Nancy Cunard was publishing George Moore, then nearing 80; and Barbara Harrison was publishing *Venus and Adonis* as well as the hardly daring tales of Bret Harte. Notwithstanding, much was done to advance the cause of mature literature; and Mr. Ford had done an admirable job in organizing a vast mass of material for those who would extend their knowledge of the 20s and 30s.

JOSEPH M. DEFALCO

Hemingway's Craft.
Sheldon Norman Grebstein.
Carbondale & Edwardsville: Southern Illinois University Press, 1973. $8.95.

The inordinate amount of attention given in both the popular and scholarly press to sensation-seeking works dealing with the personality of the artist is one of the saddest facts of Hemingway studies. Serious criticisms that attempt to probe the meaningful mechanisms of Hemingway's artistry often receive scant notices only in non-literary journals intended for the eyes of librarians. One can guess merely the degree of aesthetic illumination that some editors expect their readers to garner from information concerning Hemingway's sexual prowess or from items that hint at Hemingway's lack of a personal code of sportsmanship because he shot birds from his fishing boat.

Sheldon Grebstein's *Hemingway's Craft* is a case in point. Published in 1973, it has been ignored generally by journals that most of us have been schooled to believe would keep us informed of the appearance of serious studies of important authors. Not that it has languished in total obscurity. To the credit of the editors of the *Annual,* the first chapter appeared originally in these pages. Additionally, it has enjoyed a subterranean sort of reputation among established Hemingway scholars and students ambitious enough to ferret out for themselves all new materials that appear on Hemingway.

Grebstein's work may not be the best critical study on Hemingway to appear in the last ten years or so, but scholars will be gratified by what he has accomplished. His examination of Hemingway's employment of imaginative materials is persuasive because his critical judgments are always judicious. Most important, he has satisfied a long-standing need for a common-sense approach to some of the vital contributions that Hemingway made to American letters.

Regardless of its critical reception, this work will be of continuing interest to younger scholars. Its surface simplicity and its generalizations combine the virtues of easy reading and palatable ideas. Old hands at Hemingway criticism will find the last chapter on comedy and the appendix on the manuscripts of *A Farewell to Arms* and *For Whom the Bell Tolls* of particular interest. Grebstein's discussions of the novels and short stories through the perspective of his thesis provides many original insights, and always there is an appealing freshness of approach.

The clear and intentionally simplified statement of the thesis appears in the first chapters. Focusing upon the short stories, Grebstein reduces the structural design in Hemingway's fiction to an uncomplicated "inside/outside/toward/away from" pattern. Coincident with this design, Grebstein sees a prevailing motif of the journey. Wisely, he avoids the quagmire of psychoanalytical jargon by limiting his consideration of the motif to a kind of "control" for the larger structural patterns. Scholars at every level profit by the reminder that "fundamental to Hemingway's craft in the short story are the archetypal principles of antithesis and opposition, or, very simply, the conflict and contrast of antipodal forces and values." As we seek to extract complex symbolic patterns from Hemingway's work or try to evaluate the relationship of his themes to larger cultural issues, we need to be reminded that the elementary constituents of fiction are the bases upon which all structures are established in the fictional process. When we overlook the importance of such elements, we invite second-rate or irresponsible critical conclusions. Grebstein's discussions of the recurrent patterns of structure and conflict through a reasonable sampling of the stories takes us back to the proper starting place for all criticism.

The second chapter treats the novels and continues to trace the pattern of the journey structure. Grebstein points out that Hemingway's division of four of the novels into books or sections reveals an important structural design inherent in the novel form. Within the larger structure, he indicates, Hemingway's technique of "alternation or counterpoint" tightly controls the emotional atmosphere and the action. Such controls account for the earmarks of Hemingway's fiction: "variety, dynamism, verve, [and] swiftness of pace."

The chapter entitled "Narrative Perspectives and Narrative Voices" is devoted to a careful examination and evaluation of specific uses of narrative perspectives. Grebstein concludes that in the main Hemingway was a "practioneer, not pioneer." Following the examples of Flaubert, DeMaupassant, Twain, Chekov, James, Conrad, Proust, and Joyce, Hemingway eschewed the "obtrusive and editorializing storytelling" and perfected a focus of narration that obscured the distinction between the teller of the tale and the states of consciousness of the characters. Grebstein discerns a number of subtle variations in Hemingway's use of point of view in both the omniscient and subjective modes. For example, in the stories he finds four variations of the first person narrator: the unreliable I-witness, the relatively reliable I-witness, the I-protagonist, and the I-witness-protagonist. The brief but incisive analysis of the time-distance contrast between the narrators of *The Sun Also Rises* and *A Farewell to Arms* leads Grebstein to a hitherto unavailable way of explaining the uneveness of quality in the short stories and the almost chasmal difference in quality between *The Old Man and the Sea* and *Islands in the Stream.*

Grebstein's discussion of Hemingway's use of dialogue is not particularly distinguished, but his synthesis of past and current views and some fresh views of his own will satisfy most skilled analysts. His view that Robert Jordan's dialogue functions as a linguistic counterpart to his politics provides a new insight into the underlying tensions within the characterization. Similarly, most readers will welcome the survey of prior views of Hemingway's style along with the reexamination of some of Hemingway's basic rhetorical ploys. I cannot applaud what seems to be a tendency to blur poetic and rhetoric, nor am I convinced that definitions such as the one that follows contribute much to our understanding of Hemingway's style: " 'imitative form,' the effort to parallel the structural design of an utterance with its lexical message so that the reader apprehends two kinds of meaning simultaneously, the one translatable or paraphrasable in logical terms, the other sensory or emotive." Handbook items of this kind do not dominate the discussion, however, and it is somewhat unfair to present one out of context. Of more interest, the penultimate chapter demonstrates the importance of music and painting to the overall impact of

Hemingway's style. Grebstein's discussion amplifies considerably the implications of Emily Stipes Watts's *Hemingway and the Arts* (1971) and provides us with new directions for further exploration.

As Grebstein himself points out in the final chapter, the subject of humor in Hemingway has been overlooked for the most part. Only Jackson Benson in his excellent *Hemingway: The Writer's Art of Self-Defense* (1969) has treated the subject at length. Unfortunately, we come away from Grebstein's account feeling somewhat shortchanged. Perhaps the subject was too large for the last chapter of a book dealing with a variety of aspects of the craft of a writer of Hemingway's stature. What there is, does illuminate satisfactorily Hemingway's enormous range: parody, burlesque, farce, comic juxtapositions, and numerous variations that serve larger satiric purposes.

The inclusion of deleted passages from *A Farewell to Arms* and *For Whom the Bell Tolls* and Grebstein's analysis of these passages offers a final insight into Hemingway's mastery of his materials. As Grebstein notes, the deletions reveal Hemingway's awareness of the craft of fiction in a way that a study of what he retained cannot. The unfinished *Islands in the Stream* aside, there is no doubt, and Grebstein's study leaves no doubt, that those of Hemingway's detractors who rely upon personal reminiscences and pseudo-biography as a basis for maligning Hemingway's distinctive artistry have no conception of how profound a craftsman he really was.

Marquette University

Announcements

Editorial: A New Edition of *Gatsby*

An axiom of textual criticism holds that texts do not improve in transmission, but become instead increasingly corrupt. This year Scribners had an opportunity to reverse this process in the case of its best-selling Scribner Library paperback, when *The Great Gatsby* was completely reset.[1] A spot investigation of this new edition reveals that it is indeed more corrupt than the preceding Scribner Library edition. The following is a cursory comparison of the two Scribner Library editions.

Earlier SL Edition (R—10.70 [C])	*New SL Edition (27...39C/P40...26)*
Average 32-33 lines per page	Average 40-41 lines per page
Total 182 pages	Total 121 pages
Chapters begin on separate pages	Chapters separated only by chapter headings
137.3 Section break	91.15 No section break
160.25 Section break	107.20 No section break
161.20 Section break	107.40-108.1 No section break
167.27 Section break	111.24 No section break
175.21 Section break	116.37 No section break
179.22 Section break	119.27 No section break
181.8 Section break	120.28 No section break
181.26 No section break	121.3 Section break
182.25 orgiastic	121.28 orgiastic

The attempt to save space results, in general, in an edition that is more difficult to read, and, more seriously, in an edition that obscures Fitzgerald's complex time structure by deleting the space breaks that were intended to signal chronological shifts. This wasted chance to recover Fitzgerald's intentions is particularly disappointing in view of the body of textual information available now for *The Great Gatsby*. Apparently the publisher has chosen economy over responsibility; let the reader beware.

Margaret M. Duggan
University of South Carolina

---

[1]Professor Bruce Harkness called our attention to the publication of the new edition in October 1975.

At left Mrs. Eleanor Lanahan Hazard and Mrs. Cecilia Lanahan Kehn (the Fitzgeralds' granddaughters) holding Nathan and Zack Hazard (the Fitzgeralds' twin great-grandsons); Jack Lanahan (the Fitzgeralds' grandson, visible behind Scottie Fitzgerald Smith); Father William J. Silk at right.

Reburial of the Fitzgeralds

F. Scott and Zelda Fitzgerald were reinterred in St. Mary's church cemetery at Rockville, Maryland on 7 November 1975. In 1940 the policy of the Catholic Church was that burial in consecrated ground was limited to practicing Catholics. As a lapsed Catholic, F. Scott Fitzgerald was ineligible for burial with his parents in St. Mary's. He was buried in Rockville Union Cemetery, and his wife was buried with him in 1948. The policy of the Church has since been revised, making it possible for the Fitzgeralds to be buried where he had wanted to be.

The following words of the Fitzgeralds were read at the reinterment service.

Zelda Sayre to F. Scott Fitzgerald:

Why should graves make people feel in vain? I've heard that *so* much, and Grey is *so* convincing, but somehow I can't find anything hopeless in having lived—All the broken columnes and clasped hands and doves and angels mean romances—and in an hundred years I think I shall like having young people speculate on whether my eyes were brown or blue—of cource, they are neither—I hope my grave has an air of many, many years ago about it—Isn't it funny how, out of a row of Confederate soldiers, two or three will make you think of dead lovers and dead loves—when they're exactly like the others, even to the yellowish moss? Old death is so beautiful—so very beautiful—We will die together—I know—

F. Scott Fitzgerald:

And I wouldn't mind a bit if in a few years Zelda and I could snuggle up together under a stone in some old graveyard here. That is really a happy thought and not melancholy at all.

Zelda Fitzgerald:

He was the best friend to me that a person could have had compatible, protective, teaching and sharing. . . . and I wouldn't have traded him for anybody as so few people have so many of the desirabilities.

F. Scott Fitzgerald:

You are the finest, loveliest, tenderest, most beautiful person I have ever known, but even that is an understatement. . . .

Zelda Fitzgerald:

Life seemed so promisory always when he was around: and I always believed that he could take care of anything.

F. Scott Fitzgerald:

. . . the impression of the fames and the domains, the vistas and the glories of Maryland followed many a young man West after the Civil War and my father was of that number. Much of my early childhood in Minnesota was spent in asking him such questions as:

"—and how long did it take Early's column to pass Glenmary that day?" (That was a farm in Montgomery County.)

and:

"—what would have happened if Jeb Stuart's cavalry had joined Lee instead of raiding all the way to Rockville?"

and:

"—tell me again about how you used to ride through the woods with a spy up behind you on the horse."

or:

"Why wouldn't they let Francis Scott Key off the British frigate?"

F. Scott Fitzgerald:

Next day at the churchyard his father was laid among a hundred Divers, Dorseys, and Hunters. It was very friendly leaving him there with all his relations around him. . . . He knelt on the hard soil. These dead, he knew them all, their weather-beaten faces with blue flashing eyes, the spare violent bodies, the souls made of new earth in the forest-heavy darkness of the seventeenth century.

"Good-by, my father—good-by, all my fathers."

SARA SHERMAN WIBORG MURPHY (1883-1975)

The opening line of her *New York Times* obituary reads: "Sara Murphy, widow of Gerald Murphy and the model for Nicole in F. Scott Fitzgerald's *Tender Is the Night* died yesterday [10 October 1975] in the Arlington (Va.) Hospital." Perhaps more than any other celebrated couple of their era, they were identified less as individuals—though both were stunningly unique personalities—than as "the Murphys"—exponents of *joie de vivre* and bound together in an indissoluble union of civilized epicureanism. To the Cap d'Antibes and, later, to East Hampton came the Picassos and another woman who would become his next wife, the Count and Countess Étienne de Beaumont, the Robert Benchleys and Alexander Woollcott and Dorothy Parker, Stravinsky and the dancers of the Diaghilev company and one, Vladimir Orloff, the son of a Russian nobleman who managed the private bank account of the Tsarina and had seen his father murdered by the Bolsheviks, and the Archibald MacLeishes and John and Katy Dos Passos, the movie idol Valentino who would die young, the Charles Bracketts, the young Hemingways and the Scott Fitzgeralds, Donald Ogden Stewart and Cole Porter and Monty Woolley, the Légers to whom they gave their pet monkey when they finally left Europe, and Ellen and Philip Barry who would also make art of their lives. All these people came to the Murphys' house in the summer where "whatever happened seemed to have something to do with art." It was their style to be loyal and gracious under, at times, extraordinary pressure—even scrutiny. It was said by their friends that they had "mastered the art of living" and that "people were always their best selves with the Murphys." Hemingway wrote in 1941 of having no closer friend than Sara. But now, with nothing of their lives left save a legacy of grace and style, Fitzgerald's letter to Sara Murphy in 1935 seems a proper and prophetic requiem: "That not one thing you've done is for nothing. . . . You are part of our times, part of the history of our race. . . ."

M. M. D.

James Charters (1897-1975)

One of the most beloved and colorful characters of Montparnasse in the twenties, James Charters, more familiarly known as Jimmy the Barman, died in London on March 19, 1975 after a long illness. He suffered from very painful arthritis and was handicapped by failing eyesight. He was 78 years old.

Jimmy had served almost anyone you can think of among the artists, writers, and hangers-on of the Left Bank over a period of more than fifteen years from Hemingway to James Joyce, from Man Ray to Marcel Duchamp and Brancusi. Hemingway and Jimmy had a special affinity because of their interest in boxing, the barman having been a professional fighter in his early years. When Jimmy wrote his memoirs, it was Hemingway who stepped forth to write the introduction—which was the second time he wrote an introduction.

Jimmy's greatest asset was his warmth of personality, his interest in all the diverse characters who stood in front of his bar, his desire to be helpful to everyone. He was the confidant of Montparnasse.

Jimmy had another quality which played an important role in the Quarter in those days, a knack of knowing how to bring people together. Complete strangers who sat alone at his bar soon found themselves talking to each other without ever realizing that Jimmy had "arranged" the encounter. Jimmy handled this so adroitly and without the least pretension on his part that he and his bar became the center for much of the Montparnasse evening life. "Let's go to Jimmy's for a drink first," many would say, or perhaps "Let's go to Jimmy's and see what is going on."

When life in Montparnasse began to fade away, Jimmy moved back to London and in his later years gave up bartending for small character parts in the movies. He carried on with this until his last days.

Jimmy was born in Wales of Irish parents. His father had been a fairly successful comedian with billings all over the country, including the old Haymarket in a black-face skit with another actor called the Two Macks. Jimmy inherited his father's talents and more.

Morrill Cody

News Briefs

The French national television in cooperation with Bavarian television is preparing a six-hour series of programs on Hemingway's life. . . . Archibald S. Alexander's Hemingway collection has been acquired by the Princeton University Library. . . . The Hemingway collection of C. E. Frazer Clark, Jr. has been acquired by the University of Maryland Library. . . . John Huston is planning a movie version of *Across the River and Into the Trees*. . . . An advance copy in wrappers of *Tender Is the Night* brought $800 at Swann Galleries on 11 September 1975. . . . Typescript copies of "Apparatus for a Definitive Edition . . . *The Last Tycoon*" by Matthew J. Bruccoli have been deposited at the following libraries: Caroliniana (University of South Carolina), Library of Congress, British Library, Princeton University Library, Lilly Library (Indiana University). . . . Bruccoli's *The Last of the Novelists: F. Scott Fitzgerald and The Last Tycoon* will be published by Southern Illinois University Press in spring 1977. . . . A Hemingway Conference was held at the University of Alabama, 14-16 October; the speakers were: Jo August, Jackson J. Benson, Matthew J. Bruccoli, Scott Donaldson, Leo Gurko, Mary Hemingway, Richard B. Hovey, Alfred Kazin, Frank M. Laurence, Michael S. Reynolds, Robert O. Stephens, and Philip Young. . . . 5-21 October the Great Neck Library sponsored an Exhibition on "The Lardners of Great Neck"; the speakers were: Matthew J. Bruccoli, James T. Farrell, Roger Kahn, Frances Chaney Lardner, Ring Lardner, Jr., and Richard Layman. . . . Matthew J. Bruccoli (Department of English, University of South Carolina, Columbia, S. C. 29208) is seeking unpublished letters from or to F. Scott Fitzgerald for an edition of Fitzgerald's correspondence.

To Ring Lardner, from his early imitator and always admirer,

Ernest Hemingway

Cooke, Montana

September 17, 19

Death in the Afternoon. Collection of Ring Lardner, Jr.